MIMESIS
INTERNATIONAL

C000171166

ITALIAN FRAME
n. 4

directed by Andrea Minuz (Sapienza Università di Roma) and Christian Uva (Università Roma Tre)

CATHOLICISM AND CINEMA

Modernization and Modernity

Gianluca della Maggiore
Tomaso Subini

MIMESIS
INTERNATIONAL

This book was funded by PRIN 2012.

This book was peer-reviewed.

This book was proofed and corrected by Dom Holdaway.

Cover illustration (with permission from Archivio dell'Istituto per la storia dell'Azione Cattolica e del Movimento Cattolico in Italia Paolo VI / Archive of the Institute for the History of Catholic Action and the Catholic Movement in Italy Paul VI): during the electoral campaign for the 1948 elections, Pastor Angelicus was screened, using vans solemnly blessed by Pius XII, in the villages of southern Italy where the parish still did not have any movie theatres.

© 2018 – Mimesis International
www.mimesisinternational.com
e-mail: info@mimesisinternational.com
Book series: *Italian Frame*, n. 4
isbn 9788869770760
© MIM Edizioni Srl
P.I. C.F. 02419370305

TABLE OF CONTENTS

INTRODUCTION
BY GIANLUCA DELLA MAGGIORE AND TOMASO SUBINI

This volume originates in the interdisciplinary dialogue between two historians, one contemporary and the other of film, on the relationship between religious phenomena and media. More specifically, it investigates the ways in which the Catholic Church used cinema in particular – since it occupied a central position in the media system during the period taken in consideration – as a space for action within the complex dynamics of modern mass society. Following a handful of isolated and at times contradictory efforts, the Church's engagement with cinema became institutionalized between the end of the thirties and the beginning of the forties, before changing in many ways towards the end of the seventies. The latter moment can be represented on the one hand by the emergence of explicit pornography, which in turn resulted from the fall of taboos related to obscenity, despite – but perhaps also as a consequence of – the rigid censorship of representations of sexuality promoted by the Church. On the other, it is embodied in the Church's new and increasingly conscientious investment in the mass media. This book investigates the historical process that lead to this change.

The presence of the Vatican on the Italian territory is key to understanding the exceptionality of the Italian case, both for its direct or indirect consequences on the general development of the film industry and for the way it influenced the Italian Catholic Church's film policy. This volume intends to provide an outline of the relationship between Catholicism and cinema with a specific focus on Italy. It relies on new sources and employs an entirely original approach which combines the analysis of archive materials – an approach typical to historical studies of institutional apparatuses – and the analysis of cultural formation and representation – an approach typical to cultural studies.

The most productive way to address the complexity of the questions that underlie this volume is to focus on the couplet of modernization/modernity, conforming thus to recent trends in historiography. With this in mind, it is necessary to offer a preliminary definition of the use of these concepts within our analysis.

The paradigm of modernity, which oriented historical studies for much of the previous century as a genuine "grand narrative" of historical development, on the one hand "emphasizes the effects of continuous technological progress, of the growing density of communication [...], of the increasing variety of types of knowledge and social functions;" on the other "it explains the conflicts underlining the rift between the push to modernize and those traditional groups which are left behind, or which resist assimilation into the modern world."[1] This paradigm has naturally provided a starting point for studies of the relationship between the Catholic Church (a stronghold of tradition that is two thousands years old) and cinema (the previous century's modern technology *par excellence*).[2] Gian Piero Brunetta's early studies in this area – which painted a radically antithetical and conflictual image of the two sides, centred on the Church's great refusal of cinema's modernity – are deeply influenced by this paradigm.[3]

By now it is widely accepted that modernity cannot provide a category for unambiguous, rigidly defined historical interpretation. We know that the concept can be analysed

---

1   Lynn Hunt, *La storia culturale nell'età globale* (Pisa: ETS, 2010), p. 12.
2   Francesco Casetti, *L'occhio del Novecento. Cinema, esperienze, modernità* (Milano: Bompiani, 2005).
3   Gian Piero Brunetta, *Tattiche della negazione e del consenso nei giudizi del Centro Cattolico Cinematografico (1934-1945)*, in *Retorica e politica* (Bressanone, 1974), ed. by Daniela Goldin (Padova: Liviana, 1977), pp. 245-268; Id., *Mondo cattolico e organizzazione del consenso: la politica cinematografica*, in *La Democrazia cristiana dal fascismo al 18 aprile. Movimento cattolico e Democrazia cristiana nel Veneto 1945-1948*, ed. by Mario Isnenghi and Silvio Lanaro (Padova: Marsilio, 1978), pp. 425-434; Id., *Cattolici e cinema*, in *Il cinema italiano degli anni '50*, ed. by Giorgio Tinazzi (Padova: Marsilio, 1979). These essays have since been reproduced, without any significant changes, in the various editions of Brunetta's history of Italian cinema.

and employed from multiple perspectives: from economic transformations to social, cultural, gender or political ones, and so forth. As a result, studies must differentiate between the effects of modernity at the different levels of individual consciences, groups and institutions. As Giovanni Filoramo has written,

> today, in the light of globalization and the profound transformations in the multiculturalism of our societies, the comparative study of these processes leads us to underline, much more decisively than in the past, the fact that communities, societies, states and therefore also religious traditions experience very different rhythms of development and responses to the challenges of modernity.[4]

As an effect of this new approach, we are able to go beyond the notion that religion and modernity are two irreconcilable entities, and introduce interpretative frameworks that reveal their interactive and surprisingly dynamic connections.[5]

In place of facile interpretative models that are situated at the polar ends of a spectrum – whereby religion is intended as a "refusal of modernity and its values" or, vice versa, as "a dynamic, propulsive push for change" – today scholarship gives greater credit to a "third kind of response [...] halfway between the two previous ones," that seeks "a reasonable compromise between the need for change and conservation."[6] Modernization is the historiographic concept that is more useful when defining this third model of interpretation: in essence, it refers to the creation of a new research perspective that invites us to "understand the modernity of religions in modernity."[7] This approach aims to capture the dynamic processes through which Catholicism has interacted with modernity, creating parallels between the evolution of the Catholic movement and those of contemporary mass

---

4   Giovanni Filoramo, "Introduzione generale all'opera," in *Le religioni e il mondo moderno*, ed. by Giovanni Filoramo, I, *Cristianesimo*, ed. by Daniele Menozzi (Torino: Einaudi, 2008), p. 23.
5   Staf Hellemans, "From 'Catholicism against Modernity' to 'the Problematic Modernity of Catholicism'," in *Ethical Perspectives*, a. VIII, n. 2, 2001, pp. 117-127.
6   Giovanni Filoramo, p. 24.
7   Staf Hellemans, p. 121.

movements. In turn, this enables a more precise understanding
of the "ever possible bind between Catholicism's modernization
and the persistent refusal of modernity."[8] There is a fundamental
assumption taking place at the basis of these analyses: before the
changes following the Second Vatican Council forged new modes
of interacting with the modern world, the Catholic Church –
which persisted in its intransigent objective of Christian social
restoration, following the model of medieval *christianitas*[9] – was
simultaneously an integral part of modernity and nonetheless
critically disposed towards it. According to Daniele Menozzi,
between the two Wars Catholicism came to elaborate a clear and
composite method of defining what attitude to adopt in relation
to the modern world:

> the point-blank refusal of the principles of modernity was bound
> to the tendency to subsume all of modern culture's tools under the
> vigilant eye of the hierarchy, the only authority entitled to make sure
> that the intended modernization would not turn into modernism,
> that is, in the insidious infiltration into the Church structure of
> those modern values that were to be uncompromisingly opposed.[10]

This method captures Catholicism's dual, ambiguous
"performance" in the modern world, that Church historian and
sociologist of religion Staf Hellemans summarizes as follows:
"objectively rooted in, and yet subjectively stubbornly resisting
modernity."[11]
    In light of these academic trends, how can we examine the
relationship between Catholicism and cinema? Scholarship by
Francesco Casetti decisively moves beyond the oppositional

---

8   Renato Moro, "Il caso italiano," in *La modernità e i mondi cristiani,* ed. by
     Francesco Margiotta Broglio (Bologna: Il Mulino, 2010), p. 169.
9   For a clarification of this interpretative framework, we refer to the
     canonical works Giovanni Miccoli, *Fra mito della cristianità e secolarizzazione.
     Studi sul rapporto chiesa-società nell'età contemporanea* (Casale Monferrato:
     Marietti, 1985); Daniele Menozzi, *La chiesa cattolica e la secolarizzazione*
     (Torino: Einaudi, 1993).
10   Daniele Menozzi, "Cristianesimo e modernità," in *Le religioni e il mondo
     moderno,* ed. by Giovanni Filoramo, I, *Cristianesimo,* ed. by Daniele Menozzi
     (Torino: Einaudi, 2008), p. XXXV.
11   Staf Hellemans, 122.

perspective represented by Brunetta's work, elaborating instead a negotiational perspective. In a 2003 essay focused on the Fascist period, Casetti and Elena Mosconi observe the Catholics' need to "rethink" their interest in cinema "within the furrow of modernization and massification processes that affect society in its entirety."[12] The two academics, both affiliated to the area of Film and Media Studies, thus inserted themselves into an ongoing debate in historical studies of Catholicism that perceives the concept of modernization as a hermeneutic category,[13] which allows us to transcend rigid dichotomies in analyses of the relationship between Catholicism and modernity.[14] Casetti and Mosconi interpret the Catholics' experience with the mass media in terms of "a prudent modernization."[15] In another important essay written by Casetti

12   Francesco Casetti and Elena Mosconi, "Il cinema e i modelli di vita," in *Chiesa, cultura e educazione tra le due guerre*, ed. by Luciano Pazzaglia (Brescia: La Scuola, 2003), p. 148.

13   Some of the more recent references include: Étienne Fouilloux, *Une église en quête de liberté: la pensée catholique française entre modernisme et Vatican II* (Paris: Desclée de Brouwer, 1998); *Il modernismo tra modernità e modernizzazione*, ed. by Alfonso Botti and Rocco Cerrato (Urbino: Quattro Venti, 2000); Daniele Menozzi, "La Chiesa e la modernità," *Storia e problemi contemporanei*, a. XIII, n. 26, 2000, pp. 7-24; *Chiesa cattolica e modernità*, ed. by Franco Bolgiani, Vincenzo Ferrone, Francesco Margiotta Broglio (Bologna: Il Mulino, 2004); *Le religioni e il mondo moderno*, ed. by Giovanni Filoramo, I, *Cristianesimo*, ed. by Daniele Menozzi (Torino: Einaudi, 2008); *La modernità e i mondi cristiani*, ed. by Francesco Margiotta Broglio (Bologna: Il Mulino, 2010); *Towards a New Catholic Church in Advanced Modernity. Transformations, Visions, Tensions*, ed. by Staf Hellemans and Jozef Wissink (Münster: LIT Verlag, 2012); *La Chiesa tra restaurazione e modernità*, ed. by Giorgio Fabre, Karen Venturini (Bologna: Il Mulino 2018).

14   Casetti and Mosconi refer explicitly to the essay Renato Moro, "Il 'modernismo buono.' La modernizzazione cattolica tra fascismo e postfascismo come problema storiografico," *Storia Contemporanea*, a. XIX, n. 4, 1988, pp. 625-716. Moro developed this terminology further in other pieces: "La religione e la 'nuova epoca.' Cattolicesimo e modernità tra le due guerre mondiali," in *Il modernismo tra modernità e modernizzazione*, ed. by Alfonso Botti and Rocco Cerrato (Urbino: Quattro Venti, 2000), pp. 513-573; Id., "Nazione, cattolicesimo e regime fascista," *Rivista di storia del cristianesimo*, a. I, n. 1, 2004, pp. 129-147; Id., "Il caso italiano," in *La modernità e i mondi cristiani*, ed. by Francesco Margiotta Broglio (Bologna: Il Mulino, 2010), pp. 145-192.

15   Francesco Casetti and Elena Mosconi, "Il cinema e i modelli di vita," p. 148.

and Silvio Alovisio, on the relationship between the Church and
early cinema, the Catholics' pedagogical approach to the new
medium is demonstrated to be the way in which they came to
"accept modernity" as expressed by cinema. In particular, the
shift from a "scheduling pedagogy" to a "textual pedagogy" with
which the Church accompanied the parallel transition from early
to institutionalized cinema reveals how it had began to "regulate"
and "discipline" the movie-going experience according to its own
methods and objectives: the birth of Catholic censorship of (filmic)
texts according to the Church's moral magisterium implied not
"the refusal and the fear of what is new and modern but, on the
contrary, the full legitimation of 'healthy modernity'."[16]

However, there is little doubt that one of the central aspects
of Catholic modernization in this light was, as various studies
reveal, the desire to appropriate several elements of scientific and
technological modernity. This desire is "extremely evident"[17] when
it comes to means of mass communication. This is the context of
that "conservative modernization," the terminology used by Renato
Moro for the Italian case between the two Wars, according to which
Catholicism, over a backdrop that was broadly conditioned by
Fascism, realized "a selective openness to modernity," privileging
its "technological aspects," and therefore looking to "an attempt
at an organizational 'update' rather than a cultural and religious
one."[18] Broader studies of the relationship between the Catholics
and the development of mass communication (from older
work on mass culture,[19] the press and public opinion,[20] to more

---

16   Francesco Casetti and Silvio Alovisio, "Il contributo della Chiesa alla
     moralizzazione degli spazi pubblici," in *Attraverso lo schermo. Cinema e cultura
     cattolica in Italia,* ed. by Ruggero Eugeni and Dario E. Vigano, 3 vols (Roma:
     Ente dello Spettacolo, 2006), I, *Dalle origini agli anni Venti,* pp. 97-127.
17   Renato Moro, "Il caso italiano," p. 169.
18   Renato Moro, "Il 'modernismo buono'," p. 714.
19   Stefano Pivato, "L'organizzazione cattolica della cultura di massa durante
     il fascismo," *Italia Contemporanea,* n. 132, 1978, pp. 3-25; Id., *Clericalismo e
     laicismo nella cultura popolare italiana* (Milano: Franco Angeli, 1980).
20   Mario Marazziti, *I papi di carta. Nascita e svolta dell'informazione religiosa
     da Pio XII a Giovanni XXIII* (Genova: Marietti:1990); Marc Agostino, *Le
     pape Pie XI et l'opinion* (Rome: École française de Rome, 1991); Id.,"Pie
     XI et les médias," in *Achille Ratti, pape Pie XI,* Actes du colloque organisé
     par l'École Française de Rome (Roma, March 15-18, 1989) (Rome: École
     française de Rome, 1996), pp. 825-837.

recent contributions on publishing,[21] radio and television[22]) do
not contradict these interpretative frameworks: in approaching
modern culture and its new tools, the actions of the Church
confirmed less a transformation that enabled it to recognize new
social attitudes and needs than a process of technological updating.
Nevertheless, developments in thought on the transnational
dimension of cinema,[23] the identification of new periodizing
markers in the development of modern mass culture,[24] and
especially the evolution over the past fifteen years of what has

21 Maria Iolanda Palazzolo, *Gli editori del papa. Da Porta Pia ai Patti Lateranensi*
    (Roma: Viella, 2016).
22 John Pollard, "Electronic Pastors: Radio, Cinema, and Television, from
    Pius XI to John XXIII," in *The Papacy since 1500. From Italian Prince to
    Universal Pastor*, ed. by James Corkery and Thomas Worcester (Cambridge:
    Cambridge University Press, 2010), pp. 182-203; Federico Ruozzi, "Voci e
    immagini della fede: radio e tv," in *Cristiani d'Italia. Chiese, società e Stato,
    1861-2011*, ed. by Alberto Melloni (Roma: Istituto della Enciclopedia
    Italiana, 2011), pp. 471-486; Id., *Il concilio in diretta. Il Vaticano II e la
    televisione tra partecipazione e informazione* (Bologna: Il Mulino, 2012);
    Massimo Scaglioni, "I cattolici e la televisione, vettore di unificazione
    nazionale," in *Non lamento, ma azione. I cattolici e lo sviluppo italiano nei 150
    anni di storia unitaria*, ed. by Maria Bocci (Milano: Vita e Pensiero, 2013);
    Mariagrazia Fanchi, "Specchio di virtù. Il mondo cattolico e l'arrivo della
    televisione," in *Televisione. Storia, immaginario, memoria*, ed. by Damiano
    Garofalo and Vanessa Roghi (Soveria Mannelli: Rubbettino, 2015);
    Raffaella Perin, *La radio del papa. Propaganda e diplomazia nella seconda
    guerra mondiale* (Bologna: Il Mulino, 2017).
23 Tim Bergfelder, "National, Transnational or Supranational Cinema?
    Rethinking European Film Studies," *Media, Culture & Society*, n. 3, 2005,
    pp. 315–331; *Transnational Cinema, The Film Reader*, ed. By Elizabeth Ezra
    and Terry Rowden (London-New York: Routledge, 2006); Will Higbee
    and Song Hwee Lim, "Concepts of Transnational Cinema: Towards a
    Critical Transnationalism in Film Studies," *Transnational Cinemas*, n. 1,
    2010, pp. 7-21; *La storia internazionale e il cinema. Reti, scambi e transfer nel
    '900*, ed. by Stefano Pisu and Pierre Sorlin, *Cinema e Storia*, a. VI, n. 6,
    2017.
24 David Forgacs, *L'industrializzazione della cultura italiana (1880-2000)*
    (Bologna: Il Mulino, 2000); Victoria de Grazia, *Irresistible Empire: America's
    Advance through Twentieth-Century Europe*, (Cambridge: Belknap Press of
    Harvard University Press, 2005); David Forgacs and Stephen Gundle,
    Mass Culture and Italian Society from Fascism to the Cold War (Bloomington:
    Indiana University press, 2007); David E. Ellwood, *Una sfida per la
    modernità. Europa e America nel lungo Novecento* (Roma: Carocci, 2012);
    Ferdinando Fasce, *Le anime del commercio. Pubblicità e consumi nel secolo
    americano* (Roma: Carocci, 2015).

been called New Cinema History[25] demand further verification
of these interpretative frameworks, enhancing our approach
through an interdisciplinary perspective in view of new questions
and new sources.

Studies on the fall of taboos related to obscenity, on the
progressive sexualization of cinema and on the appearance of
pornography in Italy[26] have provided a crucial element in our
understanding of the non-linear relationship between the Church
and cinema's modernity. This relationship cannot be represented
as a progressive acceptance (no matter how prudent and
instrumental) of the tools (more than the values) of modernity, but
rather it alternates between episodes of slow progress and abrupt
retreats. On certain issues in particular (like the aforementioned
case of the representation of sexuality), the fundamental
contradictions at the base of the Church-cinema relationship
literally explode, undermining the reassuring syntheses that were
established through the "negotiation approach." In this line of
research, and in line with the methodology proposed by New
Cinema History, it is vital to develop interpretative models that
can integrate the normalizing pressures of high-level institutions
which act "top down" on the faithful (the Secretary of State of the
Holy See, the Pontifical Council for Social Communications, the
CCC), with those that move in the opposite direction, rising up
from the bottom to the hierarchy, pushing for difficult (and not
always possible) renegotiations (through film criticism, popular
reception, parish cinema communities, organized collective and
individual dissent). In other words, it is necessary to investigate
the phenomenon considered in this volume in its entirety and
complexity; one must create interpretative models for Church
policy that account for doctrinal and regulatory development as

---

25   *Explorations in New Cinema History. Approaches and Case Studies*, ed. by
     Daniel Biltereyst, Richard Maltby and Philippe Meers (Oxford: Wiley-
     Blackwell, 2011); Eric Smoodin, "As the Archive Turned: Writing Film
     Histories without Films," *The Moving Image*, n. 2, 2014, pp. 96-100.
26   Callisto Cosulich, *La scalata al sesso* (Genova: Immordino, 1969); Peppino
     Ortoleva, *Il secolo dei media. Riti, abitudini, mitologie* (Milano: Il Saggiatore,
     2008); Giovanna Maina and Federico Zecca, "Le grandi manovre. Gli
     anni Settanta preparano il porno," *Bianco e nero*, n. 572, 2012; *La sessualità
     nel cinema italiano degli anni Sessanta*, ed. by Federico Zecca and Giovanna
     Maina, *Cinergie*, n. 5, 2014.

much as for its concrete effects on beliefs and practices, and for the support of religious film production as much as the efforts to tackle obscene cinema. The clamorous failures in the latter area upset the "negotiation model," raising several doubts about the responsibility of the Church itself for the progressive pornification of society from the second half of the '70s. For Peppino Ortoleva, the rapid and intense process that led to the fall of taboos related to obscenity in very few years (which he describes as the "breaking of a dam that many would have defined unbreakable until few years before"[27]) was also a consequence of the Church's rigid approach to the crucial issue of the representation of sexuality.

By focusing on the relationship between the Catholics and cinema's modernity, our interpretation therefore revisits not only Brunetta's "oppositional model," but in some ways also the "negotiation model" proposed by Casetti (which had first surpassed the oppositional one). The concept of "modernization without modernity" (that is, the idea that Catholic culture's negotiation with modernity inspired no real exchange of values, but was instead mostly instrumental) and the non-linearity of negotiation processes (which had substantial inconsistencies and abrupt steps backwards when it came to some particularly thorny issues) force us to critically examine the "negotiation model" in light of several new questions. On a political and geopolitical level: in what way did cinema's genetically transnational character influence the approach of the Catholic Church – whose perspective was, by nature, global? What was its attitude towards macroscopically transnational phenomena such as the cinematic experiences that developed in the Soviet Union and the United States? Are there continuities or discontinuities in its relationship with cinema in Fascist Italy and Christian-Democratic Italy? On a social and anthropological level: in what way did cinema influence the redefinition of the pedagogical models or the social and sexual morals of the Catholic Church? How did the Church address cinema's ability to modify the Catholics' frame of mind, aspirations and points of reference? On a theological and devotional-religious level: how was cinema integrated into the Catholic Church's traditional use of images? What theological issues did the

---

27 Peppino Ortoleva, pp. 170-171.

cinematographic apostolate pose in relation to cinema? Under what conditions could a cinematic image become a devotional means? These essential questions will provide the guiding thread for our proposed interpretation. By relating the debate on modernization and modernity to the specific issue of the cinematographic representation of the sacred on the one hand, and of sexuality on the other (the two main problems that inspired the Holy See's film policy, especially in Italy) this book questions the aforementioned oppositional and negotiation approaches in light of several unpublished sources. The analysis in the first part of this book (focused on the 1930s) reveals certain foreshadowing dynamics that were to characterize the post-war years – which is subsequently the focus of the second part. This included: first of all, the increasing centralization of decision-making processes and Catholic film policy, marked, as they were, by very evident clericalization; secondly, the emergence of the strategic role played by the Jesuits, the cultural, Catholic *intelligentsia par excellence*, with their concrete experience in media and culture; thirdly, the Holy See's clear intention to invest in the autonomous production of documentaries centred on the living Pontiff, which then become the only entirely legitimate cinematographic products to represent the savcred in a theologically correct way; and finally, the Holy See's stance on censorship in its multifarious expressions (classification, lobbying with state institutions, the establishment of a network of parish cinemas in order to influence production) as a crucial issue for Catholic film policy, given the power exerted by cinema on the viewer's conscience.

Although the structure of the volume originated from constant, interdisciplinary dialogue between the two authors, this interpretive approach necessitated a two-part structure for the volume, each focusing on a determined period, in order to exploit and enhance fully the specificity of each research perspective and the different sources used. The first part was written by Gianluca della Maggiore, the second by Tomaso Subini.

Note

Documents in Italian are quoted in English (the translation is ours). The orginal Italian text is reported in the corresponding footnote. Documents in Latin have been left in Latin (the English translation is available in the corresponding footnote). Documents in French have been left in French. With regard to the documents available online (https://users.unimi. it/cattoliciecinema/) in the database of the PRIN research project on Catholics and cinema, coordinated by Milan Statale University: documents available in the PRIN database come both from indexed archives and from archives which have not yet been ordered: in the former case, source verification can be carried out on the scans available in the database as well as in the archive in which the documents are preserved. Documents are therefore identified in the footnotes by a double description: one with which they are indexed in real archives (if available) and another referring to the PRIN database (indicated within parentheses). After the first occurrence, each document is identified solely through database abbreviation.

Document numbers are indicated in English, with the single exception of documents from the Vatican Secret Archives, which explicitly requested that document numbers be left in Italian.

Volumes and articles in Italian are quoted in English (the translation is ours, if no English translation was available). Volumes and articles in French have been left in French.

List of abbreviations

ACEC: Associazione Cattolica Esercenti Cinema (Catholic Exhibitors' Association)
ACI: Azione Cattolica Italiana (Italian Catholic Action)
ANEC: Associazione Nazionale Esercenti Cinema (Commercial Exhibitors' Association)
CCC: Centro Cattolico Cinematografico (Catholic Cinematographic Centre)
CEI: Conferenza Episcopale Italiana (Italian Episcopal Conference)
CUCE: Consorzio Utenti Cinematografi Educativi (Consortium of Educational Cinema Users)
DC: Democrazia Cristiana (Christian Democracy Party)
ECER: Ente per la Cinematografia Educativa e Religiosa (Office for Educational and Religious Cinema)
IECI: International Educational Cinematograph Institute

LUCE: L'Unione Cinematografica Educativa (Educational Cinematographic Union)
MPPDA: Motion Picture Producers and Distributors of America
NCWC: National Catholic Welfare Council
OCIC: Organization Catholique Internationale du Cinéma (International Catholic Office for Cinema)
ONB: Opera Nazionale Balilla (National Youth Club)
OND: Opera Nazionale Dopolavoro (National Recreational Club)
PCA: Production Code Administration
PSI: Partito Socialista Italiano (Italian Socialist Party)
RAI: Radiotelevisione italiana (Italian Radio and Television)
SCAEC: Società Cattolica Assistenza Esercizi Cinema (Catholic Society for Support to Cinematographic Exhibition)

s.d.: *sine data*
Pos.: Posizione (position)
Fasc.: Fascicolo (folder)
f: foglio (sheet)
ff: fogli (sheets)
r: recto
v: verso
a: anno (year)
rubr.: rubric

Archives

AA.EE.SS.: Congregrazione degli Affari Ecclesiastici Straordinari presso l'Archivio Segreto Vaticano (Sacred Congregation for International Affairs at Vatican Secret Archive)
ACEC Archive: Archivio Associazione Cattolica Esercenti Cinema (Catholic Exhibitors' Association Archive)
ACS: Archivio Centrale dello Stato (Centrale State Archive)
AFMER: Archivio storico della Provincia di Cristo Re dei frati minori dell'Emilia Romagna (Historical Archive of the Provincia di Cristo Re dei frati minori dell'Emilia Romagna)
ANT: Archivio Nazareno Taddei (Nazareno Taddei Archive)
ASDMI: Archivio Storico della Diocesi di Milano (Historical Archive of the Milan Diocese)
ASILS: Archivio Storico dell'Istituto Luigi Sturzo (Historical Archive of the Luigi Sturzo Institute)
ASV: Archivio Segreto Vaticano (Vatican Secret Archive)

CEI Archive: Archivio Conferenza Episcopale Italiana (Italian Episcopal Conference Archive)

ISACEM Archive: Archivio dell'Istituto per la storia dell'Azione Cattolica e del Movimento Cattolico in Italia Paolo VI (Archive of the Institute for the History of Catholic Action and the Catholic Movement in Italy Paul VI)

S.RR.SS.: Sezione per i Rapporti con gli Stati presso l'Archivio Segreto Vaticano (Section for Relations with States at Vatican Secret Archive)

CATHOLIC RECONQUESTS, TOTALITARIAN PROJECTS, GLOBAL PERSPECTIVES
BY GIANLUCA DELLA MAGGIORE

1. *A Healthy Modernity*

At the beginning of 1940, news from Hollywood spread in the international press: a major production on the life of Pope Pius XI was underway. The scoop, which appeared in the *Los Angeles Examiner*, came from influential columnist Louella Parsons, "Hollywood's first lady," whose ever-well-informed articles were often given further visibility subsequently in newspapers throughout the world.[1] Between March and August 1940, from the United States to Australia, many newspapers reported that same news. For instance, the 9 May issue of Melbourne-based *Advocate* wrote:

> "I hope Arthur Hornblow's negotiations with Danton Manfredo for 'The Life of Pope Pius XI' are successful," miss Parsons says. "The asking price is 75,000 dollars, and the present Pontiff has given his approval of the story, which is based on the biography of this great Catholic leader. With the world in its present state of turmoil and hatred, it seems fitting that such a picture should be made now, for the late Pope worked unceasingly for world peace. His memory will live in the hearts, not only of Catholics, but of all those who appreciated his efforts for world peace. Those of us who were fortunate enough to have had an audience with him will never forget his fine spiritual face and his gentle bearing. Born Achille Ratti, of poor people, his

---

1   Samantha Barbas, *The First Lady of Hollywood: A Biography of Louella Parsons* (Berkeley and Los Angeles: University of California Press, 2005).

rise to the place at the head of the great Catholic Church is filled with dramatic interest, and Paramount should be able to produce an inspiring picture.[2]

Although the project was not carried out, probably due to worsening of the World War, it remains extremely relevant. Indeed, little more than one year after Pius XI's death, Paramount was eager to produce a biopic on the Pope; one of the most authoritative voices of American film journalism spent very kind words on him; and Pius XII endorsed the project: together these elements reflect the deep transformations that occurred in the relationship between the Catholic Church and cinema during the twenty years of Pius XI's pontificate.

In fact, the most important document of teaching that Ratti explicitly addressed to the US episcopate – and, therefore, implicitly to North American society at large – was the 1936 *Vigilanti Cura*, the first (and, until now, the only) encyclical entirely dedicated to cinema. For pundits in the USA, the most striking element of Pius XI's teaching was represented by a new kind of Catholicism that, by using 'American' methods and languages, had a profound impact on key sectors of the nation's society, and thus increased the number of believers. In fact, when the Pope died in 1939, the American press did not fail to underline that one of the major achievements in Ratti's pontificate had been his fight against Hollywood. On the very day of his death, February 10, 1939, the Pennsylvania daily *The Pittsburgh Press* described his pontificate with the following words:

> During his entire tenure as Supreme Pontiff of the Roman Catholic Church the world was in torment. Like the plagues of Egypt, various "isms" spread over the earth, following the World War. Implacable foe he was to all of them – atheism, agnosticism, Communism, Nazism – yes, and even Fascism, that sprang from his own native soil.

---

2   "Film of Pius XI. Planned," *Advocate*, Melbourne, May 9, 1940. The same news is found in other newspapers including *The Fresno Bee* (Fresno, California, March 5, 1940), *The Courier-Journal* (Louisville, Kentucky, March 6, 1940), *The Observer* (Rockford, Illinois, March 28, 1940), *The Telegraph* (Brisbane, Australia, June 8, 1940) and *Southern Cross* (Adelaide, Australia, August 2, 1940).

And last, but hardly the least – "Hollywood-ism." For it was on the authority of Pope Pius XI that the Catholic hierarchy of the United States launched its crushing crusade against screen indecency and forced the greatest entertainment industry since the world began to scurry to cover. His thundering encyclicals against all manner of evil, wars, antireligious movements, immorality, the divorce menace, time after time stirred a dormant Christianity to militant action, and will most certainly echo down succeeding centuries as masterful documents in defense of the rock-hewn verities.[3]

That same day, the much more authoritative *New York Times* featured five pages on Pius XI's death, and synthesized in one sentence the features and style that had characterized his pontificate: "while conservative – rationally conservative – where the conduct of the Church was concerned, Pope Pius XI was progressive in art and science."[4] The same feature writes that the Pope of "conservative progressivism" succeeded in extending the Church's influence in an unprecedented way, which moreover triggered a great leap forward for Catholicism in North America: "He became the head of a church having 250,000,000 communicants, 17,000,000 of them in the United States; he left it with 330,000,000, of whom 20,000,000 are in this country."[5]

Pius XI's clearly modernizing attitude attracted attention throughout the world. In his postwar *memoir*, Luigi Freddi, who from the thirties onwards became the *deus ex machina* of fascist film policy and was in regular contact with Vatican circles, saw Ratti's 'modernity' as one of the hallmarks of his pontificate. "He was," the fascist leader writes, "among the most vigilant, sensitive, modern and far-sighted [Pontiffs] of the Roman Church: he founded the first Vatican radio station, he empowered the Vatican Observatory, he reformed the science Academy and loved the cinema."[6] Indeed, Pius XI was not scornful of new technologies,

---

3   "Pontiff Made Frequent Attacks on Communism, Hollywood-ism," *Pittsburgh Press*, February 10, 1939.

4   "Pius Progressive in Art and Science," *New York Times*, February 10, 1939.

5   "Principal Events Involving Catholic Church During Incumbency of Pope Pius XI," *New York Times*, February 10, 1939.

6   Luigi Freddi, *Il cinema: il governo dell'immagine* (Roma: L'Arnia 1949; Gremese, 1994), p. 43.

instead he was receptive of the novelties introduced by modern mass society. Ratti believed in a fruitful alliance between science and faith – likely thanks to a religious and cultural education that was characterized by wide-ranging scientific interests[7] – so for instance, during his tenureship as its director, he promoted a radical renewal of the Ambrosian Library.[8] When he became Pope he acted in much the same way with Vatican institutions: he inaugurated the Vatican Pinacoteca and the railway station, he had the Vatican Apostolic Library modernized and the Vatican Observatory renovated. Pius XI's most sensational change was probably the transformation of the Lincean Academy into the Pontifical Academy of Sciences, in 1936. The institution became a sort of Scientific Academy for the Church, which united more than eighty scholars from diverse academic and research backgrounds.[9] This was an open response from Pius XI, that aimed at silencing those who believed that "science, when it is real cognition, is [...] in contrast with the truth of the Christian faith."[10]

However, Ratti's optimism about scientific modernity did not accompany its unconditional acceptance. Tracing out the evolution of his attitude towards cinema enables us to unravel the specific design underlying Pius XI's modernizing statements. These marked a significant departure from his predecessors' actions. During the eighteen years of his pontificate, the Holy See changed its once wary and defensive attitude towards the cinema by devising a clear and refined strategy to align its function to the Church's religious aims. The final goal of the Holy See, though, did not change, and was conveyed by the motto that Pius XI chose for his pontificate – *Pax Christi in regno Christi*: the ecclesiastical authorities repeatedly tried to put the cinema's steady technical

7   Giorgio Vecchio, "Achille Ratti, il movimento cattolico, lo Stato liberale," in *Achille Ratti, pape Pie XI*, Actes du colloque organisé par l'École Française de Rome (Roma: École française de Rome, 1996), pp. 77-82.

8   Carlo Marcora, *Achille Ratti e la Biblioteca Ambrosiana*, in *Achille Ratti, pape Pie XI*, pp. 52-67.

9   Marcelo Sánchez Sorondo, *I papi e la scienza nell'epoca contemporanea* (Milano: Jaca Book, 2009), pp. 15-16.

10   Pio XI, motu proprio *In multis solaciis*, October 28, 1936, in Mario Gargantini, *I Papi e la scienza: antologia del magistero della Chiesa sulla questione scientifica da Leone XIII a Giovanni Paolo II* (Milano: Jaca Book, 1985), pp. 129-31.

and linguistic innovations at the service of this goal, against the background of deep geopolitical transformations, which in turn enhanced the role and significance of mass media.

Until Ratti's era, the relationship between the Church and cinema had developed erratically, with significant differences between centre and periphery. The film portraying Leo XIII in 1898, strolling in the Vatican gardens and blessing the American Mutoscope & Biograph Company's camera, in a highly symbolic gesture, implied the strict control by the Holy See, and its demand to establish the modes and venues of distribution.[11] It thus pre-empted the line of action that characterized the Catholics' attitude in the following years: not a preconceived closure to cinema but instead a conditional opening, one that matched the Church's plans. However, this perspective produced relevant papal teachings only in the second half of Pius XI's pontificate. Before the twenties, the Holy See's few statements were mostly defensive and had one of two aims: either to dictate the terms of a response to a general wave of activism, for or against the new medium, that had characterized the attitudes of Catholics in Europe and America; or to regulate the excessive commercial appetite for images of the Pontiff and Vatican treasures. Pius X, who did not personally sign any instructive documents on cinema, entrusted the catholic curia with the implementation of two significant actions. First, in November 1908, a regulation that reverberated in the international press: photography and film footage in the Vatican and in St. Peter were prohibited unless under the strict control of the Curia. The regulation was issued after the death of photographer Francesco De Federicis. De

---

11   Charles Musser, *The Emergence of Cinema: The American Screen to 1907* (Berkeley/Los Angeles: University of California Press, 1994), pp. 218-21; Elena Mosconi, "Un potente maestro per le folle. Chiesa e mondo cattolico di fronte al cinema," in *Attraverso lo schermo. Cinema e cultura cattolica in Italia*, ed. by Ruggero Eugeni, Dario E. Viganò (Roma: Ente dello Spettacolo, 2006), I, *Dalle origini agli anni Venti*, pp. 145-71; Patrick Loughney, "1898-1899: Movies and Entrepreneurs," in *American Cinema, 1890-1909: Themes and Variations*, ed. by André Gaudrealt (New Brunswick, Rutgers University Press, 2009), pp. 66-90 (pp. 78-80); Federico Ruozzi, "Le fotografie dei pontefici: dal dagherrotipo ai selfie," in *Santi in posa. L'influsso della fotografia nell'immaginario religioso*, ed. by Tommaso Caliò (Roma: Viella, in print).

Federicis had been granted an exclusive to photograph and film
the Vatican, and his passing triggered his relatives to initiate a legal
fight over the usage of pontifical images.[12] Second, in December
1912 the Sacra Congregazione Concistoriale [Sacred Consistorial
Congregation] issued through a decree on "actiones scenicas
in ecclesiis" a further ban, which would never be suppressed.
The Congregation stated that churches consecrated to God,
"in quibus divina celebrantur mysteria et fideles ad caelestia et
supernaturalia eriguntur, ad alios usus et praesertim ad scenicas
actiones etsi honestas piasve agendas converti non debere,
quaslibet proiectiones et cinematographicas repraesentationes
prohibendas omnino esse in ecclesiis censuere."[13] This regulation
should be read in connection with contemporary innovations
in cinematographic language: until that moment the nature of
filmic texts had been, in a certain sense, open and unstable, which
enabled the cinema to enter into sacred spaces. Until then, cinema
had represented a "mixed device,"[14] through which the viewer
was part of an experience that was still largely oriented by the
presenter's commentary. This practice was the modern version of
a typical catholic formula, whereby the words of the preacher had
for centuries been the mediator, presenting images to the wider
public.[15] The emergence of feature films, which occurred at the
beginning of 1910s and provided a visual code for the consumption
of a "homogeneous text, one that was increasingly 'closed' and
structured in its representational autonomy,"[16] signalled more
clearly the impossibility of reaching a compromise between

---

12   "Vatican's Ban Put on Photographers," *Moving Picture World*, November
      28, 1908, p. 425.
13   *Acta Apostolicae Sedis*, vol. IV, 1912, p. 722: "where divine mysteries are
      celebrated and believers are directed towards spiritual and supernatural
      life, should not be used for other activities, and least of all for shows, be
      them also genuine and pious, have decided to strictly forbid any kind of
      cinematographic show in churches."
14   Francesco Casetti and Silvio Alovisio, "Il contributo della Chiesa alla
      moralizzazione degli spazi pubblici," in *Attraverso lo schermo. Cinema e
      cultura cattolica in Italia*, I, pp. 97-127.
15   Lina Bolzoni, *La rete delle immagini: Predicazione in volgare dalle origini a
      Bernardino da Siena* (Torino: Einaudi 2009, 2nd edn).
16   Francesco Casetti and Silvio Alovisio, pp. 120-21.

"traditional sacred rituals and [the] modern ones"[17] represented by cinema. The Church thus shifted its focus to strategize means of controlling an increasingly pervasive medium that had the potential to forge a new mass culture inspired by secular values and habits. The boom of the Hollywood industry and the use of propaganda film during World War I clearly demonstrated that cinema posed a significant threat to the role of the Church in society, by spreading new ideologies, depicting immoral lifestyles or simply ignoring religion. Through the 1910s, the combination of these factors caused frenetic activity: a huge number of pastoral documents and epistles through which national episcopates either condemned immoral movies or encouraged 'good films', the establishment of institutions entrusted with the task of influencing distribution and production, and the proliferation of catholic film journals featuring classification film lists, reviews and articles.[18]

During the first years of his pontificate, Ratti's attitude towards cinema did not radically depart from that of his predecessors. His most striking interventions addressed the burgeoning phenomenon of Hollywood star worship. For example, in 1924, Pius XI granted an audience to Jackie Coogan, the very young star of Charlie Chaplin's *The Kid* and collaborator of the Near East Relief Foundation.[19] This was a clear sign of his gradual and balanced approach to the world of cinema, which he confirmed further two years later, in 1926, when he refused to receive the Hollywood 'perfect couple' – Mary Pickford and Douglas

---

17   *Ibid.*
18   For an outline of the relation between Catholics and cinema from the origins to the twenties see: *Une invention du diable? Cinéma des premiers temps et religion*, ed. by Roland Cosandey, André Gaudreault and Tom Gunning (Lausanne-Québec: Payot/Université de Laval, 1992).
19   The Pontiff awarded Coogan with the golden cross of the Order of Jerusalem and committed itself to bring aid to the kids of an orphanage in Athens. See: "Jackie Coogan's Diary," *Photoplay*, XXVII, February 1925, p. 53; Gian Piero Brunetta, *Il ruggito del Leone. Hollywood alla conquista dell'impero dei sogni nell'Italia di Mussolini* (Venezia: Marsilio 2013), p. 68; Diana Serra Cary, *Jackie Coogan. The World's Boy King: A Biography of Hollywood's Legendary Child Star* (Oxford: The Scarecrow Press, 2003), p. 102.

Fairbanks[20] – during their triumphal journey to Italy, since their "marital status did not perfectly comply with the norms of the catholic doctrine."[21] However, in those same years the Pontiff did not fail to provide clear guidelines on the ways in which the Pope could appear on screen. On the occasion of the great 1925 Jubilee he permitted the private shooting of religious ceremonies excluding those officiated by the Pope himself. Consequently, he entrusted the Central Committee for the Holy Year with the task of "strictly forbidding the cinematic reproduction of any event involving the person of the Pope"[22] in his guise as the supreme minister of Catholic liturgy. At the same time, however, he actually encouraged the use of cinema to foster a new kind of devotion to the Pope, on the condition that this would happen under the strict control of Vatican circles.

As *L'Osservatore Romano* reports, in the immediate aftermath of his coronation, in February 1922, Ratti authorized screenings of the event in the Vatican's Sala Pia.[23] These images then enjoyed broader distribution in the documentary *Nella Roma dei papi*. The film was produced by the Moral and Educational Cinematographic Institute,[24] which had been established in Rome in 1920 by the Salesians with the active support of Ratti's predecessor, Benedict XV.[25] The same production, with the title of *His Holiness Pope Pius XI*, was also widely distributed in the United States from 1923, thanks to the Cleveland Catholic Film Syndicate: as the American press tended to stress, the documentary had been made possible "by the benevolent concession of the holy father so that Catholics throughout the

20 "Mary Pickford e Douglas Fairbanks visti da vicino," *Corriere della Sera*, April 17, 1926.
21 "Il Papa riceverà Fairbanks e la Pickford?," *La Stampa*, April 30, 1926. On the two stars' visit to Italy see, Lorenzo Quaglietti, *Ecco i nostri: l'invasione del cinema americano in Italia* (Torino: Eri-Edizioni Rai, 1991), pp. 41-45.
22 *Cronistoria dell'Anno Santo MCMXXV*, ed. by Segreteria Generale del Comitato Centrale (Roma: Tipografia Poliglotta Vaticana, 1928), p. 87.
23 The news was reported in two short articles entitled 'Sala Pia' in *L'Osservatore Romano*, February 23 and 27-28, 1922.
24 *National Film Archive Catalogue: Part II Silent Non-Fiction Films 1895-1934* (London: The British Film Institute, 1960), p. 127.
25 "Una bella iniziativa benedetta dal S. Padre," *Bollettino Salesiano*, a. XLIV, n. 2, 1920, p. 55.

world might have an opportunity to view these wonderful scenes and the supreme Pontiff himself in his official life."[26] Nevertheless, ecclesiastical authorities struggled in their attempts to control efficiently the circulation of images of the Pontiff, even in the American press. In November 1927, for example, the popular magazine *Variety* broke the news of the sensational protest by "dignitaries of the Catholic Church" against the presentation of a film produced by the Salesians at Syracuse Savoy theatre, "heretofore used for stock burlesque." The dignitaries' "strong disapproval" resulted in the film being screened in a more suitable location: "The Catholic leaders, […] could not see pictures of the faith's sacred ceremonies and ritual flashed on the same stage where thinly garbed dancers and red-nosed comics had just finished scampering."[27] These events illuminate well the increasing concerns of Vatican leaders about cinema, which resulted, on the one hand, in the refusal to authorize footage of the Pontiff in the exercise of sacred liturgy; and on the other in the difficulty to secure adequate usage conditions for 'official' images of the Pope that would not jeopardize the sacredness of his figure.

The Church's increasing interest in cinema would soon become evident even in papal teachings. Indeed, at the turn of the decade Pius XI issued the first magisterial provisions on cinema. These references to the new mass medium can be framed within the important doctrinal output through which the Pontiff responded to the 1929 crisis and to its major financial and social consequences. Previously, in the programmatic encyclical *Ubi arcano*, issued on December 23, 1922, Ratti had maintained that apostasy from the Church was at the origin of the most obscure disasters: "the tremendous sufferings" of World War I had infected the social body with "new horrors;" the "cancer" of class struggle and the "revolutionary spirit" had infiltrated "that sanctuary of peace and love, the family;" "great spiritual misfortunes" were

---

26   "Beautiful Scenes Mark Papal Film," *Altona Tribune*, July 31, 1929. The circulation of the film in the United States was reported also in "His Holiness Pius XI," *Fitchburg Sentinel*, June 9, 1923; "Pope's Pictures Available," *Exhibitors Trade Review*, July 14, 1923, p. 289; "An Impressive Religious Film," *The Educational Screen*, vol. VI, n. 1, 1927, p. 108.

27   "Vatican Film's Wrong Spot," *Variety*, November 9, 1927, p. 22.

caused by the drastic reduction of the clergy and of missionaries;
"we behold with sorrow society lapsing back slowly but surely
into a state of barbarism."[28] For Pius XI such a situation could be
addressed only by restoring the power of the Church, by fulfilling
the kingdom of Christ and therefore by subjecting modern
society to the moral guidance of ecclesiastical hierarchies.[29]
Ratti's ascent to the papal throne and his receptiveness to
technology, science and industrial society had doubtless dimmed
the anti-Modernist legacy that had deeply influenced the first
two decades of the twentieth century.[30] Nevertheless, as far as
concerned the belief that mankind was able to give itself rules,
that is to say the possibility of a modernity that was fully reconciled
with Catholicism, nothing had actually changed. When the
Great Depression came about, the post-War apocalyptic scenario
described in Ratti's first documents was aggravated by further
aspects of capitalistic collapse: the unrestrained accumulation of
wealth and an equally unrestrained consumption, in both private
and public spheres.[31] The cinema was quoted in three encyclicals
denouncing the effects of the abandonment of God by society:
the *Divini Illius Magistri* (December 31, 1929) on the Christian
education of youth, the *Casti connubii* (December 31, 1930) on
Christian marriage, and the *Caritate Christi compulsi* (May 3, 1932),
which for the first time denounced militant and mass atheism.[32]

---

28   Pio XI, *Ubi arcano dei consilio*, December 23, 1922, <http://w2.vatican.va/
     content/pius-xi/it/encyclicals/documents/hf_p-xi_enc_19221223_ubi-
     arcano-dei-consilio.html> [last access July 24, 2017].
29   On the significance of Pius XI's reference to the theology of the regality
     of Christ, see Daniele Menozzi, "Liturgia e politica: l'introduzione alla
     festa di Cristo Re," in *Cristianesimo nella storia. Saggi in onore di Giuseppe
     Alberigo*, ed. by Alberto Melloni, Daniele Menozzi, Giuseppe Ruggieri
     and Massimo Toschi (Bologna: Il Mulino, 1996), pp. 607-56. See also:
     Lucia Ceci, *L'interesse superiore. Il Vaticano e l'Italia di Mussolini* (Roma-Bari:
     Laterza, 2013) pp. 68-74.
30   Renato Moro, "La religione e la 'nuova epoca.' Cattolicesimo e modernità
     tra le due guerre mondiali," in *Il modernismo tra cristianità e secolarizzazione*,
     ed. by Alfonso Botti and Rocco Cerrato, Atti del Convegno internazionale di
     Urbino, October 1-4, 1997 (Urbino: QuattroVenti, 2000), 513-73 (p. 562).
31   Guido Verucci, *La Chiesa nella società contemporanea* (Roma-Bari: Laterza,
     1988), pp. 87-100.
32   *Acta Apostalicae Sedis*, vol. XXII, 1930, pp. 55-86; vol. XXII, pp. 539-92; vol.
     XXIV, 1932, pp. 177-94.

The *Caritate Christi compulsi* saw the origin of all evils in greed, and emphasized that the financial and moral disorder caused by the crisis posed the grave danger of widespread atheism, which, then more than ever, was able to infiltrate a society thanks to modern means of entertainment and communication, through theatre, cinema, the gramophone and the radio. Such a menace could be overcome, once again, solely by returning to God, by devoting oneself to the Sacred Heart, and through atonement. Implicit in Ratti's argument was the notion that the disastrous effects of cinema – not only for Catholics, but to society as a whole – depended on the fact that the Church's pre-eminent role in defining its correct usage had not been acknowledged. Therefore, even in the case of cinema, it was crucially important to draw a distinction between "healthy modernity" and the refusal of the alternative, the modernity that did not reconcile the Church's plans.[33]

2. Radio and Cinema: Producing the First "Talkie" on the Pope

In the meanwhile, on February 12, 1931, the Vatican Radio station was inaugurated, marking a very significant innovation. The radio station was Ratti's ambition, and it came about thanks to his collaboration with Guglielmo Marconi. The event clearly demonstrates the Holy See's attempts to embrace modern communication techniques in order to master them and to use them for the Church's specific needs.[34] The fact that such a task was entrusted to Marconi, by then a symbol of modern inventiveness, was significant in more than one way. The Church seized the opportunity to create a direct channel between the Holy See and believers all over the world, and to let the Pope's voice – his *real* voice – be heard worldwide. This implied the

---

33   Renato Moro, "La religione e la 'nuova epoca'," p. 563.
34   Raffaella Perin, *La radio del papa. Propaganda e diplomazia nella seconda guerra mondiale* (Bologna: Il Mulino, 2017); Alberto Monticone, "La radio vaticana tra fascismo e guerra, in Chiesa e società dal secolo 4° ai nostri giorni," in *Studi storici in onore di p. Ilarino da Milano*, ed. by the Istituto di Storia della Facoltà di Magistero dell'Università di Perugia (Roma: Herder, 1979), pp. 681-727.

highest degree of technical innovation, which would set Vatican Radio well above national radio stations, and, especially Italian radio, which was still in its embryonic stages. Secondly, the entire operation was deliberately presented as scientific, demonstrating the Holy See's desire to "stress the compatibility between the Word inspired by the Gospel and advances in sciences."[35] It is no coincidence, therefore, that the inauguration of the radio station should take place in the Casina Pio IV in the Vatican Gardens, on the very same day as Marconi's nomination at the Lincean Academy.[36]

Furthermore, Jesuit Giuseppe Gianfranceschi's appointment as director of the Vatican's radio provided a further indication of the Holy See's shift to modern means of communication.[37] The famous mathematician and physicist, Gianfranceschi, who had been chaplain of Umberto Nobile's team during its first expedition to the North Pole in 1928, had also been president of the Lincean Accademy since 1921 – an appointment that Pius XI renewed, since he wanted Gianfranceschi to control the internationalization process leading to the Pontifical Academy of Sciences. Gianfranceschi's appointment, therefore, meant that the radio activities would be managed by the Vatican's scientific institution: and in fact one of Gianfranceschi's first decisions was to launch the *Scientiarum Nuncius Radiophonicus*, "spoken news" that reported on a regular basis, and exclusively in Latin, scientific research and new discoveries.[38] Despite the fact that

---

35   Alberto Monticone, p. 683. On the technological advances of Vatican
      Radio (compared to other radio stations) see Giuseppe Gianfranceschi,
      "La Stazione Radiotelegrafica a onde corte della Città del Vaticano,"
      L'Elettrotecnica, vol. XVIII, n. 29, October 15, 1931, 733. In Italy, the State
      begin to play an active role in radio production only in the thirties:
      regular broadcasting began in 1924, in 1927 the number of subscribers
      (called "licenze") was 41,000, rising to 241,000 in 1931, 997,000 in 1938
      and 1,800,000 in 1943. See David Forgacs, *L'industrializzazione della cultura
      italiana (1880-2000)* (Bologna: Il Mulino, 2000), pp. 94-101.
36   Fernando Bea and Alessandro De Carolis, *Ottant'anni della radio del Papa
      (1931-2011)* (Città del Vaticano: Libreria editrice vaticana, 2011), pp.
      45-49.
37   Sabino Maffeo, "Padre Giuseppe Gianfranceschi e Guglielmo Marconi.
      A cinquant'anni dall'inaugurazione del primo ponte radio," *La Civiltà
      Cattolica,* a. 136, vol. 1, n. 3229, January 5, 1985, 62-67.
38   Alberto Monticone, p. 684.

it clashed somewhat with the technological modernity of the medium, Pius XI chose Latin as the language for his first speech on the radio, thus cloaking the modern medium in old and traditional clothes.[39] Cardinal Carlo Confalonieri, who was then Ratti's personal assistant, later remembered that "when asked why he had spoken in Latin, using almost exclusively the Scripture's words," the Pope answered "that Latin was the Church's universal language and that, on such a genuinely ecumenical encounter, the word of God – '*Pater et Dominus universae creaturae*' – would reach everyone, undisputed and welcome."[40]

However, the radio station's inauguration on February 12, 1931 was not only the moment when this "conservative modernization"[41] became mostly apparent; it also marked the occasion when the Roman Curia became aware of the bewildering tangle of financial interests surrounding the Pope's figure within the film industry, and the significant difficulties that they faced in efficiently controlling it.

A note from the State Secretariat dated November 1930 clearly shows that big American newsreel companies were genuinely interested in producing the first "sound movie"[42] about the Pope. "To gauge the value that a movie about the Holy Father would have," – the note reads – "suffice it to think that the 'Augusto Pontefice' [Venerable Pontiff] is the only person who had not accepted to be filmed in a sound movie."[43] It emphasizes that many film studios

---

39 Pio XI, *Qui Arcano Dei*, in *Acta Apostalicae Sedis*, vol. XXIII, 1931, p. 65. The Italian text was published in *Il primo radiomessaggio a tutte le genti e ad ogni creatura*, 12 febbraio 1931, in *Discorsi di Pio XI*, ed. by Domenico Bertetto (Città del Vaticano: Libreria Editrice Vaticana, 1985, 2nd edn), II, *1929-1933*, pp. 479-83.

40 Carlo Confalonieri, *Pio XI visto da vicino* (Torino: SAIE, 1957; Cinisello Balsamo: Edizioni Paoline, 1993), p. 99.

41 The expression "conservative modernization" (modernizzazione reazionaria) is borrowed from Renato Moro, "Il 'modernismo buono'. La modernizzazione cattolica tra fascismo e postfascismo come problema storiografico," *Storia Contemporanea*, a. XIX, n. 4, 1988, 625-716 (p. 714).

42 Segreteria di Stato, S.RR.SS., Archivio Storico, AA.EE.SS., Stati Ecclesiastici, IV, Pos. 445, Fasc. 406, f. 17r, Vatican City Governor's note on Paramount News: "Film parlante."

43 *Ibid.*: "Per apprezzare quanto valore avrebbe un film del Santo Padre è sufficiente pensare che l'Augusto Pontefice è l'unico che finora non ha consentito d'essere preso dal cinema parlante."

had "tried in every way," for years, "to achieve this goal," they had
sent "men from America, among which S.R. Richard W. Child,
former US ambassador in Italy, who got paid 10,000 dollars for the
task."[44] The note furthermore provides details of the negotiations
that the Holy See – which, until that moment, had made the
fascist institution L'Unione Cinematografica Educativa [hereafter
LUCE] the sole agent permitted to shoot footage featuring the
Pope – had entered on that occasion. Though William Fox in
person had demonstrated his clear interest by declaring that "a
sound movie featuring the Pope would be of inestimable value,"[45]
and although the Pope had explicitly expressed his preference
for LUCE (which, however, had not invested in technology yet),
the State Secretariat made Paramount News the sole agent after
long negotiations with Bixio Alberini, the Italian correspondent
of the American company. The Vatican was, however, aware of the
risks that such an operation entailed. "The film," we read in the
notes of the State Secretariat, "would be shown in movie theatres
worldwide together with immoral movies. The company with the
privilege of producing it could profit from it extraordinarily."[46]
The Vatican office, however, estimated that the financial potential
of the Los Angeles studio would guarantee a high investment in
the project and "ensure a successful outcome."[47] The American
studio therefore came to film the historical event, which was
shown in US movie theatres.

Nevertheless, once the Pope's image began to be available
worldwide through the Paramount newsreels, Vatican circles were
not at all satisfied with the final results. The risks outlined by the
State Secretariat's note proved to be prescient, as reveals another
of its memoranda written some years later, on the occasion of
the extraordinary Holy Year 1933-1934. On that circumstance the

---

44   *Ibid.*: "Provato in tutte le maniere di riuscirvi;" "uomini dall'America tra i
      quali S. R. Richard W. Child, l'ex ambasciatore degli Stati Uniti in Italia il
      quale riceveva dollari 10.000 a tale scopo."
45   *Ibid.*: "Il valore della Film parlante del Santo Padre sarebbe inestimabile."
46   *Ibid.*: "Il film sarebbe di certo esposto nei teatri del mondo insieme con
      altre film poco buone. La Compagnia che avesse il privilegio di fare
      questa film potrebbe specularvi sopra in maniera straordinaria."
47   Segreteria di Stato, S.RR.SS., Archivio Storico, AA.EE.SS., Stati
      Ecclesiastici, IV, Pos. 445, Fasc. 406, f. 16r, Memorandum Paramount
      News, s.d.: "Sicura garanzia del buon esito."

Holy See opted to produce and distribute its own Jubilee film, recalling the "serious inconveniences generated by the film of the inauguration of the short-wave Vatican radio station."[48] The memorandum specifies that the film produced by the "Paramount Picture Corporation" "was shown in movie theatres together with other movies that were not decent enough, and alongside vaudeville shows."[49]

Nonetheless, two years after the radio inauguration, Paramount was again appointed to shoot footage of a new phase in the alliance between Marconi and the Vatican. In February 1933 the ultra-short wave station connecting the Vatican City with the Pontifical Palace at Castel Gandolfo was inaugurated.[50] This was probably the first time that a Pontiff spoke spontaneously in front of a camera. In the film, which was later included in a LUCE newsreel,[51] the contrast between pontifical solemnity and Ratti's non-linear, improvised clauses clearly emerges. The mixture of modernity and tradition in the words that the Pontiff directly addressed to Marconi conveyed the very gist of his approach:

> We asked you to give us some...some notion, some experience or experiment of how you... and in which snares of science you found the way to these waves that no one sees and no one hears. [...] In fact, our curiosity remains, our desire to know why the human mind sees, so to speak, sees such a distinct vision, why it measures, with such exact measurements, what eyes cannot see and hands cannot reach. [...] We must therefore congratulate you again for what divine bounty, divine power has allowed you to achieve and to do, so that the secrets of divine omnipotence and of divine knowledge,

---

48   Segreteria di Stato, S.RR.SS., Archivio Storico, AA.EE.SS., Stati Ecclesiastici, IV, Pos. 445, Fasc. 409, ff. 11-12r, Memorandum s.d.: "I gravi inconvenienti sorti in occasione del film dell'inaugurazione della Stazione Radio Vaticana ad Onde Corte."

49   *Ibid.*: "nei cinema venne presentato al pubblico unitamente ad altre produzioni non sufficientemente castigate ed al Varietà."

50   "Visita del Santo Padre alla Radio," *L'Osservatore Romano*, March 1, 1933, see also *1929-2009: ottanta anni dello Stato della Città del Vaticano*, ed. by Barbara Jatta (Città del Vaticano: Biblioteca Apostolica Vaticana, 2009), p. 410.

51   Luce Historical Archive, "S. S. Pio XI e S. E. Marconi inaugurano la nuova stazione a onde ultra corte che collega la Città del Vaticano e il Palazzo pontificio di Castelgandolfo," Cinegiornale Luce B0211, 02/1933, b/n, sonoro, 5' 30".

which governs everything so amazingly, will truly bring benefits for
humankind, significant benefits considering what our endangered
humankind has already experienced. [52]

The Pope's curiosity and wonder for the "snares of science" had
a necessary corollary, that is, the need to bring everything back to
supreme divine law. Only by acknowledging that human inventions
were gifts bestowed, through science, by divine knowledge could
they become "true benefits" for "our humankind in danger."

3. The Pacelli-Pizzardo Axis and the Jesuit Network

The change in the Pontiff's attitude was therefore determined
by sound doctrinal reasons. Still, at the beginning of the thirties,
two further events, albeit quite apart from one-another, were
crucial in framing the very question of cinema from a wider
perspective. [53] The technological revolution within the film

52   *Ibid.*: "Le chiedevamo di darci qualche... qualche senso, qualche esperienza
       o esperimento del come ella, e da quali agguati della scienza, ella sorprenda
       il cammino di queste onde che nessuno vede e nessuno ode. [...] Resta
       tuttavia, resta intera la nostra curiosità, il nostro desiderio di sapere come
       mai la mente umana veda, per così dire veda, di una visione così distinta,
       misuri, con misurazioni così esatte, quello che l'occhio non vede e che la
       mano non raggiunge. [...] Non possiamo almeno che rinnovarle tutta la
       nostra... la nostra... le nostre congratulazioni per quello che la divina bontà,
       la divina potenza ha concesso a lei di raggiungere e di fare affinché i segreti
       appunto della divina onnipotenza e della divina sapienza che tutto così
       mirabilmente governa diventino dei veri benefici per l'umanità, benefici
       già grandi per quello che l'umanità pericolante ne ha esperimentato." The
       official text was published by *L'Osservatore Romano*: "L'inaugurazione della
       Stazione Radio a onde ultracorte," February 13-14, 1933.
53   Recently, scholars have shed new light on the Papacy in the thirties, having
       been able to work on the documents on Ratti's pontificate available at
       the Vatican Archive since 2006. Historians have progressively abandoned
       the mainly national perspective that had characterized the study of
       nineteenth and twentieth-century pontificates, instead embracing a
       transnational and at times global perspective and revising contemporary
       Church history. The most recent outcome of this line of research is to be
       found in *Pio XI nella crisi europea*, Atti del Colloquio di Villa Vigoni, May
       4-6, 2015, ed. by Raffaella Perin (Venezia: Edizioni Ca' Foscari, 2016);
       Gouvernement pontifical sous Pie XI. Pratiques romaines et gestion de l'universel,
       ed. by Laura Pettinaroli (Roma: Ecole Française de Rome, 2013).

industry, on the one hand, and the solution to the age-old 'Roman question' on the other, lay the foundations for a new, international film policy.

The expansion of the film industry caused by the emergence of sound movies made much clearer, also to the Hierarchy, the challenge that cinema posed to the Roman Church's universal design. The flexibility of the new medium and its ability to accompany or even to emphasize the great transformations of those years struck Vatican observers: with its billionaire income, the cinema was clearly becoming the main actor in the entertainment business and the bridge-head for the "irresistible" rise of the US "market empire."[54] The cinema was at the same time an innovative teaching instrument, which was used by several educational institutions, both public and private, and an extraordinary means of propaganda – crucial for the "aestheticization of politics" by burgeoning totalitarian regimes.[55]

In such a context, the finalization of the Lateran Pacts with the Italian State in 1929, which improved the negotiations between the Church and modern societies that were initiated under Leo XIII's pontificate and intensified during the years of World War I, made Vatican leaders more receptive to contemporary changes. The Lateran Pacts with Fascism, in fact, allowed the Pontiff – who was finally released from secular concerns – to find new ways to exert his proclaimed universal *auctoritas*.[56] We can therefore speak of the Holy See's new global charisma, which took on the question of cinema and had immediate institutional consequences.

Soon after the signing of the Lateran Pacts, two figures, whose cultural background and scope of action reached well beyond the precinct of St. Peter, played a key role in the Church's appropriation of cinema: Cardinal Eugenio Pacelli, appointed Secretary of State on February 7, 1930, and Monsignor Giuseppe Pizzardo, a very influential member of the Roman Curia. Just a

---

54 Victoria de Grazia, *Irresistible Empire: America's Advance through Twentieth-Century Europe* (Cambridge: Belknap Press of Harvard University Press, 2005).

55 Mario Pezzella, pp. 26-28.

56 This question has been widely investigated. For a general survey, see Manlio Graziano, *Il secolo cattolico. La strategia geopolitica della Chiesa* (Roma-Bari: Laterza, 2010), pp. 43-51.

few months before Pacelli's nomination, Pizzardo reached the highest stage in his career at the Secretariat of State (where he had begun in 1912 in the capacity of drafter) by becoming secretary to the Sacra Congregazione per gli Affari Straordinari [Sacred Congregation for Extraordinary Ecclesiastical Affairs]. Pacelli proved immediately receptive to cinema by designing and implementing a series of initiatives which provided the foundations of his subsequent approach to the field when he was elected Pontiff. Yet in certain aspects Pizzardo's contribution was even more strategic: though he maintained a low-profile, an informative note by the fascist police (dated 1929) defines him as "the most important and dominant figure" after Cardinal Pietro Gasparri, the "primary confidant and advisor" to Pius XI:[57] in fact, following the 1923 statutory reform, the Pope had appointed the prelate as ecclesiastical assistant at Italian Catholic Action, thus assigning him a key role as leader of the association that most shaped his policy. Pizzardo's two-fold role within the Church hierarchy proved to be of crucial importance in Catholic film policy, too: a policy that was based in Italy but developed at an international level, two sides that together characterized pontifical actions in the field from the thirties onward.[58] Pizzardo, who ran a sort of Ministry of Foreign Affairs that answered directly to the Secretariat of State, shaped the Holy See's involvement in cinema as an issue of foreign policy.[59]

The Pacelli-Pizzardo axis, therefore, shaped a complex institutional architecture that, in-keeping with the general trend in Vatican affairs, was structured on the dialectics between

---

57   State Central Archives of Italy, Ministry of Internal Affairs, Public Security Division, Political Police Division, Personal folders, Series B, envelope 19, folder: "Pizzardo, monsignore," Roma, August 13, 1929: "il personaggio più importante e dominante;" "primo confidente e consigliere." See also Carlo M. Fiorentino, *All'ombra di Pietro: la Chiesa cattolica e lo spionaggio fascista in Vaticano 1929-1939* (Firenze: Le Lettere, 1999), pp. 85-101.

58   On the significance of Pizzardo's 'double career' within the Holy See, see Giuliana Chamedes, "Contro il totalitarismo di Stato. Il Cardinal Pizzardo e l'internazionalizzazione dell'Azione cattolica," in *Gouvernement pontifical sous Pie XI. Pratiques romaines et gestion de l'universel*, pp. 359-77.

59   On the Holy See's international policy under Pius XI's pontificate see, among others, *Diplomazia senza eserciti. Le relazioni internazionali della Chiesa di Pio XI*, ed. by Emma Fattorini (Roma: Carocci, 2013).

internationalization and Romanization. On one side, the axis empowered the government structures that dealt with the process of global transformations, on the other it promoted centralization as well a monarchization of ecclesiastical institutions, so that catholic policies could be safely controlled from Rome. This centralized organization was accompanied by the strong clericalization of the governance in charge of film policy. Hence Pacelli's and Pizzardo's central positions and the appointment of men coming from the ecclesiastical apparatus acted as tools for the Roman authorities: on the one hand, pontifical representatives tasked with establishing and maintaining relationships with foreign episcopates and civil governments; on the other, the transnational network of Jesuits, which traditionally represented the catholic *intelligentsia*, with a long-standing experience in culture, the media and education.

Under the shrewd and authoritarian guide of Superior General Włodzimierz Ledóchowski – who had a close relationship to Pius XI – and having secured the management of a key asset of Vatican communication that was its radio station, the Jesuits succeeded in placing their people in strategic positions within the field of cinema. This was the case for Daniel A. Lord, among the ablest policy-makers in the United States, and the German Friedrich Muckermann, who played an important role in several cinema-related issues in Europe and who, together with French-American Joseph H. Ledit, was an expert on the Soviet cinema system. Not to forget, in Italy, Pietro Tacchi Venturi who, despite being less of an expert on cinema, was nonetheless able to exploit his role as the unofficial *trait d'union* between Mussolini and the Holy See on more than one occasion, to meet Pius XI's demands.

In fact, the Jesuits' awareness of cinema's importance is also evident in the attention they dedicated to the medium in their journals and magazines. From the twenties, several articles had appeared in French *Études* that aimed to warn readers against the "social danger" posed by "corrupting movies."[60] The journal

---

60 Michel Lagrée, "L'encyclique Vigilanti Cura sur le cinéma (1936)," in *Achille Ratti, pape Pie XI*, 839-853 (p. 841); Laura Pettinaroli, *La politique russe du Saint-Siège (1905-1939)*, PhD dissertation, Université Lumière Lyon 2, 2008 (tutor Prof. Claude Prud'homme), pp. 738-39.

America, directed by Father Wilfrid Parson, strategically supported the campaign launched by the American episcopate against Hollywood films.[61] The Italian journal, *La Civiltà Cattolica,* paid constant attention to cinema from a very early stage. Between 1914 and 1919, with remarkable advances within the Catholic cultural field, the journal dedicated a significant series of articles to the new medium, with a special focus on the reform of censorship.[62] Its engagement with issues related to film did not diminish in the following years, when, with the emergence of sound, cinema acquired even greater importance at a global level. In this sense, Father Mario Barbera's 1934 article is particularly relevant: Barbera surveyed the rapid development of the cinema as one of the key factors influencing public opinion. The new medium was so pervasive that it had almost superseded the press, undermining the latter's predominance in the media system. With his at times apocalyptical tone, the Jesuit prophesied the advent of a technological monster, the "tele-cine-radio," which would undermine the three powers – legislative, judicial and executive – of the State.[63]

4. *Vatican Film Geopolitics*

Within the complex institutional architecture described in the previous section, it is possible to outline the map of pontifical film geopolitics. The United States, the Soviet Union and Europe were the three areas of focus for the Vatican offices, each one with a specific strategy. America, with its great Hollywood "dream factory" was undoubtedly on top of the Vatican's agenda. This was partly due to the fact that, during the Fascist period, Rome – as anybody who ventured for a walk outside the Leonine walls would have noticed – underwent major transformations, in which the

---

61   See Stephen Vaughn, "Film Censorship in America. The Motion Picture Production Code of 1930, Before the Codes 2. The Gateway to Hays" ed. by Giuliana Muscio, XLVIII Mostra internazionale d'arte cinematografica (Milano: Fabbri, 1991), pp. 81-86.

62   Francesco Casetti and Silvio Alovisio, pp. 113-19.

63   Mario Barbera, "Il I Congresso internazionale del cinema educativo," *La Civiltà Cattolica,* a. 85, vol. 2, n. 2016, June 16, 1934, p. 578.

lure of the new "Hollywood religion" actually played a key role, in spite of Mussolini's attempts to promote "integral education" for Italians. Furthermore, the advent of sound cinema animated the American film industry's interest in Vatican affairs. This was the moment, therefore, when the Pontiff and the Curia understood the true power of cinema. As such, from the early thirties the Holy See sought to establish direct contact with the main influential figures in the Hollywood film industry by building a diplomatic network, thanks to the joint efforts of Pacelli and Pizzardo, on the one hand, and on the other of Monsignor Amleto Cicognani, who, in March 1933, was appointed pontifical delegate at the Apostolic Nunciature of the Holy See in Washington DC. In one of the most detailed reports on cinema that he sent to Rome, Cicognani presented an alarming picture of the situation, which solicited the papacy's interest in the issue. In his view, American cinema was becoming one of the most insidious hindrances to the social restoration of the Kingdom of Christ – which was one of the key points of Pius XI's pontificate. As Cicognani wrote to Pacelli in July 1934:

> As far as cinema is concerned, America rules the world: more than 84% of films produced worldwide come from the United States; and 90% of the American production is provided by eight big companies based in Hollywood, California, which, in fact, all go by the name of Hollywood. In general, it can be said that producers have lost all moral sense, and that cinema has become a school for perversion and immorality for the 70 million people going to the movies every week in North America.[64]

---

64 ASV, Segreteria di Stato, a. 1934, rubr. 325, fasc. 6, "Campagna dell'Episcopato nord-americano contro il cinematografo immorale," report 9070, Amleto Cicognani to Eugenio Pacelli, July, 27, 1934: "L'America domina il mondo per quel che riguarda la cinematografia; - più dell'84% di tutte le pellicole che si producono nel mondo vengono dagli Stati Uniti; - e il 90% di questa produzione Americana è confezionato da otto grandi società che hanno centro ad Hollywood in California e sono chiamate col nome generico di Hollywood; - si può dire in generale che i produttori hanno perduto ogni senso morale, e il cinema è divenuto scuola di pervertimento e d'immoralità ai 70 milioni di persone che in media vi assistono ogni settimana, nell'America del Nord."

From that moment, the Holy See undertook two types of action. On one side Cicognani acted behind the scenes, promoting a crusade to moralize Hollywood, beginning in November 1933 when the American Episcopate established the Legion of Decency.[65] From August 1934 to April 1936 at least ten reports on the matter were sent to the Vatican by Cicognani. On the other side, the prelate attempted to enter the Hollywood control room by maintaining personal relationships with its most influential members. This included Joseph I. Breen, a conservative Catholic who, in June 1934, had been appointed chief of the Production Code Administration [hereafter PCA]; Martin Quigley, catholic editor of an important magazine by movie exhibitors – the *Exhibitor's Herald World* –; and the influential promoter of the Hollywood's self-censorship code and of the Motion Picture Producers and Distributors of America [hereafter MPPDA], Will H. Hays. The latter, a Presbyterian with a "religious spirit" but inspired by "moral principles" that were not "fully compliant" with Catholic ones, as Cicognani wrote to the Vatican after meeting him in October 1935,[66] was received for a private audience with Pius XI in November 1936.

On that crucial occasion, the Pontiff made it clear that the Holy See's interest in establishing direct contact with the American entertainment industry was also an attempt to unite against the expansion of Soviet cinema. As Hays himself writes in his memoir:

> In the midst of the conversation the Pope picked up a big loose-leaf book, two or three inches thick, lying on his table, and pushed

65   The Legion of Decency is the subject of several studies, mainly by American historians, who, therefore, have worked mainly on American sources. Recent studies include Alexander McGregor, *The Catholic Church and Hollywood. Censorship and Morality in 1930s Cinema* (London: I.B. Tauris & Co. Ltd, 2013); and Gregory Black, "The Legion of Decency and the Movies" in *Silencing Cinema: Film Censorship around the World*, ed. by Daniel Biltereyst and Roel Vande Winkel (New York: Palgrave, 2013), pp. 241–54.

66   Segreteria di Stato, S.RR.SS., Archivio Storico, AA.EE.SS., Stati Ecclesiastici, IV, pos. 445, fasc. 416, ff. 31-36r, Amleto Cicognani to Giuseppe Pizzardo, report n. 12902/35, October 28, 1935: "dotato di spirito religioso;" "criteri morali;" "del tutto conformi."

it toward me. He explained that this volume of reports contained the series of original communiqués sent out from the Comintern in Moscow to comrades and fellow travelers all over the world, and that one of the most emphatic orders was to "go out get hold of the cinema of the world."[67]

The Vatican considered Soviet cinema as a fatal alliance between ideology and media, that could amplify the effects of anti-religious campaigns. Its awareness of the power of Soviet propaganda techniques was, in fact, one of the central aspects that characterized the change in the Holy See's attitude towards Communism during the thirties. The failed attempts to empower a clandestine Catholic hierarchy in Russia, under the control of Jesuit Michel D'Herbigny (president of the *Pro Russia* pontifical commission), brought to an end a phase in which the Holy See had tried to take a prevailingly diplomatic and pastoral approach towards the Soviet regime. At the same time, episodes of anti-religious violence in Mexico and Spain (territories newly conquered by Bolshevism) had increased, in-keeping with the growing consensus for communist parties in several countries.[68]

Papal teaching therefore began to account for the danger represented by the Communist power system. Thanks to its concentration of the nexus between mass society and a transnational notion of politics, it was the "first genuinely 'anti-religious' phenomenon in modern world history,"[69] one that could potentially grip Catholicism in a deadly embrace. In this regard, in April 1932, the international inquiry on communism

---

67   William Harrison Hays, *The Memoirs of Will H. Hays* (New York: Doubleday & Company, 1955), p. 522. On Ratti's audience with Hays from the Vatican's point of view, see Ernesto Ugo Gramazio, "Colloquio con William Hays. Lo 'zar del cinematografo'," *L'Osservatore Romano*, November 20, 1936.

68   In addition to the recent studies that draw on current archival discoveries (which are cited in the following footnotes), a useful and ever valid reference that reconstructs the relationship between the Church and Communist Russia in the interwar period remains Antoine Wenger, *Rome et Moscou. 1900-1950* (Paris: Desclée de Brouwer, 1981).

69   Daniele Menozzi and Renato Moro, "Conclusioni," in *Cattolicesimo e totalitarismo. Chiese e culture religiose tra le due guerre mondiali (Italia, Spagna, Francia)*, ed. by Daniele Menozzi and Renato Moro (Brescia: Morcelliana, 2004), p. 378.

promoted by the Secretariat of State included, in its focus, the use of cinema for propaganda: Pacelli sent a circular letter to all pontifical representatives, demanding that they inform the Holy See "on the manifestations, means of propaganda, and progress of Communism in various countries."[70] Another document, enclosed with the letter and entitled *Notes on Communist Propaganda*,[71] outlines an organizational system that had its main seat in Moscow and was entrusted to the International League of Militant Atheists, which was "actively extended to all countries in the world" and intended to "encourage a simultaneous social and political revolution throughout the world."[72] It devoted particular attention to the "anti-religious efforts of the Third International," whose specific targets were "monotheistic religions, therefore also Judaism and Islam, but above all the Catholic Church."[73] The document described in detail the guidelines that oriented the Soviet propaganda network; among the "ways of taking people away from any religions" were listed "the press, conferences, and above all the cinema."[74] The answers that nuncios and delegates were to send to Rome were to report: "Propaganda spread through the press, flyers, bills, caricatures, films. Please signal

---

70   Segreteria di Stato, S.RR.SS., Archivio Storico, AA.EE.SS., IV, Stati Ecclesiastici, Pos. 474, Fasc. 475, f. 24r: Pacelli's circular is dated April 14, 1932: "circa le manifestazioni, i mezzi di propaganda, i progressi del comunismo nei diversi paesi."

71   *Ibid.*, ff. 25rv-26r: "Note circa la propaganda comunista." The document has been analysed in several recent studies: the general context is outlined in particular by L. Pettinaroli, *La politique russe du Saint-Siège (1905-1939)*, pp. 733-36. See also: Filippo Frangioni, "L'URSS e la propaganda contro la religione. Per una definizione dell'anticomunismo nella Santa Sede degli anni Trenta," in *Pius XI: Keywords. International Conference Milan 2009*, ed. by Alberto Guasco and Raffaella Perin (Berlin/Munster/Vienna/Zurich/London: LIT Verlag, 2010), pp. 300-03.

72   Segreteria di Stato, S.RR.SS., Archivio Storico, AA.EE.SS., IV, Stati Ecclesiastici, Pos. 474, Fasc. 475, f. 24r and ff. 25rv-26r: "Attivamente in tutti i paesi del mondo;" "suscitare una simultanea rivoluzione mondiale d'ordine politico e sociale."

73   *Ibid.*: "Lo sforzo antireligioso della terza Internazionale;" "di mira specialmente le religioni monoteiste, quindi anche il giudaismo e il maomettismo, ma soprattutto la Chiesa cattolica."

74   *Ibid.*: "Mezzi per distogliere il popolo da ogni religione;" "la stampa, le conferenze, ma specialmente il cinema."

films, and in particular those of Russian origin, even if they might at first sight seem anodyne."[75]

All in all, the inquiry strengthened the belief that Soviet propaganda was spreading in several European and extra-European countries, and that it had an extraordinary ability to adapt to diverse local contexts.[76] While it was not the first time in European history that a revolutionary state was established, its novelty lay in the fact that Soviet Union was particularly good at making proselytes, in organizing them, and in animating constellations of states that were inspired by the same ideals. In this way, communism inspired new messianic and universal expectations that were inevitably perceived as the ultimate challenge, insofar as issued on their own territory, to Roman Catholic authorities.[77]

The cinema, therefore, stood to some extent for the anti-religious side of communism, as not only a mean of fiendish propaganda but also, concretely, a symbol of the Bolshevik's radical transformations in urban space that sought to establish the new religion of godless people. The destruction of orthodox and catholic churches, or indeed any other religious building, and their subsequent conversion into movie theatres, clubs, warehouses etc. was, for many years, the image used by catholic reports to convey the anti-religious fury that was passing through villages and cities.[78]

---

75   *Ibid.*: "Propaganda stampata con giornali, fogli, cartelli, caricature, films. Importa specialmente segnalare le films [sic] d'origine russa, anche se sembrano da principio anodine."

76   Elisa Giunipero, "Le inchieste sul comunismo," in *Gouvernement pontifical sous Pie XI. Pratiques romaines et gestion de l'universel*, pp. 191-202.

77   On the characteristics of the history of communism as the transnational political phenomenon *par excellence*, see in particular Silvio Pons, *La rivoluzione globale. Storia del comunismo internazionale 1917-1991* (Torino: Einaudi, 2012).

78   Evidence of this in the catholic press is for example to be found in: "La Russia infelice sotto il calcagno comunista. Non più chiese a Leningrado dopo il 1° maggio 1930," *L'Osservatore Romano*, February 28, 1930; "I vandali insaziabili. La cattedrale di Mosca distrutta con la dinamite," *L'Osservatore Romano*, December 11, 1931; "Tutte le chiese sono aperte, tutti i culti sono permessi...," *L'Osservatore Romano*, December 12, 1931; "Crisi nell'ateismo militante sovietico," *La Civiltà Cattolica*, a. 86, vol. 1, n. 2034, March 16, 1935, p. 566; Enrico Rosa, "Arti di propaganda e nuove conquiste del bolscevismo," *La Civiltà Cattolica*, a. 86, vol. 4, n. 2050, November 16, 1935, p. 268.

The burgeoning expansion of Soviet cinema across the globe, linked as it was to growing anti-religious violence in Mexico and Spain, spurred a greater involvement of the Society of Jesus. As it is known, the Society was a key actor in negotiations between the Catholic Church and Marxism; it also promoted action that aimed to reveal the inner workings of communist propaganda.[79] It is little surprise, therefore, that the inquiry promoted by Pacelli progressed steadily in part thanks to the Jesuits, who, in 1934, founded the Special Secretariat on Atheism. Directed by Father Joseph Ledit, Professor of Russian History at the Pontifical Oriental Institute, the Secretariat, where also Muckermann assiduously worked, became the main international hub for the collection and organization of information on the communist world.[80]

Drawing on his experience at the Secretariat, in *La religione e il comunismo* [*Religion and Communism*], the volume collecting the proceedings of conferences held at Catholic University of Milan in summer 1936, Ledit provided a detailed and thorough analysis of Communist cinema from a Catholic point of view.[81] Ledit maintained that Soviet films were significant propaganda materials, and extremely challenging at that, because the film industry in the Soviet Union had "won a bet, being at the same time producer of pure propaganda and of technically well-made products." Thus Ledit accounted for the worldwide success of directors Èjzenštejn's and Pudovkin's *montages*:

> According to Soviet film theory, directors should appeal to the subconscious; as one of them once said, speaking to his friends: "We have to connect four or five different elements: element A, alone,

---

79   See in particular: Giorgio Petracchi, "I Gesuiti e il comunismo tra le due guerre," in *La Chiesa cattolica e il totalitarismo*, ed. by Vincenzo Ferrone (Firenze: Olschki 2004), pp. 123-52.

80   Elisa Giunipero, p. 196.

81   Joseph Ledit, *La religione e il comunismo* (Milano: Vita e Pensiero, 1937), pp. 35-40. Ledit's analysis relies on and synthesizes some of his previous articles on the issue of cinema, including "Crisi nell'ateismo militante sovietico," *La Civiltà Cattolica*, a. 86, vol. 1, n. 2034, March 16, 1935, 561-75; "La nuova condanna del comunismo," *La Civiltà Cattolica*, a. 88, vol. 2, n. 2083, April 3, 1937, 19-32; "Il comunismo contro Dio. II. La pratica e i metodi," *L'Osservatore Romano*, April 3, 1937.

will not produce any outcome, and the same applies to elements B, C and D, if considered separately. Still, the overall result will be that the viewer will want to kick the policeman!"

Paradoxically enough, the kind of cinema promoted in the Soviet Union, controlled as it was by Soviet centralism, represented a model for the Catholics: it had been able to "almost completely resist the lure of passions, that mass of dirt" which made up "the main attraction of our entertainment." Was not there some truth, wondered Ledit, "in the Communist's reproach of us: 'for you, cinema and the theatre serve to make some people rich; for us, they serve to educate the masses'?"[82]

In this way, the director of the Special Secretariat for Atheism tackled a crucial issue, one which had never really been settled previously, regarding the relationship between the Church and cinema in those years and, more generally, the way in which the former had to deal with the major transformations imposed by secularized modernity. The extremely centralizing vocation of Pius XI's and Pius XII's pontificates, the need to regain power over society in order to establish the social Kingdom of Christ, had to confront a rapidly changing world where the centres of global power had slowly but inexorably moved from the political arena – which was easier to manage – to the more slippery spheres of the market and the mass media. Tragically, these could not be domesticated within a concordatarian logic. How could a machine such as cinema – built and compartmentalized on a complex web of financial, political and social aspects but ultimately fueled by the profits made by big industrial syndicates in the entertainment industry – be framed within the rigid catholic logic? Though it proved to be only partially successful in aligning cinema to political and ideological aims, the Communist model (and, partly, the Nazi one too) ultimately demonstrated that only draconian policing could rise to this challenge.

Ledit's analysis features the two main lines along which the relationship between Catholics and the cinema would develop under Ratti's and Pacelli's pontificates: on the one hand, the will to create a central hub that would deal with film policies

---

82   Joseph Ledit, pp. 36-37.

effectively; on the other, the search for a way to combine ethics and profit in order to promote productions inspired by Christianity.

The Vatican's strategy is apparent in its response to the inauguration first of the Office Catholique International du Cinéma [International Catholic Office for Cinema, hereafter OCIC], in April 1928 in The Hague, and second the International Educational Cinematograph Institute [hereafter IECI], in October of the same year, within the Society of Nations. Born as the outcome of coordinated efforts dedicated to cinema from its beginnings in several European countries (Germany, Belgium, the Netherlands, France and Italy first and foremost), the OCIC had some fundamental flaws from Rome's perspective: first, it had a very limited relationship with the Holy See, and, second, lay personalities occupied key positions within it. This, for example, provoked the discontent of Monsignor Lorenzo Schioppa, internuncio in the Netherlands and one of the most prominent middlemen with Roman institutions during the launch of the initiative.[83]

The OCIC's role was further downplayed, in the Vatican's point of view, by the way in which IECI's hierarchies came to be structured. There was a fear that this new body, based in Geneva, would fall under the leadership of French radicals and masonic groups, therefore corroborating Pius XI's notorious reservations about the Society of Nations.[84] This risk – which was well known in Roman circles thanks to the diplomatic work of the nuncio in Switzerland, Luigi Maglione[85] – was ultimately

---

83   Schioppa refused to attend the first OCIC conference, since, in his opinion, it had not received the approval of the Holy See. The episode has been thoroughly reconstructed in Guido Convents, "Resisting the Lure of the Modern World, International Politics and the Establishment of the International Catholic Office for Cinema (1918-1928)," in *Moralizing Cinema: Film, Catholicism and Power*, ed. by Daniel Bitereyst and Daniela Treveri Gennari (New York: Routledge, 2015), pp. 57-58 and 60-62.

84   Liliosa Azara, "Santa Sede e Società delle Nazioni," in *Pius XI: Keywords. International Conference Milan 2009*, ed. by Alberto Guasco and Raffaella Perin (Berlin/Munster/Vienna/Zurich/London: LIT Verlag, 2010), pp. 407-20.

85   *Ibid.*, pp. 47-50.

averted by Mussolini. The Fascist leader in fact saw the film institute as the right stage from which to gain consensus and international credit for the regime's policy.[86] No sooner than it entered the sphere of influence of Fascist Rome, the IECI was taken away from progressive French circles. The Holy See therefore lost its interest in the OCIC as a defense against the potential anti-Catholic policy of the new Institute, which coordinated the film policies of the Society of Nations at an international level. Consistently, the relationship between the Vatican and the IECI, during the very years of the Lateran Pacts, must be considered within the framework of the direct links with representatives of the regime (in a complex web of alliances and competition), and no longer in the murky web of indirect relationships with the Society of Nations. The words addressed to Pizzardo by Luciano De Feo, the General Secretary of the Institute, on occasion of the international congress held in Rome in 1934 are revealing: De Feo declared himself "available for any collaborations that [...] might be inspired by the necessity to contribute to the improvement of cinema, on the one hand, and to its popularization as a means of moral, civil and Christian education."[87] The Vatican's strategy was already clear: the central hub of Catholic film policy could not be based in the Netherlands, since every aspect had to be decided and managed in Rome, included relationships with international institutions.

---

86   For an analytical contribution on the IECI within the wider context of fascist policies see Christel Taillibert, *L'Institut International du cinématographe éducatif. Regard sur le role du cinéma éducatif dans la politique internationale du fascisme italien* (Paris: L'Harmattan, 2000).

87   Segreteria di Stato, S.RR.SS., Archivio Storico, AA.EE.SS., Stati Ecclesiastici, IV, Pos. 445, Fasc. 406, f. 92r, Luciano De Feo to Giuseppe Pizzardo, May 10, 1934 : "di essere a totale disposizione per ogni collaborazione che potrebbe [...] essere suggerita dalla necessità di contribuire al miglioramento del cinema da una parte e alla divulgazione dello schermo come mezzo di educazione morale, civile, Cristiana."

5. *From Rome to the World. The Failure of Catholic Production*

The key role played by Rome in the Vatican's changing positions on cinema is not confined to institutional issues. In the thirties, Rome was like a work in progress. On the one hand, the Lateran Pacts had created an unprecedented political situation, with two capitals in the same urban space, which generated increasing tensions and contrasts as well as attempts to reconcile the needs of the "sacred city"[88] with those of the "Fascist capital."[89] Such a situation led to the coexistence of rituals and symbols inspired by a flexible version of the "Roman myth," and a polysemic one too.[90] On the other hand, as an increasingly refined historiography has illustrated, Rome faithfully mirrored the great transformations that were taking place in the whole country and Italian society more widely, as it was pervaded by contrasting drives such as repression and modernization, regulation and transgression. Images, sounds, objects and lifestyles – typical of foreign consumerist societies – progressively invaded the background of this complex scenario, torn between Catholicism and Fascism.[91] The burgeoning culture of commerce and leisure modelled on the "American dream," which pervaded films, fashion magazines,

---

88   Andrea Riccardi, *Roma "città sacra"? Dalla Conciliazione all'operazione Sturzo* (Milano: Vita e Pensiero, 1979).

89   Vittorio Vidotto, "La capitale del fascismo," in *Storia di Roma dall'antichità ad oggi. Roma capitale*, ed. by Vittorio Vidotto (Roma-Bari: Laterza, 2002), pp. 379-413.

90   Andrea Giardina and André Vauchez, *Il mito di Roma. Da Carlo Magno a Mussolini* (Roma-Bari: Laterza 2016, 3rd edn), in particular pp. 213-87.

91   In this sense, Victoria de Grazia's work was pioneering: *Consenso e cultura di massa nell'Italia fascista: l'organizzazione del dopolavoro* (Roma-Bari: Laterza, 1981); "La sfida dello 'star system'. L'americanismo nella formazione della cultura di massa in Europa 1920-1965," *Quaderni Storici*, a. XX, n. 58, April 1985, pp. 95-133; *How Fascism Ruled Women: Italy, 1922-1945* (Berkeley: University of California Press, 1992). More recent contributions are: Bruno P. F. Wanrooij, "Italian Society under Fascism," in *Liberal and Fascist Italy, 1900-1945*, ed. by Adrian Lyttelton (Oxford/New York: Oxford University Press, 2002), pp. 175-95; David Forgacs and Stephen Gundle, *Mass Culture and Italian Society from Fascism to the Cold War* (Bloomington: Indiana University press, 2007). On cinema: *Hollywood in Europa. Industria, politica, pubblico del cinema 1945-1960*, ed. by Gian Piero Brunetta and David Ellwood (Firenze, La Casa Usher, 1991); Gian Piero Brunetta, *Il ruggito del Leone.*

department stores, commodities, advertising and the radio, knocked insistently at the door of St. Peter's. Initial surprise soon turned into alarm and finally into scandal: a poster or a bad film were enough to trigger the sensation that the sacred space in the very heart of the Eternal City was being violated, desecrated. Emblematic in this sense was the note sent by Luigi Maglione, the apostolic nuncio in Paris, to the Secretariat of State in March 1935, a few weeks after the closure of the Extraordinary Holy Year. Here Maglione quotes a letter send to him by a friend:

Last night I took a desolating walk (through Rome): at the Alhambra (the variety theatre near the railway station) they were screening a Roman film, entitled "Pius XI spricht zu dir" that was licensed – so read the gigantic bills attached on all spots of the poster – by His Holiness. Now, apart from the painful fact that such badly shot, chaotic views, with no concept behind them are offered to innocent viewers, and with such a high patronage at that, with a most unsuitable soundtrack, apart from the inconvenience of having the Pontiff's name featured in such a profane venue, the religious part of the movie is a real disaster. The film is about the Pontiff's visit to St. John Lateran. The Pope is shown in the external Loggia, while he is blessing people and uttering incomprehensible words. For some technical error that I am not able to figure out the image is slanted, so that the Holy Father seems to totter. His gestures are ape-like, his voice is somewhat altered…a real shame. The laughter and comments of the public were so unbearable to me that I had to leave before the end of the show.[92]

---

92   Segreteria di Stato, S.RR.SS., Archivio Storico, AA EE. SS., Stati Ecclesiastici, IV, Pos. 445, Fasc. 409, f. 26rv, Luigi Maglione to Giuseppe Pizzardo, March 4, 1935: "Ho fatto ieri sera (a Roma) un viaggio desolante: davano qui all'Alhambra (quel teatro di varietà che è vicino alla stazione) un film di Roma, intitolato "Pius XI spricht zu Dir" e munito – dicevano gli affissi giganteschi incollati dappertutto – dell'approvazione di Sua Santità. Ebbene, a parte la pena di vedere offerte agli ignari, sotto così alto patrocino, vedute mal prese, peggio concepite e caotiche, con un accompagnamento musicale assolutamente inadatto, a parte la sconvenienza di permettere l'apparire del nome della persona del Pontefice in un locale tanto profano, la parte propriamente religiosa del film è un disastro. Si tratta della visita del Pontefice a San Giovanni in Laterano. Si vede il Papa sulla loggia esterna, intento a benedire ed a pronunziare parole incomprensibili. Non so per via di quale errore tecnico l'immagine è di traverso, onde pare che il Santo Padre barcolli.

Information on the global advance of cinema's 'soft power' from all over the world, from pontifical representatives and the Jesuit congregation, illustrated to the Holy See a concrete danger, albeit one which was perceived as removed from the quotidien life in Rome. More striking, for the Vatican, was probably the fact that certain habits and traditions were suddenly disappearing in a city that had not changed in the least for centuries. Just a few steps away from Bernini's colonnade, the world's pace was being dictated by the opening of one movie theatre after the other.

The international information network on which the Vatican relied was widespread; equally diffused and efficient was the machine set up in Rome and in Italy to monitor transformations in public morals. As early as 1923, a reform at Azione Cattolica Italiana [Italian Catholic Action, hereafter ACI] led the Central Board to appoint a national Secretariat for morality, which sent daily reports to the Vatican.[93] Among the most regular visitors at the Vatican was professor Carlo Costantini, who was probably the most committed Catholic in the crusade for morality in the thirties.[94] Between January 1931 and December 1936, working for the Secreatariat in Rome, he carried out an impressive amount of work, combing the streets of the capital and of other major Italian cities. At the national Conference on morality, organized by ACI in January 1937, besides his report on *Lo stato attuale del problema della moralità* [*The Current State of the Issue of Moralitys*], he presented a thorough statistical report on his very detailed – almost obsessive – work: in the "six years between 1931 and 1936" Costantini had carried out 4,405 inspections and inspections. With an apocalyptic tone, he underlined the urgent need to "check efficiently the appalling corruption that was menacing faith and

I gesti sono scimmieschi, la voce è non so come alterata... Una vera pena. Le risa ed i commenti del pubblico mi furono così intollerabili che dovetti allontanarmi prima della fine dello spettacolo."

93   The Secretariat was established in October 1923 and Father Francesco Gavotti (Congregation of the Mission) was appointed as its first director. See Luigi Civardi, *Manuale di Azione Cattolica. La pratica* (Pavia: Casa Editoriale Vescovile Artigianelli, 1927, 2nd edn), pp. 26-29.

94   Pacelli's audience with the Italian ambassador at the Holy See, January 9, 1931: *I "Fogli di udienza" del cardinale Eugenio Pacelli Segretario di Stato*, ed. by Giovanni Coco and Alejandro Mario Dieguez (Città del Vaticano: Libreria Editrice Vaticana, 2014), vol. II, p. 19.

humankind in a terrible way."[95] Rome, as described by Costantini in his over-two-hundred page document, was hard to recognize: immorality had flooded the city, and stemming it was becoming impossible. The main, "undisputable"[96] consequence of all this was that the Italian people were swiftly and inexorably drifting away from God: "in Rome, in the very heart of Catholicism, more than half of the 1,200,000 inhabitants do not attend mass on festive days, and for every one thousand men, three quarters never take holy communion. Such figures are bewildering!"[97] Such a major transformation was due – the ACI delegate had no doubt – to the cultural commodities that had gradually, but steadily, conquered the leisure time of Italian people, and among these the cinema had the lion's share.

Reliable calculations show that in Italy 500,000,000 tickets are sold annually and that the takings are over one million Lira. The 72 movie theatres in Rome sell a monthly average of one and a half million tickets. The Capranica alone, last March, was attended by 55,549 people. In Milan, in 1931, cinema goers exceeded 25,000,000 people, with takings amounting to 50 million Lira. The number of tickets sold annually worldwide is 12 and a half billion. How can soul healers avoid meditating on such figures, in particular when they realize that cinema, nowadays, is left to the speculative fever of unscrupulous entrepreneurs?[98]

---

95 ISACEM Archive, PG XII Secretariat for Morality, envelope 99, "Relazione sulla Moralità compilata dal prof. Carlo Costantini, sessennio 1931-1936:" "Arginare efficacemente la spaventevole corruzione che in maniera impressionante minaccia la fede e la stessa stirpe."

96 *Ibid.*: "Incontestabilmente."

97 *Ibid.*: "Nella stessa Roma, centro della Cattolicità su 1.200.000 abitanti, più della metà nei giorni festivi non vanno a Messa e su mille uomini, tre quarti non prendono Pasque. Cifre sbalorditive!"

98 *Ibid.*: "Da calcoli attendibilissimi, in Italia si vendono annualmente 500.000.000 di ingressi e l'incasso supera notevolmente il miliardo. Nei 72 cinematografi di Roma ogni mese vengono acquistati circa un milione e mezzo di ingressi. Il solo cinema Capranica, nel mese di marzo us. è stato frequentato da 55.549 persone. A Milano, nel 1931 gli spettatori dei cinema hanno superato i 25.000.000, con un incasso per gli impresari per oltre 50.000.000 di lire. Annualmente in tutto il mondo si vendono 12 miliardi e mezzo di ingressi ai cinematografi. Possono i curatori di anime non fermarsi a meditare su queste cifre, quando si pensi che la cinematografia oggi è abbandonata alla febbre speculatrice

The Holy See proved very flexible in responding to such constant pleas, which came both from the centre and the periphery of the Catholic world. Hollywood remained the central problem, since the Holy See was well aware of the need to undermine the machine of the main producer of "immorality." The large-scale action scheme, in those democratic countries where Church was separate from the State, was largely founded on the mobilization of public opinion, and on specific lobbying activities that aimed to establish relationships with the most influential figures in the film industry, the government, and related associations. Thanks to the Vatican's privileged relationship with the Italian government and consequently with the IECI, on the other hand, provided the ideal laboratory to test out an effective strategy for totalitarian or concordatarian regimes, a strategy based on politic deals made with high-level authorities. In both cases, the two main objectives were the same: to moralize cinema and to domesticate it within a Christian restoration of society, and to implement a larger, more refined plan, which saw cinema working as a powerful ally in the fight against communism.

Soon after the inauguration of the Vatican radio station, another initiative by Pius XI in the world of media, one that culminated in the clamorous collapse of the OCIC, persuaded the Church leaders that this two-fold strategy was the most efficient in such a complex scenario. In December 1931, the International Eidophon Company was founded in Amsterdam in close collaboration with the OCIC.[99] Its aim was to establish a film company that was

---

di industriali senza coscienza?" The data quoted by Costantini on the number of movie theatres in Italy does not perfectly match the SIAE numbers in the same period: the 1936 *Annuario statistico* reports a total of 4,049 theatres and a total of 1,643,161 seats: *Lo spettacolo in Italia. Annuario statistico: anno 1936* (Roma: Società Italiana degli Autori ed Editori, 1937). Cfr. also Mariagrazia Fanchi, "Sale e pubblici," in *Storia del cinema italiano* (Venezia: Marsilio, 2006), V, *1934-1939*, ed. by Orio Caldiron, pp. 176-82.

99   The main stages of the Eidophon development have been outlined by Karel Dibbets, who draws on sources from the Dutch episcopate. See "A Catholic Voice in Talking Pictures: The International Eidophon Company (1930-1934)," in *Moralizing cinema: film, Catholicism and power*, pp. 225-54. Dibbets' essay is a slightly revised version (with no major updates) of his previous "'Een prachtkans voor een katholiek rilmkartel'. Internationale Eidophon NV, 1932-1934," *Jaarboek Mediageschiedenis*, 2, Amsterdam

completely controlled by Catholics, which could compete with US majors as well as communist producers. The fact that the Vatican embarked on such an enterprise relatively late (i.e. when the film industry was already well developed) gave a clear sign of the Vatican Hierarchy's shifting perspective with regard to film policy. During the transition from silent to sound cinema, Pius XI, with the support of Pacelli, seemed to cherish the dream of launching a major film production company, so as to deploy the cinema in his project of Christian restoration. The ultimate failure of this plan and subsequent conflicts within ecclesiastical hierarchies seem to have affected his later choices quite profoundly.

A detailed note from May 1936, in which the Secretariat of State outlines the different stages of this enterprise, reveals the Hierarchy's position on it. The note states that Eidophon was an international public limited company "headed" by Mr B.J. Brenninkmeyer from Amsterdam, that sought to "put sound and talking films at the service of Catholic ideals by exploiting the technical discoveries of Münster priest Heinrich Könemann."[100] The Eidophon thus served a two-fold aim: on the one hand, it was a response to the Communists' propagandistic activities in cinema; on the other, it was the synergetic outcome of intellectual and financial efforts, from the Catholics, to embrace the challenge posed by the advent of sound cinema.

In 1926, the tycoon Brenninkmeyer, co-owner of the clothing company C&A, invested in a patented invention made by physicist and abbot Heinrich Könemann, who in turn collaborated with Tri-Ergon, a leading German group of researchers in sound cinema.[101] His intention was clear: Könemann's product could be employed by the Church in order to build a major international film company.

1990, 15-39, trad. it. "L'EIDOPHON. Il sogno di un impero cattolico del cinema: la storia della 'Internazionale Eidophon,' 1932-34," *Cinegrafie*, n. 5, Bologna 1992, 81-94.

100 Segreteria di Stato, S.RR.SS., Archivio Storico, AA.EE.SS., Stati Ecclesiastici, IV, Pos. 445, Fasc. 408, ff. 94-96r, "Eidophon. Riassunto della questione fino al 1936, 14 maggio:" "di mettere a servizio dell'idea cattolica il Film sonoro e parlante, applicando perfezioni tecniche scoperte dal Sac. Enrico Koenemann, di Münster."

101 Karel Dibbets, "A Catholic Voice in Talking Pictures," p. 226.

Discussions within circles connected to the OCIC provided the testing ground for the idea. Two clear positions emerged, which would continue to influence Catholic debates for a long time. Some, like Jesuit Muckermann, maintained that Catholics should not enclose themselves in a fortress, but instead foster relationships with existing film companies, in order to influence their production and to make it compliant with the Church's needs. Such behavior would moreover preclude the danger of risky financial operations, which were very likely to fail.[102] Others, and in particular the Dutch Dominican Hyacinthe Hermans, advocated the creation of a large-scale Catholic film company.

A prominent and active OCIC man from its foundation, Muckermann publicly stated his position at the "Catholic Press, Cinema and Radio Week" held in Cologne in June 1929. The Jesuit urged Catholics to change their attitude toward cinema. Once they had overcome a "religious and purely prohibitive attitude," Catholics could influence cinema's development only by positioning themselves at the centre of the field." Conversely, the formation of a "ghetto" within the field of cinema would not provide a helpful solution. While the idea of Catholic film companies could be a welcome option, for Muckermann it was more important to participate actively in the existing film industry, by involving "people who bring new ideas, who could promote new content that moves away from materialism."[103] A keen advocate of the Dutch Catholics' engagement in cinema, Hermans instead saw the Eidophon as the last real chance for the Church to strike back and not surrender the field to the 'enemies'. The project was extensively discussed at the OCIC conference in Zürich, in June 1931,[104] but Hermans had prepared the ground

---

102   Friedrich Muckermann: *Im Kampf zwischen zwei Epochen. Lebenserinnerungen* (Mainz: Matthias-Grünewald-Verlag, 1973), p. 282. The Jesuit hoped to establish an agreement with the UFA film company in Germany.

103   "L'Opera dei cattolici per il cinematografo," *Rivista del Cinematografo*, a. I, n. 8, August 1928, pp. 117-118. The Jesuit was also entrusted with the task of delivering the inaugural speech at the second OCIC conference in Munich, in June 1929: Dcc [Don Carlo Canziani], "2° Congresso Cattolico Internazionale pel Cinematografo, Monaco 12-20 giugno 1929," *Rivista del Cinematografo*, a. II, n. 6-7, June-July 1929, pp. 155-57.

104   Robert Molhant, *Les catholiques et le cinéma: une étrange histoire de crainte et de passions: les débuts 1895-1935* (Bruxelles: Signis, 2000), pp. 23-28. See

with a series of articles published in the Dutch Catholic magazine *De Maasbode*. On February 15, 1931 he launched an ultimatum to the Catholics, referring to the Soviet case and expressing regret that the Catholics had been indifferent to the new medium for too long: "Just look at Russia!" There, many resources were dedicated to film, "which, apparently peacefully and without the clamour of war, is transcending the boundaries of countries and nations in order to win over the whole of a new humanity to her ideas, thereby winning their allegiance." As such Hermans asks: "Can we catch up? Can we as Catholics, and as a world power, still make ourselves heard in the area of cinematography?" The answer was provided by Könemann's patent: thanks to this invention, this "Godsend," the Catholic Church would have a last chance to grasp a stake in the international film industry. It was now or never.[105] Hermans succeeded in involving Dutch bishops in the initiative, exploiting the relationships he had established with the episcopate in his capacity as member of the State-controlled censorship board. Together with Brenninkmeyer and Könemann, the Dominican launched the Eidophon project in December 1931, as a reaction "against this deluge of brash materialism that is inundating the world through the cinemas." With an initial share capital of around 3 million guilders (around 30 million dollars in 2017), later downsized to 1,7 million, the public limited company (which was about to be founded) was to be entrusted with the production of Catholic films for the European market, and to manage their distribution network. However, fundraising proved more difficult than expected: in May 1932, board members complained to the episcopate that they had not been able to raise even half of the necessary capital.[106]

Talks with Rome intensified, in search of support. The Vatican's answer came in the summer of 1932, at a crucial moment for later developments in the Holy See's attitude towards cinema. A 1936 memorandum from the Secretariat of State declared that "on

        also: "L'opera dei cattolici per il cinematografo," *Rivista del Cinematografo*, a. IV, n. 4, April 1931, pp. 99-101.
105   Hyachinte Hermans, "Nu of nooit meer... nogeenmaal: een Katholiek filmkartel," *De Maasbode*, February 15, 1931. Quoted in: Karel Dibbets, "A Catholic Voice in Talking Pictures," pp. 227-28.
106   Karel Dibbets, "A Catholic Voice in Talking Pictures," pp. 230-34.

June 17, 1932, after a long inquiry into the issue, a letter was sent
to the Archbishop of Utrecht in support of the initiative."[107] The
letter, written by cardinal Pacelli on that same day and addressed
to Monsignor Johannes H.G. Jansen, had a particularly genuine
and resolute tone which left no room for equivocal interpretation.
The arguments used by the Secretary of State moreover echoed
the alarming information that had begun to reach Rome, once
the inquiry into communist propaganda had commenced in
April of the same year.

> We must say that distressing circumstances impose on Catholics
> the duty to put admirable inventions produced by the progress of
> civilization to the service of the Glory of God and the spreading
> of Christian faith. God's sworn enemies have become masters of
> cinema – the influence of which has increased since the advent
> of sound – and, using it in an evil and impious way, they are
> destroying the divine and religious passion and inspiration in
> every soul. If, therefore, the Catholics – sustained as they are by
> their zeal for God and for the Church – should get hold of such
> a powerful means, they will provide an invaluable contribution to
> the Catholic cause, and create a new and splendid force of social
> apostolate.[108]

The subsequent steps taken by the ecclesiastical authorities, and
by Pius XI himself, provided further confirmation of the purposes
stated in the letter. In the course of 1932 Eidophon opened a
Berlin branch and managed to produce five films. However,
despite pontifical support, Eidophon had great difficulty getting
off the ground: at the end of the year, a further 280,000 guilders
were required in order to reach the initial share capital. Hitler's
rise to power further complicated the scenario, creating a period
of stagnation for German cinema. In April 1933 Eidophon was

---

107 Segreteria di Stato, S.RR.SS., Archivio Storico, AA.EE. SS., Stati
    Ecclesiastici, IV, Pos. 445, Fasc. 408, ff. 94-96r, "Eidophon. Riassunto
    della questione fino al 1936, 14 maggio:" "il 17 giugno 1932, dopo
    lungo esame della cosa, fu inviata all'Arcivescovo di Utrecht, una lettera
    d'incoraggiamento per l'iniziativa."
108 The text of the letter is published in M. M. [Mario Meneghini], "Due
    documenti di Pio XII sui problemi del cinema," *L'Osservatore Romano*,
    March 11, 1939.

forced to plea to a group of Dutch bishops for a 500,000 guilders loan that would save the company.[109]

The Holy See's subsequent moves illustrate both the constancy of its intentions and the risk that Ratti was ready to take in order to save the whole operation, despite the strong opposition of ecclesiastical authorities. In May and June of the following years, Eidophon delivered to Cardinal Pacelli a series of documents that had been produced in the negotiations between the company and the Dutch episcopate. These included a letter from the archbishop of Utrecht, reassuring Eidophon that the episcopate would vouch for the requested loan if the Holy See allowed each bishop to "retain 10,000 guilders per year plus interest on Peter's pence."[110] In the memorandum issued on the subject by the Secretary of State, we read that in audiences on August 3 and 4 Pius XI confirmed that Peter's pence would pose no difficulty, though he also expressed his strong disapproval regarding the direct involvement of the episcopate as guarantor of the financial operation. The bishops had instead to find a trustworthy bank that would negotiate with Eidophon, and, without any public knowledge, "let the bank understand that they backed the operation anyway, with any necessary support."[111]

The Secretariat of State therefore drafted a letter for Jansen which contained the Pope's orders, which was sent on August 9. Nevertheless, before Ratti's decisions reached the Utrecht curia, the Holy See had to deal with the strong opposition of the pontifical representative in the Netherlands. Schioppa, to whom, as usual, pontifical correspondence was initially sent before being forwarded to bishops, wrote to Rome on August 16, stating that he thought that he considered such a message inadvisable due to the "insufficient financial safety of the project."[112] This inspired a significant confrontation between Ratti and Schioppa. During

---

109 Karel Dibbets, "A Catholic Voice in Talking Pictures," pp. 230-34.

110 Segreteria di Stato, S.RR.SS., Archivio Storico, AA.EE.SS., Stati Ecclesiastici, IV, Pos. 445, Fasc. 408, ff. 94-96r, "Eidophon. Riassunto della questione fino al 1936, 14 maggio:" "potesse trattenere 10.000 fiorini annui ed interessi sulla raccolta dell'Obolo di S. Pietro."

111 *Ibid.*: "facessero capire alla Banca che essi stavano dietro con i dovuti affidamenti."

112 *Ibid.*: "Per l'insufficiente sicurezza finanziaria del progetto."

the August 20 audience, the Pontiff, despite acknowledging that the internuncio had presented him with "reasonable observations," ordered that he should be given the following response: "'In decisis'; no difficulty should be made for Peter's pence, nor should the Episcopate commit itself financially. The bishops alone should decide for the best."[113] Yet, before the Pontiff's reply (sent from Rome on August 28) could reach the internuncioship in The Hague, Schioppa sent his proposal to the Vatican on August 26, in which he more openly contravened pontifical provisions: he reported that he had managed to obtain a "a submissive agreement" with his position from Dutch bishops and therefore proposed to reduce the amount of money that the Holy See would grant to Eidophon to a "a one-time sum."[114] This greatly irritated the Pope, who replied on September 5: Schioppa's proposal should not be accepted, as not to "set a precedent and not to be inconsistent with what the Church was about to do."[115] The Pontiff's orders were eventually adopted: in October, Eidophon representatives were received for an audience at the Secretariat of State, and subsequently declared their willingness to apply for a loan with a bank; in December Pius XI wrote to the bishop of Utrecht, confirming that the "requested loan had been granted."[116]

The Eidophon operation nevertheless compelled the Holy See to recognize the complexity and risk of direct involvement in the film industry: despite the ecclesiastical funding, the company's rescue proved to be an egregious failure. The alliance between major capital and the Church ultimately surrendered to the laws of market: Könemann's patent proved obsolete and was superseded by sound technologies used by large-scale American companies. At the beginning of 1934, Brenninkmeyer announced that he would leave Eidophon, and in March 1934 he informed C&A's shareholders that he intended to close down the film company.

---

113 *Ibid.*: "'In decisis'; né si faccia difficoltà per l'Obolo, né si consenta che l'Episcopato si impegni finanziariamente. Facciano i Vescovi quello che credono meglio."
114 *Ibid.*: "Remissiva adesione;" "una somma una volta tanto."
115 *Ibid.*: "Per non creare precedenti e per non essere incoerenti con quanto s'era sul punto di fare."
116 *Ibid.*: "la concessione del sussidio richiesto."

At the end of December, with ill-concealed satisfaction, Schioppa wrote to Pacelli that, as he had "modestly foreseen" in his August 1933 report, "not only did Eidophon have no success, but it was also forced to put an end to its miserable and obscure existence."[117]

6. *The Downsizing of the OCIC*

Eidophon's failure had major repercussions on the Holy See's relationship with the OCIC, which in any case had never been particularly straightforward. By that time, the OCIC had chosen Brussels for its headquarters and changed leadership: in 1933 the resourceful Leuven Canon Abel Brohée was appointed president, where he would remain until 1947. At the beginning of the twenties, Brohée had been president of Belgian distributing company Brabo Films and had established close links with the Office National Catholique du Cinéma in Brussels. He was one of the promoters of the OCIC, and doing so could rely on his experience in the field of cinema, in both France and Germany.[118] At the public audience that Pius XI granted to OCIC heads during an international symposium held in Rome, organized in April 1934 by the IECI, Brohée handed a document over to the Pontiff, which he had co-signed with the members of his secretariat. The document stressed the need to deal with "un des plus difficiles problèmes qui se soient jamais posés à l'Apostolat catholique."[119]

---

117 Segreteria di Stato, S.RR.SS., Archivio Storico, AA.EE.SS., Stati Ecclesiastici, IV, Pos. 445, Fasc. 408, ff. 101-102rv, Lorenzo Schioppa to Eugenio Pacelli, The Hague, December 30, 1934: "modestamente preveduto;" "l'Eidophon non solo non ha avuto successo alcuno, ma è stata costretta a mettere fine alla sua magra ed oscura esistenza." On the failure of the rescue plan see Karel Dibbets, "A Catholic Voice in Talking Pictures."

118 Louis Picard, *Un pionnier. Le chanoine Brohée* (Brussels: Editions Universitaires, 1949). The context of Brohée's action is outlined in Daniel Biltereyst, "'I Think Catholics Didn't Go to the Cinema'. Catholic Film Exhibition Strategies and Cinema-Going Experiences in Belgium, 1930s-1960s," in *Moralizing Cinema: Film, Catholicism and Power*, pp. 398-423.

119 Segreteria di Stato, S.RR.SS., Archivio Storico, AA.EE. SS., Stati Ecclesiastici, IV, Pos. 445, Fasc. 410, ff. 3-13r. The April 18 (1934) letter was signed by Brohée, general secretary Jean Bernard (Luxembourg) and by secretariat members Richard Muchkermann (Germany), Carlo Canziani (Italy) and by Henri Caffarel (France).

Le cinéma exerce sur les mœurs une incalculable influence. Il peut avilir ou élever les âmes. Et ce pendant son action est bien plus redoutable encore dans le domaine des idées. C'est que le cinéma enseigne et propage une doctrine, une véritable philosophie, une conception totalitaire de la vie et du monde. Et, en ce moment, en raison précisément de la carence pour ainsi dire absolue des catholiques, la conception de vie qu'expose et répand le cinéma est purement païenne, elle se résume en un évangile qui n'est autre chose que le contrepied de l'Evangile du Christ.

For the OCIC heads, production was the most pressing issue. In fact, they quoted Pacelli's June 1932 letter to Jansen to argue that influencing production by intervening solely on distribution was not enough, and that the Catholics should act "comme l'a fait l'Eidophon, au cœur même de l'industrie du film."[120] During the 23 April audience, by giving his "approval" to OCIC actions and emphasizing the need for "close links" in the field of cinema, the Pope also touched on production: "if everybody, even less wealthy people, contributed, [...] much could be achieved." It was therefore necessary to "inspire the good will of people, especially of wealthy people," to foster "Catholic action in this field, too."[121] The Holy See's desiderata for the OCIC regarding production, however, were clearly stated in a letter that Secretary of State Pacelli sent to Brohée few days later.[122] Although not an official declaration, the document did convey the Vatican

---

120 *Ibid.* The document also states, as had been said during OCIC's Third Symposium, held in Bruxelles in May 1933, that "il est peut être impossible que des hommes absolument étrangers à nos croyances, puissent arriver à fixer comme il convient sur l'écran le pur idéal chrétien; et il est en tout cas inadmissible que tout notre effort se borne à mendier ces réalisations auprès de producteurs qui ne partagent pas nos convictions. C'est à nous, a déclaré très justement Mr. Bidault, un de ces catholiques français qui ont bien mérité de l'Église dans le domaine du cinéma, <u>c'est à nous à créer la genre, et on nous imitera</u>," underlined in the original text.

121 "L'Office Catholique International du Cinématographe in udienza dal S. Padre," *Rivista del Cinematografo*, a. VII, n. 4, April 1934, 23-24.

122 Segreteria di Stato, S.RR.SS., Archivio Storico, AA.EE. SS., Stati Ecclesiastici, IV, Pos. 445, Fasc. 410, ff. 62-76r, Eugenio Pacelli to Abel Brohée, general OCIC secretary, April 27, 1934. The letter is published in *Cinema e Chiesa: i documenti del magistero*, ed. by Dario E. Viganò (Roma: Effatà, 2002), pp. 220-22.

Hierarchy's will to control the activities of an organization that, despite several evident limitations, was indeed strategic for the Holy See, and for this very reason could not be granted too much independence from Rome. The cardinal provided an outline of cinema's harmful effects on society as well as the Church's hierocratic project: warnings against the "moral and religious dangers caused by cinema" were reaching the Pope from all over the world. He wrote that cinema had an "irresistible influence on the population, especially on young people," making their souls drift "towards world and life views that could in no way be reconciled with the rules of Christian wisdom." "Positive and concerted action" was therefore urgent, in order to "reconvert cinema into the means of a healthy education."

> Scientific advances are also gifts from God that must be used for His glory and to expand His kingdom. Catholics of all countries must therefore deal with this increasingly central issue, which should become their duty of conscience. Cinema is about to become the first and most powerful influencing medium, more efficient than the press, for it is proved that certain films had several millions of viewers.

The Secretary of State then focused on practical aspects. He urged the Catholic Action groups in various countries to engage with cinema, and Catholic magazines to feature film columns ranking good and bad films. The letter also stated that the Pontiff praised the OCIC's intended policy: that the Office was right to favour the "development of a network of big, modern movie theatres," although it should not "take on financial responsibilities." In this way, the Office would serve two aims: to "offer instructive and entertaining shows inspired by Christian values" and to generate the demand for good films, thus "attracting the interest of potential producers." The final passage, however, with its focus on production, lent itself to controversial interpretations:

> Furthermore – and this should be our main goal – this [the OCIC's] programme is likely to inspire good people, who should therefore understand that, by securing, with their coordinated action, the wide circulation of good films, they will be able to deal competently and

with the necessary training with the production of high-level films. This will ensure the success of an enterprise that, by safeguarding moral habit and by standing out for its technical, artistic and human value, will yield good, tangible results in the industrial field.

The OCIC's leaders interpreted this statement as the Pontiff's encouragement to engage in fundraising within the Catholic world, even in the wake of the events surrounding Eidophon's previous attempts. In reality the Vatican had been deeply disappointed by that very experience, and wanted rather to change its course of action radically.

When Brohée and the new general OCIC secretary Jean Bernard were received by Pizzardo in September 1935, little more than a year after Pacelli's letter, and Brohée handed him a long memorandum, the mood had changed. In the meantime, the secretary of the Sacred Congregation for Extraordinary Ecclesiastical Affairs had become supervisor of all matters regarding cinema. In June 1935 Brohée had written to Pizzardo, to outline the positive effects that Pacelli's letter had, in his opinion, already produced, including in particular the creation "d'une firme internationale de Distribution et de Production de films."[123] At the same time, Brohée wanted to create a holding for the distribution and, at a later stage, production of films, that would be based in Luxembourg, and would collaborate with Catholic associations in Belgium, France and Switzerland.[124]

---

123   Segreteria di Stato, S.RR.SS., Archivio Storico, AA.EE. SS., Stati Ecclesiastici, IV, Pos. 445, Fasc. 410, f. 16rv. Abel Brohée to Giuseppe Pizzardo, Louvain, June 5, 1935, text in French. The letter also listed: the foundation of a limited company for production and distribution based in Spain; the foundation, in Austria, of the magazine *Der Gute Film*; the attendance, by the OCIC, of the Berlin International symposium in April 1935; the foundation of a "bureau international" for film press; the first draft of a major Crusade of Prayer; an increase in the activity of Catholic Action in France, Italy, Poland and the United Kingdom; and new OCIC connections in Poland, Czechoslovakia, Lithuania, Columbia and the United States.

124   The initiative is outlined in Father Carlo Canziani's letters; Canziani was the director of the CUCE in Milan and the Lux Films company, which was a part of Geneva Catholic Action. The letters provide evidence that Canziani intended to promote the holding project through these two organizations. Segreteria di Stato, S.RR.SS., Archivio Storico, AA.EE. SS., Stati Ecclesiastici, IV, Pos. 445, Fasc. 413, ff. 59r e 60r.

Brohée's aim was clear: he intended on the one hand to influence production indirectly, increasing the demand for 'moral films', and on the other to market films produced by Catholic companies. The intended implementation of his plan was outlined in a memorandum submitted to Pizzardo on September 25, 1935, in which Brohée envisages the creation of a "Denier de St. Paul," a kind of Peter's Pence dedicated exclusively to film. Brohée defined the financial question as the "primordial issue," and therefore demanded that funds for cinema be raised on a regular basis in Rome, and in all Catholic countries. As in the case of Peter's Pence, money would have to be collected in Rome and subsequently be distributed externally. In addition to providing the means to finance the industrial and commercial enterprise, the new "St. Paul's Pence," Brohée and Bernard explain, would also serve to educate the Catholic masses by making an explicit claim for Catholic cinema.[125] Brohée's and Bernard's proposal was vehemently rejected by the Holy See. An anonymous note from the Secretariat of State that addresses each point of the OCIC's memorandum reads: "as regards the financial aspects, money transfer is the most delicate issue;" "*il danaro di S. Paolo* demanded for Rome, sent to Rome and distributed in Rome" was "not a viable option...No one must be put in the condition to say that Rome wants to make money... with all the apostles."[126]

On the question of the holding, Pizzardo replied to the OCIC heads by outlining the many difficulties that such an operation would engender: Brohée and Bernard's plan, wrote the bishop, would be difficult to carry out without an adequate network of movie theatres to ensure effective distribution.

---

125 Segreteria di Stato, S.RR.SS., Archivio Storico, AA.EE. SS., Stati Ecclesiastici, IV, Pos. 445, Fasc. 413, ff. 65r-96r, Memorandum on the OCIC drafted on occasion of the visit to, September 25, 1935, original text in French. The paragraph entitled "Denier de St. Paul" is to be found on f. 79r.

126 Segreteria di Stato, S.RR.SS., Archivio Storico, AA.EE. SS., Stati Ecclesiastici, IV, Pos. 445, Fasc. 413, ff. 54-55rv, pen-written note, dated 24.9.1935, the original text is underlined: "quanto al lato economico, le difficoltà attuali sono enormi specialmente per lo scambio di danari;" "il danaro di S. Paolo chiesto per Roma, mandato a Roma e diviso poi da Roma;" "scartato senz'altro... Anche perché non si dica che Roma vuol far soldi... con tutti gli apostoli."

There were further clear difficulties in finding movies that were suitable for all countries, and locating the necessary money to translate talking films into different languages. The project would encounter too many problems, and first and foremost the major social, cultural and religious differences between the countries in which the holding intended to operate. To sum up, there was no single method to moralize cinema in all Catholic countries and for all audiences. While in the United States, some moralization of Hollywood production had been enabled by the episcopate's involvement in the Holy See's campaign, France and Spain had chosen to establish Catholic companies but had avoided promoting an explicitly Catholic model. Not to mention the fact that Hitler's rise to power in Germany hindered the OCIC's actions there, and that the European organization had no chance of carrying out effective work further afield, in South America.[127]

Financial aspects were not the only issues considered by Brohée and Bernard. In a document enclosed with the memorandum, entitled *Ce que nous demandons à S. E. Mgr Pizzardo,* they summarized their requests: a more explicit moral endorsement from Rome, as well as considerable financial support and the approval of the OCIC's new statutes; close collaboration with Catholic Action groups as well as the most important Catholic magazines; the appointment of a national and international theological authority, who would be entrusted with the aesthetic and moral evaluation of films and whose judgment would be valid through all countries; and the recognition of the OCIC's President and Secretary by the Holy See.[128] In the anonymous notice by the Secretariat of State mentioned earlier, the Vatican clearly stated its stance on the OCIC. The existence of an international Catholic office for cinema was defined as "an excellent thing;" however, the office should have the sole aim

---

127 Segreteria di Stato, S.RR.SS., Archivio Storico, AA.EE. SS., Stati Ecclesiastici, IV, Pos. 445, Fasc. 413, ff. 121-123r, text in French. A penwritten note in the margins reads: "Observations communicated by Monsignor Pizzardo" ("Osservazioni comunicate di Mgr. Pizzardo)."

128 Segreteria di Stato, S.RR.SS., Archivio Storico, AA.EE. SS., Stati Ecclesiastici, IV, Pos. 445, Fasc. 413, f. 96. The main points were also summarized, in Italian, in an unsigned and undated note: f. 103r.

of "supporting initiatives in various countries (by establishing research institutes and by providing information and advice, etc) and coordinating actions undertaken in different countries."[129] The OCIC, however, should have no "executive" role, because, 1) it has no authority to present itself as the Catholic point of view on the matter; 2) because the central authority, for all Catholic matters, is Rome and only Rome."[130] The OCIC, therefore, could provide suggestions and advice, but never give orders: should its heads consider it is necessary that directions be provided to Catholics in different countries, they would have to submit them first to Rome. The possibility to maintain the Office's seat in Brussels, far from St. Peter, furthermore, was seen in a positive light: "outside the precinct of St. Peter the Office is less authoritative but has more freedom of movement. In Rome it would be too authoritative (due to the greater involvement of the Holy See) and it would therefore have very little freedom to act. And since cinema is all about movement…"[131]

Brohée replied to Pizzardo in person during the 26 September audience, where the project of a large-scale Catholic film company was addressed in greater detail. A document drafted by Pizzardo at the end of the encounter clearly indicates how Pacelli's letter of April 1934 should be interpreted. The purpose of the OCIC was so well outlined in the Pacelli's letter, he contends, that it was hard to understand how its heads had intended to modify it on "purely financial grounds," given that the Holy See would be unable to support such a change. "Film production" implied such "financial efforts" that the Brussels Office, as its Statute confirms, could not possibly undertake, even indirectly.

---

129 Segreteria di Stato, S.RR.SS., Archivio Storico, AA.EE. SS., Stati Ecclesiastici, IV, Pos. 445, Fasc. 413, ff. 54-55rv, pen-written note dated 24.9.1935, original text is underlined: "cosa ottima;" "di aiutare le iniziative delle varie Nazioni (Centro di studi, informazioni, consigli, ecc.) e coordinare il lavoro che si svolge nelle varie Nazioni."

130 *Ibid.*: "direttivo perché 1) non ha – dal punto di vista cattolico – alcuna autorità al riguardo; 2) perché l'autorità centrale, per tutto ciò che è cattolico, è soltanto Roma."

131 *Ibid.*: "fuori ha meno autorità, ma più libertà di movimento. In Roma avrebbe troppo autorità (perché coinvolgerebbe troppo la S. Sede) perciò avrebbe pochissima libertà di movimento. E siccome nel cinema, quello che conta è il movimento…"

The film industry has developed so much and in such a way that it is unthinkable that a Catholic company (such is the OCIC, given the modifications to its statute that have been proposed) could directly influence production. The few films that the company could effectively market – with considerable financial effort – would not be influential enough in moral terms, and in fact, it would cause bigger companies, those which dominate almost entirely the world of the press, to launch a smear campaign against the new company, with predictable financial consequences. The remark in H.E. Pacelli's letter on the possibility to generate in good people an interest in the production of films with a high level of morality means that the OCIC's duty is to inspire the production of moral films without being financially involved in the operation, especially given the present state of the film industry.[132]

Pizzardo's conclusion eloquently summed up the Vatican's stance:

Now more than ever it is of the utmost importance to outline a simple and readily implantable policy: to put Catholics in a condition to understand the moral and social influence of cinema as well as the responsibility they are taking by letting their families watch immoral films; to put producers in a condition to see the

---

132 Segreteria di Stato, S.RR.SS., Archivio Storico, AA.EE. SS., Stati Ecclesiastici, IV, Pos. 445, Fasc. 409, ff. 57-59r, Note "in relazione alle spiegazioni complementari sottoposte dal Can. Brohée a S. E. Mons. Pizzardo in data 26 settembre" [on further details provided by Brohée to H.E. Monsignor Pizzardo on September 26], orginal text underlined: "Il campo dell'industria del film à oggi tali sviluppi che non si vede come una editrice cattolica (e tale risulterà al pubblico date le interferenze proposte dallo statuto) possa influire direttamente sulla produzione. I pochi film che la Casa potrebbe lanciare sul mercato – pur rappresentando uno sforzo economico considerevole – non avrebbero certo una influenza morale sufficiente mentre spingerebbero le altre case produttrici – che dominano la quasi totalità della stampa – ad inscenare una campagna denigratoria della nuova produzione con conseguenze economiche facilmente prevedibili. La frase della lettera di S. E. Pacelli relativa ad eccitare nei buoni l'interessamento alla fabbricazione dei film di alto valore morale va interpretata come l'incarico all'O.C.I.C. di eccitare nell'ambiente industriale il desiderio di editare dei films morali senza che l'O.C.I.C. né direttamente né indirettamente rimanga coinvolto nell'operazione e ciò vista l'attuale situazione del mercato cinematografico."

opportunity to produce films that are suitable for all audiences; to coordinate the activity of Catholic movie theatres in each country, by providing lists of films that are suitable for their audiences; to influence the press so that it does not favour immoral films; to collaborate with Hierarchy always; and to maintain a watertight separation of the bodies that depend on Catholic Action from commercial companies.[133]

7. The Cinematographic "Concordat"

The first five years of the thirties proved to be vital when it came to a clear definition of the Holy See's film policy. The Eidophon vicissitude, the inquiry into Soviet propaganda and the cantankerous relationship with OCIC were key events in this process, however it was the initiatives that the Holy See promoted in those same years, in Italy and in the United States, that provided the real foundation for the its wide-ranging actions. In other words, a comprehensive international survey of cinema, and a solemn pronouncement by the Pontiff – the *Vigilanti Cura* encyclical – in June 1936. We have already highlighted the centrality of both Mussolini's Italy and Roosevelt's United States in the definition of alternative (yet complementary) policies, each in relation to the needs and difficulties of Catholics in both countries. In each case, it was in those crucial first five years of the thirties that relationships were established and various associations and projects were promoted that together came to influence the Holy See's attitude towards cinema for at least four decades.

---

133 *Ibid.*: "Quello che oggi è più urgente è di tracciare un programma semplice e di immediata applicazione. Far comprendere ai cattolici l'influenza morale e sociale del cinema. Far comprendere loro la responsabilità che si assumono lasciando che i loro famigliari visionino films immorali. Far comprendere ai produttori l'opportunità e gli interessi che essi hanno nell'eseguire una produzione visibile a tutti. Coordinare in ogni nazione l'attività delle sale cattoliche segnalando loro la produzione adatta al loro pubblico. Influire sulla stampa perché non favorisca i films immorali. Agire sempre in collaborazione con la Gerarchia. Mantenere completamente distinti gli organismi dipendenti dall'Azione Cattolica e le Società Commerciali."

70 Catholicism and Cinema

For Italian Catholics, the major point of reference was the laboratory of the Ambrosian diocese.[134] Albeit from different perspectives, Agostino Gemelli and Carlo Canziani had laid the (respectively, cultural and administrative) foundations for the Italian Church's film policy. In the mid-twenties Gemelli (Chancellor of the Catholic University of Milan) introduced film technology into his psychology labs, thus contributing to the cultural legitimization of the new medium.[135] In the articles that he had published with *Vita e Pensiero* from 1926, Gemelli had begun to investigate the aspects related to perception and emotions in film reception, the illusion of reality produced by film vision, and the problematic social and psychic effects of the new medium.[136] For Gemelli, films were comparable to dreams, in which images are so arresting that they inhibit rational judgment. Hence the threat that cinema presented to the theocratic project of societal "rechristianization," and the necessity to reform cinema by moralizing its contents.[137] Rallying Catholics in the field of cinema, too, was part of Gemelli's plan to educate a new ruling class that would obey the Church, in-keeping with Pope Ratti's ideas.[138]

---

134 Dario E. Viganò, *Un cinema ogni campanile: Chiesa e cinema nella diocesi di Milano* (Milano: Il Castoro, 1997).

135 See Andrea Bellavita and Massimo Locatelli, "Padre Agostino Gemelli," in *Figure della modernità nel cinema italiano (1900-1940)*, ed. by Raffaele De Berti and Massimo Locatelli (Pisa: Ets, 2008), pp. 211-34; Massimo Scaglioni, "Agostino Gemelli: a Pioneer from Cinema to Audiovisuals" and Massimo Locatelli, "The Educational Question and the Filmological Enterprise in Italy," in *Can We Learn Cinema? Knowledge, Training, the Profession,* ed. by Anna Bertolli, Andrea Mariani and Martina Panelli, XIX Convegno Internazionale di Studi sul Cinema (Udine: Università degli Studi di Udine, 2012), pp. 85-91 and pp. 63-73.

136 Agostino Gemelli, "Le cause psicologiche dell'interesse nelle proiezioni cinematografiche. Il fondamento scientifico per la riforma del cinematografo," *Vita e Pensiero,* April 1926, pp. 205-215 and Id., "Contributo allo studio della percezione. IV. Il comparire e lo scomparire della forma," in *Contributi del Laboratorio di Psicologia e Biologia della Università Cattolica del Sacro Cuore* (Milano: Vita e Pensiero, 1928); see also Silvio Alovisio, *L'occhio sensibile: cinema e scienze della mente nell'Italia del primo novecento* (Torino: Kaplan, 2013).

137 See Elena Mosconi, "Un potente maestro per le folle," pp. 169-71.

138 *Agostino Gemelli e il suo tempo. Storia dell'Università Cattolica,* ed. by Maria Bocci (Milano: Vita e Pensiero, 2009).

In addition to Gemelli's academic activity, several Catholic associations in the field of cinema inaugurated a phase of joint and coordinated activity, thanks to Canziani's painstaking work. In 1926 the Consorzio Utenti Cinematografi Educativi [hereafter CUCE] was established in Milan, and its press organ the *Rivista del Cinematografo*, was founded two years later. The magazine supported the rapid development of a wide-ranging programme of movie theatre expansion and control of.[139] With the Concordat with Fascism, however, the Consortium's operational centre moved progressively from Milan to Rome, generating some contrasts within the ecclesiastical structure.

The issue of cinema had by no means been underestimated in the capital, but, as observed above, the central offices of Catholic Action approached the medium in a less direct and refined way. Before being acknowledged as a matter of cultural, didactic and artistic relevance, or in terms of its economic-industrial significance – that is say, as a field that necessitated the coordination of a networked distribution and management infrastructure – cinema had essentially been seen as an issue of public morality, encouraging more of a defensive attitude than a proactive one. Pacelli's appointment as head of the Secretariat of State, the double role that Pizzardo played in the Vatican and in Italy's Catholic Action, and the global vision of cinema that both men had caused a sudden change, which came to hone rapidly the ecclesiastical leaders' strategies and accelerate the Italian Catholics' centralization of cinematographic policy, in some ways embracing Gemelli's political project. In the context and atmosphere created by the Lateran Pacts, the conditions for implementing a sort of parallel "Concordat" on cinema between the Church and Fascism were thus created. Ecclesiastical and Fascist leaders established several agreements on some crucial points of the politics against cinema, which, albeit unofficial, defined the regulations that remained in place almost until Mussolini's fall. It was not, of course, a comprehensive convergence of the two bodies, but rather a series of reciprocal agreements that existed

---

139 *Nero su bianco, le politiche per il cinema negli ottant'anni della "Rivista del Cinematografo,"* ed. by Elena Mosconi (Roma: Ente dello Spettacolo, 2008).

in a delicate balancing act: the moral issue of cinematographic production was at the heart of this relationship with Fascism, but the range of covered themes and interests also included the fields of production, distribution and management. These agreements – which ensured the Church and its organizations a key role in censorship, on the one hand, and on the other the autonomy to consolidate an infrastructural and distribution networks – created a rift even in the film industry with regard to Fascism's hegemonic tendency, by instead sanctioning the presence of another power that the regime would not be able to incorporate.[140] The Church took advantage of the Fascist's lack of a systematic and rational plan: indeed the "schizophrenia" of the regime towards the film industry alternated – once the total inertia of the twenties had been overcome – between vain ambitions of nationalization in-keeping with the Nazi model, and policies that favoured autonomy of production, in-keeping with the American "individualist" system.[141] For other aspects related to cinema – such as institutional and didactic communication – the precocious birth of the LUCE Institute in 1924 was perhaps misleading: the political direction imposed by the regime and the aims and necessities of LUCE's managers and technicians never found any real harmony, failing to strike a balance between educational vocation and propagandistic intent. This was even more so when the Goebbelsian model, on the one hand, and the birth of the IECE on the other forced the institution to change its policy and increase its political relevance, as well as its international status.[142]

---

140 Gian Piero Brunetta, *Il Cinema italiano di regime. Da "La canzone dell'amore" a "Ossessione"* (Roma-Bari: Laterza, 2009), pp. 49-68.

141 Vito Zagarrio, *L'immagine del fascismo. La re-visione del cinema e dei media nel regime* (Roma: Bulzoni, 2009), specialmente pp. 186-87; Alfonso Venturini, *La politica cinematografica del regime fascista* (Roma: Carocci, 2015).

142 Gabriele D'Autilia, "Il fascismo senza passione. L'Istituto Luce," in *L'Italia del Novecento. Le fotografie e la storia*, ed. by Giovanni De Luna, Gabriele D'Autilia and Luca Criscenti (Torino: Einaudi 2005-2006), 1/I, *Il potere da Giolitti a Mussolini (1900-1945)*, pp. 91-114; Christel Taillibert, "Le cinéma, instrument de politique extérieure du fascisme italien," *Mélanges de l'Ecole française de Rome. Italie et Méditerranée*, 110, n. 2, 1998, pp. 943-62.

By alternating a firm will to pursue their aims and the subtle art of compromise, ecclesiastical leaders were able to progress within the interstices left by the regime, in order to consolidate their role in the cinema sector, in a way that would eventually yield results in the long run, especially in the complex post-War scene. The necessary conditions for a clearer convergence between governmental and ecclesiastical policies matured with the institutional turn taken almost simultaneously by both Catholic and Fascist fronts: Freddi's appointment as head of the new Direzione Generale per la Cinematografia [hereafter General Film Office] in September 1934, and the institution of the ACI's General Secretariat for Cinema some months later, in April 1935. The duties of the latter were soon after transferred to the Centro Cattolico Cinematografico [Catholic Cinematographic Centre, hereafter CCC]. Pizzardo's actions led the Italian Church to take on the "issue of cinema" and, benefiting from the dialectic relationship with Fascism, to translate the Holy See's aims into an organizational model that could be adopted by ecclesiastical institutions all over the world. Of course, America remained a model, but it had to be accommodated under new coordinates, where the main impulse for any initiative was no longer the Episcopate but Catholic Action. Soon after the promulgation of *Vigilanti Cura*, a brief report on the activity of the CCC for the Secretariat of State clarified the sense of renewal and the centrality of the Italian project:

> As film organizations were gradually established in several other countries, in Italy, Catholic Action, which, closer to the Pontiff See, felt bound to comply with the Pontiff's August Desires, became quickly concerned with coordinating what was taking place in this field, providing consistent direction and organization to the whole movement.[143]

---

143 Segreteria di Stato, S.RR.SS., Archivio Storico, AA.EE. SS., Stati Ecclesiastici, IV, Pos. 445, Fasc. 414, ff. 15-16r, Note "Il Centro Cattolico Cinematografico Italiano," s.d. The document was also published, with some amendations, in *Bollettino Ufficiale dell'A.C.I.*, n.8, 1936, p. 172 and it was entitled "L'Enciclica 'Vigilanti Cura' e l'Azione Cattolica Italiana." It was also published in *L'Assistente Ecclesiastico*, n. 8, August 1936: "Come in molti altri paesi si erano andate gradatamente costituendo le organizzazioni cinematografiche, così anche in Italia l'Azione Cattolica,

Alongside Pizzardo, ACI president Augusto Ciriaci played a pivotal role in these processes. He was an irreplaceable pawn in forging a network of political relationships with the regime as far as cinema was concerned, which would later become one of the main "unofficial" tasks that the Holy See assigned to the CCC.[144] Appointed head of Catholic Action by Pius XI in 1929, he vowed to revitalize the Secretariat for Morality immediately, endowing the campaign against immoral cinema a strategic role. He found a staunch ally in Ferdinando Prosperini, who would go on to play a leading role in Catholic film policy up to the fifties. With Prosperini as director of the Secretariat for Morality, the central board of ACI relaunched its campaign against cinema, specifying the subordination of Canziani's CUCE to the Roman institution. The circular dated June 30, 1930 set the terms for the centralization of film policy: the document claimed that the Secretariat for Morality considered it appropriate to give "moral support" to the Milanese consortium and its attempt to reorganize parish movie theatres, so as to gain, from distributors, "a repertoire that corresponded to the educational purposes of their screenings."[145]

The importance of this initiative did not escape the Central Board, which regarded it as a suitable means to obtain, thanks to the close union of many of our theatres, a lavish and genuine cinematographic production from religious, moral and education points of view, one that would indirectly impact upon production

---

che per essere più vicina alla sede del Pontefice sente il dovere di essere anche la più vicina nell'obbedienza ai Suoi Augusti Desideri, si è preoccupata subito di poter coordinare quanto in questo campo si stava facendo, imprimendo a tutto il movimento uniformità di indirizzo e di organizzazione."

144 On Augusto Ciriaci see Luciano Osbat's biographic profile, in *Dizionario biografico degli italiani*, vo. 25 (Roma: Istituto della Enciclopedia Italiana, 1981), pp. 781-83.

145 ISACEM Archive, PG XII, envelope 1, *Alle Giunte Diocesane e ai Segretariati Diocesani per la Moralità*, June 30, 1930. The circular was signed by ACI general president Augusto Ciriaci and by the General Secretary of the General Secretariat for Morality, Rev. Ferdinando Roveda: "Appoggio morale;" "un repertorio corrispondente agli scopi educativi delle loro proiezioni."

itself.[146]

For this reason, the Secretariat deemed it appropriate to report CUCE's "merits and achievements at all times," and recommend the *Rivista del Cinematografo*. Canziani's invitation to become a member of the central Secretariat for Morality marked the moment when central Vatican bodies officially took control of issues related to distribution and management.[147]

ACI's direct involvement in the issue of parish movie theatres was a clear signal. The question of a Catholic infrastructure was, not by chance, one of the most delicate aspects of the relationship between the Church and the Fascists. In fact, we know very well that a network of Catholic movie theatres, which the regime itself contributed to develop, entered into direct competition with that of the Opera Nazionale Dopolavoro [National Recreational Club, hereafter OND].[148] Therefore, frictions and tensions were not rare, particularly once the regime became aware of the hidden danger that Catholic pedagogy – which was promoted through the widespread network of parish movie theatres – posed to the edification of the new Fascist man. The most explicit instance of this took place in April 1933, when Canziani was officially

---

146   *Ibid.*: "L'importanza di questa iniziativa non sfuggì alla Giunta Centrale, che vide in essa un mezzo adatto per ottenere, grazie all'unione compatta delle numerosissime nostre sale, una produzione cinematografica copiosa e sana sotto ogni punto di vista religioso, morale ed educativo, sia per influire indirettamente sulla produzione generale."

147   *Ibid.*: "ogni volta le benemerenze e i successi;" "plaudendo ed incoraggiando quelle Giunte che si erano adoperate per il suo sviluppo."

148   It is worth noting that figures presented in Catholic sources significantly differ from those published by SIAE. For example, in the year 1936 the *Rivista del Cinematografo* published the following figures: 2,175 commercial theatres, 600 theatres reporting to the Opera Nazionale Dopolavoro, 860 theatres reporting to the Opera Nazionale Balilla and other cultural institutions, 1,600 theatres reporting to catholic associations and/or institutions ("Le sale cinematografiche in Italia," *Rivista del Cinematografo*, a. IX, n. 1, January 1936, p. 3). Data provided by SIAE for the year 1936 reports 2,641 commercial movie theatres, 629 belonging to the OND, 118 controlled by other organizations of the PNF and 537 parish theatres (or cinemas that otherwise report to catholic organizations). *La vita dello spettacolo in Italia nel 1936* (Roma: SIAE, 1937), quoted in Stefano Pivato, "L'organizzazione cattolica della cultura di massa durante il fascismo," *Italia Contemporanea*, 132, 1978, pp. 17-18.

fobidden by the Royal Police Headquarters of Milan to use the name CUCE: the acronym, as the police order reads, "is too close to LUCE." Thus, from that moment the CUCE sacrificed a vowel to the needs of the regime and adopted the new name of Consorzio per il Cinema Educatore [Consortium for Educational Cinema, CCE].[149]

Some months earlier, the bishop of Milan, Ildefonso Schuster, troubled the Secretariat of State for what was, in his opinion, an evident injustice against the Catholic cinematographic organization. From 1932, in fact, a provision by the Autorità di Pubblica Sicurezza [Public Security Authority] required that parish movies theatres pay to have their building inspected, in order to verify their stability and safety.[150] The same inspection was free of charge for theatres and cinemas of the Opera Nazionale Balilla [hereafter ONB] given "the role of great national importance" that this Fascist association played.[151] The Secretariat of State immediately wrote to the Ministry in charge of such issues in order to have parish movie theatres placed on the same level as those of the ONB, moreover taking the opportunity to suggest that ONB programmes be controlled by "the local ecclesiastical authority, which would be ensured by chaplains."[152]

Ciriaci and Prosperini also provided other, more solid foundations for the Catholic battle over moral conditioning, by aligning their activities with the new atmosphere created by the Lateran Pacts. Indeed, as well as modernizing the organizational system of their central and peripheral associations, they also

---

149 ISACEM Archive, PG XV, envelop 1, C. Canziani to ACI's press office, 28 April 1933: "avvicina troppo alla LUCE."

150 Segreteria di Stato, S.RR.SS., Archivio Storico, AA.EE. SS., Stati Ecclesiastici, IV, Pos. 445, Fasc. 406, ff. 33-34r, Ildefonso Schuster to Giuseppe Pizzardo, February 5, 1932.

151 Segreteria di Stato, S.RR.SS., Archivio Storico, AA.EE. SS., Stati Ecclesiastici, IV, Pos. 445, Fasc. 406, f. 35r, Lettera R. Questura di Milano agli Uffici di P. S., May 31, 1928: "la funzione di alta importanza nazionale."

152 Segreteria di Stato, S.RR.SS., Archivio Storico, AA.EE. SS., Stati Ecclesiastici, IV, Pos. 445, Fasc. 406, ff. 37-38r, "Voto sulla proposta del Card. Schuster per i locali dei cinematografi," s.d.: "la vigilanza dell'autorità ecclesiastica locale per mezzo dei Cappellani."

reinforced the cultural framework that linked Catholic morals to Latin and imperial traditions:

> No one can doubt how striving to defend public morality and decency is necessary to both the well-being of civil society and the encouragement of religious life. It is both a Christian and patriotic duty. It was perceived by our earliest ancestors, who, although relying on law of nature only, in that great *Corpus juris* that brought so much light to the world, wrote several laws in defence of morals. The noble traditions of Latin civilization were propelled forward and implemented by Christianity. [...] Italian Catholics, therefore, should feel much more vividly and accutely the duty to carry on with this civilizing and moralizing mission, which, if it is a glory of the Catholic Church, it is also a great pride of our Italy and of Rome in particular.[153]

The myth of Rome as "the holy city" of both the Church and the country proved to be a very fertile ground for the reconciliation of Catholics and Fascists, creating hence the subtlest confrontation between their respective symbolical-cultural apparatuses. Its premise was that the Church and Fascism would converge to enact the rebirth of the Ancient Roman civilization, whereby Church would represented the soul, and the regime its political and social force. At the same time, however, the two counterparts aspired to bring their mutual interlocutor within their own sphere of cultural and political supremacy.[154] In general, Ciriaci, working

---

153 ISACEM Archive, PG XII, envelope 1, Direttive per i Segretariati della Moralità, March 1, 1933, circular letter signed by Augusto Ciriaci and Ferdinando Prosperini: "Nessuno può dubitare quanto sia necessario al benessere della società civile, non meno che all'incremento della vita religiosa, adoperarsi a tutela della pubblica moralità e del buon costume. È un dovere cristiano insieme e patriottico. Lo sentirono gli stessi antichi nostri antenati, che, pur basandosi sulla sola legge naturale, in quel grandioso *Corpus juris*, che tanta luce diede al mondo, accolsero numerose, provvide leggi per la tutela della moralità. Le nobili tradizioni della civiltà latina furono continuate e perfezionate dal cristianesimo. [...] I cattolici italiani quindi debbono risentire tanto più vivo e più stretto l'obbligo di continuare in tale missione, civilizzatrice e moralizzatrice, che se è una gloria di tutta la Chiesa Cattolica, è pure uno specialissimo vanto dell'Italia nostra e di Roma in particolare."

154 Andrea Riccardi, *Roma "città sacra"?*, pp. 3-58; Lucia Ceci, *L'interesse superiore*, pp. 167-175.

together with Pizzardo (although not always in a systematic way),
was one of the most fervent promoters of this approach: he looked
favourably on a union with the regime, which he saw as a historical
opportunity for Italian Catholics to overcome the minority
status to which they had been relegated after the Risorgimento.
Nevertheless, in reality the agreement was evidently founded on
the Church's higher interests. While the fact that the president of
ACI was aligned to the regime is not unexpected – indeed Cesare
Maria De Vecchi, Italian ambassador to the Holy See, regarded
him as "an agent of ours in the Vatican"[155] – it is little surprising
that he also advocated the Association's tolerant attitude towards
intellectual movements that often criticized fascism, such as
the Federazione degli Universitari Cattolici Italiani [Federation
of Italian Catholic University Students, FUCI] and Catholic
Graduates.[156] Augusto Rovigatti, who wrote the first hagiographic
sketch of Ciriaci just a few weeks after his death in 1936, suggested
the correct interpretation for Ciriaci's 'conciliation' with the
regime through the theme of morality. Ciriaci, Rovigatti writes,
blessedly and joyfully welcomed "the day of the Conciliation:
the sacrament of matrimony is granted civil law status and this
will do Italian families great good," though it was nonetheless
necessary to "translate and bring the spirit of the Conciliation
into the Nation's daily life: laws are not enough, actions are
needed most of all. Half a century of de-Christianization cannot
be erased in a day."[157] What was taking shape in Italy, therefore,
was an ecclesiastical project for a "Catholic State:" it aimed to
reinforce the Church's presence in society by exploiting the
spaces provided by the Lateran Pacts, and it sought a convergence
with the illiberal aspects of fascism in order to realize a complete
catholicization of the fascist state.[158] These general objectives

---

155 This opinion is voiced in the letter that De Vecchi sent to Mussolini on
      December 3, 1932: Cesare Maria De Vecchi di Val Cismon, *Tra papa, duce
      e re. Il conflitto tra la Chiesa cattolica e lo Stato fascista nel Diario 1930-1931 del
      primo ambasciatore del Regno d'Italia presso la Santa Sede,* ed. by Sandro Setta
      (Roma: Jouvence, 1998), pp. 38-39 e pp. 53-55.
156 Renato Moro, *La formazione della classe dirigente cattolica (1929-1937)*
      (Bologna: il Mulino, 1979), pp. 356-59.
157 Augusto Rovigatti, *Augusto Ciriaci, primo presidente dell'Unione Uomini di
      Azione cattolica* (Roma: Unione Uomini di Azione cattolica, 1936), p. 31.
158 On this question, and in view of its impact on future historiography, see

account for the different modes, despite certain similarities between the two pedagogical models, through which the Church and the fascist regime promoted their moralization campaigns. For all these reasons, the regime often followed in the wake of the Church, nevertheless distancing itself from certain themes, or if the latter's actions represented an obstacle to the fascistization of Italy. In this context, some scholars, who have focused on sexuality at that time, have highlighted the deep-seated contradiction in the regime's attitude towards the modernization of sexual morals, opposing the process to the intransigence of Catholic culture. According to Bruno Wanrooij, the dividing line between "rigor" and "liberalization" was not found between Catholicism and fascism, but rather within fascism itself. It inspired an internal tug of war between those who most strongly endorsed the position of the Church, on the one hand, and, on the other, those who favoured a notion of modernization that embraced sexual health and physical well-being, in contrast with the presumably unhealthy effects of prolonged chastity and sexual repression (onanism, nervous disorders, etc.).[159] One indication of this can be found in the varying levels of restraint of the Fascists and Catholics as regards the sexual behaviours that cinema conveyed: it was not unusual, in fact, for Catholic Revision Board (whose responsibility covered exclusively parish cinemas) to classify as "Excluded for all" or "Excluded for minors" films that had the *nihil obstat* of the Fascist Cinematographic Revision Board. The same variances can be seen in the changing attitudes of Fascist prefects: in fact, local State representatives (who had the authority to seize films) at times endorsed local Catholic opposition to specific films, and at others contested it.[160]

The frequent exchanges between Ciriaci and the Duce about cinema and morality are to be situated within this complex

---

Giovanni Miccoli's essay "La chiesa e il fascismo," in *Fascismo e società italiana*, ed. by Guido Quazza (Torino: Einaudi, 1973), pp. 185-208.

159 Bruno P. F. Wanrooij, *Storia del pudore. La questione sessuale in Italia 1860-1940* (Venezia: Marsilio, 1990).

160 David Forgacs, "Sex in the Cinema. Regulation and Transgression in Italian Films, 1930-1943," in *Reviewing Fascism. Italian Cinema 1922-1943*, ed. by Jacqueline Reich and Piero Garofalo (Bloomington: Indiana University Press, 2002), pp. 144-71, especially p. 146.

framework: they took place under Pizzardo's careful supervision, and paved the way for the foundation of the CCC. In February 1933, once the 1930 turmoil between the Church and the regime about the organization of ACI had subsided, an important event took place: the head of ACI sent a detailed memorandum to Mussolini[161], where, thanking the fascist leader for his "important appreciation" of "the work of Catholic Action in defending families from the dangers of egoism and corruption," he further reinforced the pact with the regime to re-Christianize leisure time by enclosing a list of Catholic *desiderata*[162]. ACI took on the duty of warning Mussolini "about all sorts of invasive actions against morals, familial strength and fertility, and therefore the prosperity of the Nation."[163] Ciriaci submitted a detailed file regarding "immoral magazines," "nudist propaganda," and "morals on the beach," though it was "cinematographic shows," "schools of murder and seduction," that were at the top of his list.[164] The director of ACI outlined a point-by-point programme for a 'concordat' on the moralization of cinema:

> Special advice should be given to the commission of cinematographic revision and theatre productions; this is to prevent the Royal Police force from intervening to suspend shows that central offices had previously approved. Governmental regulation should prevent the so-called "variety shows" from being represented on film. Film exhibitors themselves support this proposal for economic reasons, and it complies with the vote of the office for educational cinema. Moreover, we most heartedly wish that all of our interventions, which have been welcomed by

---

161 Segreteria di Stato, S.RR.SS., Archivio Storico, AA.EE. SS., Italia, IV, pos. 929, vol. 1, fasc. 616, ff. 31-36r, Letter from Augusto Ciriaci to Giuseppe Pizzardo, July 29, 1933. In his letter to the ecclesiastical assistant, the ACI president enclosed a copy of "the letter sent to Your Excellency the head of the Government, Rome 23 February 1933" ("lettera mandata a S.E. il Capo del Governo, Roma, 23 febbraio 1933").

162 *Ibid.*: "Alte parole di compiacimento;" "l'opera dell'Azione Cattolica nella tutela della famiglia dai pericoli dell'egoismo e della corruzione."

163 *Ibid.*: "La voce di allarme per tutto quello che si va tuttora osando in molte parti contro la moralità, la saldezza e la fecondità della famiglia, e perciò anche contro la prosperità della Patria."

164 *Ibid.*: "Riviste immorali;" "propaganda nudista;" "moralità delle spiagge;" "spettacoli cinematografici;" "scuole di delitto e di seduzione."

the Royal Police force, are always interpreted as a sincere desire to cooperate with the authority itself in order to ensure a much better observation of the laws in force.[165]

In his letter, Ciriaci, singing the praises of those who had "given back God to Italy and Italy to God," outlines further grounds for agreements and collaboration: in ACI's view, the moralizing campaign represented an important contribution to the success of the demographic battle.

Your Excellency, Catholic Action does not intend to spoil the honest comfort and entertainment of the people; yet, it wants and strives to ensure that, in a highly Catholic country, it complies with human and divine laws and is worthy of this great people. It does not ask for new laws; it only demands that the excellent laws in force – thanks to Your Excellency's strength and wisdom – will be observed and enforced more effectively by everyone; this is not only for the spiritual good, but also for the physical health of our people. In so doing, we will succeed in avoiding the weakening of the union and integrity of families – which has happened in other countries, with the consequent decrease in the birth rate, the first and immediate effect of immorality – from bringing its shameful massacre, much more fatal than war, into our Nation.[166]

---

165 *Ibid.*: "Una particolare raccomandazione riteniamo debba essere fatta alla commissione di revisione delle pellicole cinematografiche e delle produzioni teatrali; onde non avvenga più che le Regie Questure debbano intervenire a sospendere rappresentazioni, che gli impresari ottennero di vedere approvate dagli organi centrali. Una disposizione governativa dovrebbe interdire per ragioni di ordine morale, l'introduzione dei cosiddetti "numeri di varietà" negli spettacoli cinematografici, tesi alla quale sono favorevoli, per ragioni di ordine economico, gli stessi direttori dei cinematografi e che corrisponde ai voti dell'Ente per la cinematografia educativa. Desideriamo vivamente altresì che ogni nostro intervento, come ha trovato sin ora accoglienza benevola non solo, ma anche efficace ascolto presso la Regia Questura, sia interpretato sempre, quale vuol essere, un sincero desiderio di cooperare con le autorità stesse per la sempre migliore osservanza delle leggi vigenti."

166 *Ibid.*: "Eccellenza, l'Azione Cattolica non intende punto vedere impedito l'onesto sollievo e divertimento del popolo; ma vuole e si adopera che, in un paese profondamente cattolico specialmente, esso riesca conforme alle leggi divine e umane, e perché anche degno di un grande popolo. Non chiede nuove leggi; chiede soltanto che le ottime leggi vigenti — e vigenti appunto in gran parte per la saggezza e la forza dell'Eccellenza

It was only with the birth of the General Film Office in
September 1934, and Freddi's contribution, that such requests
were taken into consideration, albeit in different ways. Freddi was
a key figure in these years: he looked to Hollywood's production
model, bringing it into compliance with the corporate culture
of fascist ideology, drawing some elements even from Nazi and
Soviet cinematographic organizations;[167] he aimed to create a
sort of "nationalized MGM," that is to say, a State film company,
a far cry from the suffocating Nazi model, which could manage
production, distribution and financial activities without stifling
or damaging the private industry.[168] In Freddi's composite
strategy, relationships with the Catholics occupied a prominent
position. The Fascist director had a precise idea of how Regime-
Church relations could prove instrumental to the "fascistization
of Italian cinema:" cinematographic censorship had to be based
on a system of religious values, but, at the same time, not use
inquisitorial methods.[169] In the first weeks after his appointment
as general director, Freddi – as he wrote in his post-war memoir –
had a number of interviews with Tacchi Venturi that illuminate his
position. In his report for Galeazzo Ciano (who, at that time, was
Undersecretary of State for Press and Propaganda), he claimed
that he had conferred at length with the Jesuit, who "delivered a
long and critical speech, usually supported by evidence, about the
pervasive immorality of cinematographic products, with specific
reference to foreign ones, but also with careful and learned
allusions to national ones." The pontifical emissary's intervention
was clearly interpreted by Freddi as a "true mission:"

Vostra — siano rispettate ed applicate con maggiore vigore e realtà da
tutti; e ciò tanto per il bene spirituale che per la sanità fisica del popolo
nostro. Così ci riuscirà alfine di evitare che il rilassamento della unione
e integrità della famiglia, avveratosi in altri popoli, con la conseguente
diminuzione delle nascite che è il primo e immediato frutto della
immoralità, porti le sue stragi vergognose, più esiziali di ogni guerra,
anche alla diletta nostra Patria."

167 See Vito Zagarrio, pp. 164-72.
168 Barbara Corsi, *Con qualche dollaro in meno: storia economica del cinema
italiano* (Roma: Editori Riuniti, 2001), pp. 23-31.
169 Jean A. Gili, *Stato fascista e cinematografia: repressione e promozione* (Roma:
Bulzoni, 1981) pp. 38-42.

I have come to understand that the Vatican devotes particular attention to the moral aspects of entertainment, especially cinema, and that, with benevolent sympathy, it relies on the action of our ministry. Father Tacchi acknowledged what I explained to him as exact [...]: that is to say that we find it difficult to check faults and to intervene, as the original vice is to be found in the very organization of production, especially abroad. As for me, I reassured Father Tacchi, in compliance with higher orders, that we would follow the process of production through censorship, so that it would not betray ethical and aesthetic principles which inform state regulations.[170]

In Freddi's view, Catholic morals and Fascist perspective could find common ground only in a form of censorship that would abandon a "coldly restrictive" surveillance and embrace a more "inspiring and generative function."[171]

Of course I made it clear that our point of view refers to those principles in progress, which *also* involve, therefore, moral issues that are the sole aim of the Church. Finally, I pointed out to the reverend father that we cannot eternally persevere in our negative criticism and censorship, but we need, on the contrary, to adopt a positive attitude that can counter licentious productions with Italian and moral ones, which, nevertheless, should have an essentially spectacular and suggestive nature. And this is in agreement with previous clear and explicit declarations by the Supreme Pontiff. Father Tacchi Venturi acknowledged the propriety of my words and, being nonetheless discreet, he ensured me that he would lead people and groups in the Vatican to support my proposal.[172]

This last observation, as Freddi explains, became "a sort of obsession" for him: he constantly returned to it any time he had the "opportunity to talk with Catholic authorities."[173] Following this logic, the fascist director soon set to work to find an agreement with Catholic institutions regarding censorship. A first instance of this new turn occurred a few weeks after Freddi's installation,

---

170 Luigi Freddi, p. 48.
171 *Ibid.*, p. 47.
172 *Ibid.*, p. 48.
173 *Ibid.*

when Ciriaci informed him of ACI's strong, negative opinion
about the film *Casanova's Love-Life* [*Les amours de Casanova*], from
French director René Barberis. Distributed by Pittalunga and
premiered at the Volturno cinema in Rome in October 1934, the
film underwent a second revision at the request of ACI. Freddi
consented to have the film screened at the Under Secretariat for
Press and Propaganda; this was carried out in agreement with
Arturo Ambrosio, member of the Ente per la Cinematografia
Educativa e Religiosa [Office for Educational and Religious
Cinema, hereafter ECER] – the Roman institute that had been
founded two years earlier, and was soon to be merged with the
CCC. On that occasion, as the ECER told Ciriaci at the end of
October, "cuts" were "definitely agreed upon" in those sections
that most offended "our religious feeling," and the film was
prohibited to anyone under the age of 16.[174] From that moment
on, Pittaluga allowed the Catholic office to preliminarily inspect
new production and distribution.

It is not surprising that the above-mentioned report sent by
the CCC to the Secretariat of State in summer 1936 stated that
the Centre had "a good and lasting relationship" with both the
General Film Office and with the Federazione degli Industriali
dello Spettacolo [Federation of Entertainment Producers]
"since its foundation," "thus having the opportunity to notify
the competent authorities about the desires of the Catholics in
this field."[175] It is with "great satisfaction – it reads – that [the
Centre] can claim to have always found true understanding and
eagerness to collaborate, according to the regulations of the
government and the desire for a better and more constructive

---

174 ISACEM Archive, PG XV, envelope 2, folder 1, ECER letter to Augusto
     Ciriaci, October 28, 1934: "concordati definitivamente i tagli;" "il nostro
     sentimento cristiano." The length of the film was reduced from 2209m
     to 2045m in order to "delete licentious scenes" ("per la soppressione di
     alcune scene licenziose"): *Bollettino n. 8*, Ministero dell'Interno, October
     1934.

175 Segreteria di Stato, S.RR.SS., Archivio Storico, AA.EE. SS., Stati
     Ecclesiastici, IV, Pos. 445, Fasc. 414, ff. 15-16r, note "Il Centro Cattolico
     Cinematografico Italiano," s.d.: "fin dalla sua costituzione;" "in rapporti
     assidui e cordiali;" "avendo così modo di far giungere alle competenti
     Autorità i desideri dei cattolici in questo campo."

moral production."[176] After all, it was precisely the meeting between Freddi and the CCC's first secretary, Paolo Cassinis, in summer 1936 that sealed the deal between the Church and the regime regarding cinema: on that occasion, the leader of fascist cinema "clarified the deep desire of the General Film Office for a closer, unofficial collaboration with the CCC."[177] This covert agreement between the highest exponents of Fascist and Catholic cinematographic organizations determined that the collaboration should "specifically take place before the State Censorship approved the films."[178] In the wake of the *Casanova* affair, Freddi suggested, therefore, that the CCC "promptly" reported to him "those foreign films that Catholic offices considered immoral, in order to invite foreign productions not to import into Italy."[179] Thus, the framework of the agreement about cinema between the highest political representatives took a most definite shape, a framework within which, however, the parties concerned did not cease to pursue their own specific interests.

8. *Americans: Allies and Enemies*

1934 stood out as turning point, and not only because Freddi took charge of Fascist cinema. It was also the year of the traditional

---

176 *Ibid.*: "viva soddisfazione esso può dire di aver sempre trovato sincera comprensione e volontà di fattiva collaborazione, rientrando nelle direttive tracciate dal Governo una volontà di una produzione moralmente più sana e più costruttiva."

177 Segreteria di Stato, S.RR.SS., Archivio Storico, AA.EE. SS., Stati Ecclesiastici, IV, Pos. 445, Fasc. 408, ff. 29-30r, "Conversazione tra l'Ing. Cassinis ed il Comm. Freddi Direttore Generale per il Cinema al Ministero Stampa e Propaganda," s.d.: "Voluto precisare il vivo desiderio della Direzione Generale per una più stretta collaborazione di carattere ufficioso con il Centro Cattolico Cinematografico." The precise date of this meeting may be deduced from the note, which refers to a previous interview between Cassinis and Manlio Binna, Vice Director general for cinema at the Ministry of Press and Propaganda, on July 26, 1936.

178 *Ibid.*: "In modo speciale svolgersi prima che la Censura di Stato;" "alla approvazione dei films."

179 *Ibid.*: "tempestivamente i filmi [sic] esteri riconosciuti immorali dagli ambienti cattolici onde poter invitare le case estere ad evitare la loro importazione in Italia."

visit *ad limina* payed by North-American bishops to Saint Peter's cathedral every five years. On this occasion, the American clergy offered the Pope first-hand accounts of the power Hollywood had gained. Cardinal Denis J. Dougherty, archbishop of Philadelphia, and John J. Cantwell, who led the dioceses of Los Angeles and San Diego, did not hold back from apocalyptic tones.

As Tacchi Venturi and Freddi pointed out in their talks about the "cinematographic concordat," the core of cinema's moral issue was found in foreign productions, and in particular Hollywood ones. One notes how the Holy See viewed Mussolini's Italy as a litmus test of the kind of power that American models and lifestyles, as conveyed by cinema and more generally by mass culture, could gain if no adequate restrictions were imposed. Quantitative data about films distributed in Italy during the regime alone is telling in this respect: 56% were Hollywood products in 1930, as opposed to 4,5% of Italian films. These percentages were confirmed in the following years: in 1934 American films constituted 58% while Italian films only 10%; in 1938, they were 59% and 16% respectively.[180] Other European countries saw similar ratios, if not higher ones: from 1925, for instance, American cinema occupied the 95% of the British market and 75% of the French one.[181] It is not surprising, therefore, that Pius XI received complaints from all over the world, confirming what *L'Osservatore Romano* would define "the devastating invasion of American films."[182] Pius XI gathered together all of these suggestions during the August of the same year, when he delivered one of his most detailed speeches about cinema, pointing out and praising the resolution of the American episcopacy. Addressing the executive committee of the International Federation of Film Critics, Ratti expressed his "serious concerns:"

---

180 See the summary table in Lorenzo Quaglietti, *Storia economico-politica del cinema italiano. 1945-1980* (Roma: Editori Riuniti, 1980), pp. 245-46, where data is taken from the SIAE annual publication *Lo spettacolo in Italia*.

181 Thomas H. Guback, *The International Film Industry* (Bloomington: Indiana University Press, 1969), p. 8.

182 Federico Marconcini, "L'invasione devastatrice delle pellicole americane," *L'Osservatore Romano*, October 13, 1935.

Without mentioning the positive aspects of cinema and all the good that comes and may come from it when it spreads virtue and truth, its effects are extremely serious, when – as we all know – it becomes a vehicle of a great evil, as it usually does.[183]

What most impressed the Pontiff was the "statistical language:" on a global scale, "87 million people" went to the cinema in November 1933 alone. "What was," Ratti wondered, "the percentage of moral, didactic films within this great amount of productions? Small and quite low." The "Holy crusade against immoral cinema" launched by American bishops was a model to be imitated: even the press, in the Pope's opinion, should join that "necessary campaign." Furthermore, "would [cinema] be so evil, so depraved, if the press was against immoral films?" The Pope's tones were rather apocalyptic. To his eyes, the perversion of cinema resulted from the degeneration of capitalism:

> Here the words of Our Lord come to mind, when he refers to *mammona iniquitatis* in his gospel. How many times does mean desire for money lead to demoralization, to the moral death of whole generations! How many disasters! And it is a problem for the soul! Thinking about it is terrible, not only – of course – from a religious point of view, but also from a human one.

On the occasion, the Pope called for a clear and vocal universal mobilization: the aim was just to produce religious films and to juxtapose or alternate them with "libertine" ones: cinema as such had to be "moral, an influence for good morals, an educator." Just a few days before Pius XI's appeal to the international press, Amleto Cicognani, the apostolic deputy in Washington, had provided the Secretariat of State with a detailed account depicting a most alarming situation. In that memorandum, he summarized the recent achievements of the episcopal campaign,

---

183 Segreteria di Stato, S.RR.SS., Archivio Storico, AA.EE. SS., Stati Ecclesiastici, IV, Pos. 445, Fasc. 414, ff. 23-25r, S.S. Pio XI's speech in favour of the moralization of cinema, August 10, 1934. Now in: *Alla Federazione Internazionale della Stampa Cinematografica. Per un "film" morale*, August 10, 1934, *Discorsi di Pio XI,* ed. by Domenico Bertetto (Città del Vaticano: Libreria Editrice Vaticana, 1985, 2nd edn), III, *1934-1939,* pp. 189-92, which we quote.

highlighting its strengths.[184] Cantwell – leader of the 'diocese of Hollywood' – was among the bishops who visited the Pope in 1934 and was one of the promoters of the offensive, together with the bishops of Pittsburgh and Fort Wayne, Hugh C. Boyle and John F. Noll respectively. The year before, the Episcopal Committee on Motion Pictures had been founded within the National Catholic Welfare Council [hereafter NCWC]. John T. McNicholas, a Dominican priest of Irish origins and Archbishop of Cincinnati, was appointed leader of the committee: he proved the shrewdest and most active member of the North-American Church's campaign. In its first months of activity, the Episcopal Committee promoted the Legion of Decency: those who joined it were obliged to make a solemn pledge to "desert immoral cinemas."[185] The success of the Bishops' enterprise left Cicognani flabbergasted. Not only had the committee organized a great number of meetings, but Catholic newspapers had also played a leading role in this respect: "the Protestants and the Jews – Cicognani claimed – have echoed the Catholic campaign for the purification of cinema; I do not hesitate to claim that it has become a quotidian topic, and deserves to be acknowledged as an important event in this nation."[186] The number of Catholics who joined the Legion was rapidly growing: "at first, many thousands of people read the pledge formula, that is to say, promised not to go to these 'contaminated' places; now they are millions."[187] The result was quite tangible: "the consequences of the Bishop's action – as the prelate observed – have bewildered people in Hollywood. A considerable decrease in box office receipts made

184 ASV, Segreteria di Stato, a. 1934, rubr. 325, n. 6, "Campagna dell'Episcopato nord-americano contro il cinematografo immorale," report n. 9070, Amleto Cicognani and Eugenio Pacelli, July 27, 1934. Pacelli received the letter on August 12, as reported in the document.
185 *Ibid.*: "disertare i cinematografi immorali."
186 *Ibid.*: "I protestanti e i giudei hanno fatto eco alla campagna dei cattolici per la purificazione del cinema; non esito a dirlo, l'argomento è divenuto ovunque quasi di trattazione quotidiana, e merita il nome di evento importante in questa nazione."
187 *Ibid.*: "Dapprima furono migliaia, che nelle chiese leggevano la formula del pledge o promessa di non recarsi in questi luoghi infetti, ed ora sono milioni."

them face up to the Bishops. They promised to improve and purify cinema production."[188]

Cicognani, the promoter and man behind the scenes of the whole operation, was well aware of the campaign's importance. Having an influence on Hollywood producers meant damaging the "machine" of cinema on a global scale: the American episcopacy paved the way to retrieving power over a product of modernity that, more than any other, was in surreptitious competion with the Roman Church for the supremacy over human consciences, as the Pontiff himself had warned. Furthermore, this model reflected Ratti's monolithic and hierarchical idea of Catholicism, as evident in the foundation of a central unit that would moralize cinema (the Legion of Decency), which was coordinated by local ecclesiastical authorities in collaboration with the Holy See. This was the basis for the model that the Pontiff would propose, with a few major adjustments, in the encyclical *Vigilanti Cura*. Rather than trying to control the phenomenon actively, in the way chosen in some European countries, the Legion of Decency adopted defensive positions. Nonetheless, it was not, as initial reports suggested, less effective. Cicognani informed the Secretary of State that the bishops had resolved to "make the means of purification permanent."[189] To support his claim, the prelate enclosed the pamphlet (written by Archbishop McNicholas, chairman of the committee) entitled *The Episcopal Committee and the Problem of Evil Motion Pictures* with the report sent to Pacelli. In it, the episcopacy outlines the structural organization of their permanent crusade: it recommends the creation of a National Council for the Legion of Decency, whose secretary should be nominated by the NCWC; each diocese was to create a local council, which would collaborate with the national equivalent; and 2,500,000 pupils in parish schools were enlisted in the Legion.[190] "Claiming that

---

188 *Ibid.*: "le conseguenze di quest'azione dei Vescovi ha sconcertato la gente di Hollywood, pel fatto che in realtà si è constatata una sensibile diminuzione d'incassi, e questo motivo li ha indotti a venire a trattative coi Vescovi, con assicurazione di fare il possibile per migliorare e purificare la produzione cinematografica."

189 *Ibid.*: "A rendere stabili i mezzi di epurazione."

190 ASV, Segreteria di Stato, a. 1934, rubr. 325, n. 6, John T. McNicholas, "The Episcopal Committee and the Problem of Evil Motion Pictures," *The*

this enterprise is a "Crusade" would be an understatement – the apostolic deputy specified in his letter to the bishops in October 1934 – since crusades are usually temporary: the nature of the present cause demands great zeal, the unity of aims, and no further setbacks."[191]

Such accurate and detailed organization was necessary, in the opinion of American bishops, especially after the negative results of the Production Code (also known as the Hays Code), Hollywood's self-censorship system established in 1930. In the absence of a federal authority on film censorship, the original American control model was based on a centralized apparatus, which relied on a series of compromises made by producers, the public, financial and entrepreneurial worlds, and pressure groups.[192] The episcopacy believed that film producers did not comply with the norms of the Code when it came into force, and that immorality in film had by no means decreased, precisely thanks to the producers, who had struck a low blow to American Catholicism. The Catholics' contribution to the Code has been documented in detail. In addition to the Presbyterian William H. Hays – after whom the Code itself is named – and a handful of protestant groups, the history of the Code counts among its promoters Martin Quigley, the Catholic editor of the *Exhibitor's Herald World*; Jesuit Father Lord, a religious consultant at Hollywood; and Cardinal George Mundelein, leader of the diocese of Chicago.[193] From 1922, Hays had directed MPPDA,

---

Ecclesiastical Review Philadelphia, Pennsylvania, August 1934. L'opuscolo è vergato da frequenti appunti e sottolineature stese da Pacelli.

191 Segreteria di Stato, S.RR.SS., Archivio Storico, AA.EE. SS., Stati Ecclesiastici, IV, Pos. 445, Fasc. 415, ff. 17rv-18r, Letter by Amleto Cicognani to the American episcopacy, October 18, 1934: "Dire che questa impresa è una 'Crociata' sarebbe poco perché mentre una crociata ha di solito carattere temporaneo, la natura della causa presente sembra tale da richiedere di essere condotta con fermezza di zelo, con unità di propositi e senza rallentamento di sorta."

192 Giuliana Muscio, "L'era di Will Hays. La censura nel cinema americano," in *Storia del cinema mondiale*, ed. by Gian Piero Brunetta (Torino: Einaudi, 1999), 2/I, *Gli Stati Uniti*, pp. 525-26.

193 One of the most accurate accounts is to be found in Richard Maltby, "The Production Code and the Hays Office," in *Grand Design: Hollywood as a Modern; Business Enterprise, 1930 – 1939*, ed. by Tino Balio (Berkeley: University of California Press, 1993), pp. 37-72.

the trade union that united Hollywood producers and renters, with an eye to self-regulation as an answer to the growing call for censorship from both local authorities and pressure groups. The primary aims of the MPPDA was to give a good impression of the film industry and to avoid the circumstances for federal censorship at all costs. Hays, who had directed the electoral campaign of President William G. Harding and subsequently become his Postmaster General, felt the need to root the code in a "philosophical corpus," as he called it, and for this reason he addressed Catholics in particular.[194] Quigley acted as mediator between the American film industry and the American ecclesiastical hierarchy; Lord contributed widely to the moral-philosophical character of the Code; and Cardinal Mundelein effectively provided the support of the Catholic Church.[195] The Holy See was aware of this enterprise. It was Ledóchowski, the head of the Jesuits, who signalled how the Catholics' involvement in this process should be interpreted. When he sent the Hays Code to the Vatican Secretariat of State, he described its genesis as follows:

> It is a sort of "Regulation" recently written in the United States of America to raise and purify cinema, and, following the task bestown upon him by the Most Reverend Cardinal Mundelein, one of our Fathers contributed to this enterprise. The "Regulation" had been approved by the supreme Censor, an office whose holder (Mr. Will Hays at the moment) is nominated by the President of the Republic, and accepted by the directors of cinema companies. From now on, this will be the official norm to produce new "films."
>
> It is true, of course, that with this Regulation not all films will entirely accord to the Catholic mind: this was an impossible aim to pursue. Nonetheless, our Fathers believed that they had to take this opportunity to introduce at least the main ethical norms and Cristian morals in this form of entertainment, which, nowadays,

---

194 William Harrison Hays, p. 439.

195 In the first drafts of the document, some sources mention the Jesuit Wilfrid Parson among the collaborators. He was the editor in chief of *America*, the weekly journal of the Company of Jesus in the United States: Stephen Vaughn, "Morality and Entertainment: The Origins of Production Code and the Hays Office," *The Journal of American History*, vol. LXXVII, n. 1, June 1990.

can indeed have great influence, be it positive or negative, on the public. [196]

The main players in this enterprise were well-known to the Vatican. In a note from the Secretary of State, Quigley was defined as the "Reverend McNicholas's right-hand man in the Legion of Decency: he was an "excellent Catholic" and "extremely devoted to the Church and its Catholic Hierarchy;" he received the Holy Communion every day, and had a Jesuit son.[197] Ledóchowski vouched for Father Lord, who would play a leading role in the creation of *Vigilanti Cura*: the American Jesuit taught drama at the University of St Louis and had been a consultant to Cecil B. DeMille in the production of *The King of Kings* (1927).

---

196 Segreteria di Stato, S.RR.SS., Archivio Storico, AA.EE. SS., Stati Ecclesiastici, IV, Pos. 445, Fasc. 415, ff. 69-70r, Włodzimierz Ledóchowski to Giuseppe Pizzardo, March 27, 1930: "Si tratta di una specie di "Regolamento" recentemente composto negli Stati Uniti d'America per elevare e purificare gli spettacoli cinematografici, al quale, secondo l'incarico datogli dall'Eminentissimo Car. Mundelein, un nostro Padre ha cooperato. Esso fu approvato dal supremo Censore, che è un ufficio il cui titolare (attualmente Mr. Will Hays) viene nominato dal Presidente della Repubblica, ed è riuscito accetto anche ai direttori delle compagnie cinematografiche, e d'ora in poi sarà la norma ufficiale da seguire nel produrre i nuovi "films." È bene vero che con questo Regolamento non si otterrà che tutte le pellicole rifondano interamente alla mente cattolica, ciò che non fu possibile di conseguire. Tuttavia i nostri Padri hanno creduto di dover accettare la buona occasione che loro si offriva per introdurre almeno le principali norme di una sana Etica e le essenziali leggi della morale cristiana in un genere di divertimento, che ai nostri giorni può esercitare un sì largo influsso tanto in bene quanto in male." *La Civiltà Cattolica* commented upon the Hays Code in America in "L'autocensura dei produttori cinematografici in America," *La Civiltà Cattolica*, a. 82, vol. 3, n. 1878, August 11, 1931, pp. 209-17: "This is an event of great importance, for the benefits it could have on the whole world. This moral Code has nothing that goes against Christian moral principles: it so detailed, that, if followed, it could improve cinema, not only in America but also all over the world, where American films are quite popular.
197 Segreteria di Stato, S.RR.SS., Archivio Storico, AA.EE. SS., Stati Ecclesiastici, IV, Pos. 445, Fasc. 415, f. 76r, Anonymous, s.d., no signature: "L'uomo di fiducia di Mons. McNicholas nella campagna della Legion of Decency;" "ottimo cattolico;" "devotissimo verso la Chiesa e la Gerarchia Cattolica."

One of modernism's greatest enemies, Lord was a prolific writer who published more than 200 pamphlets, as well as numerous books and plays: in his writings he was against abortion, birth control, Darwinism and communism, not to mention contemporary literature, dance and art. In his autobiography, he wrote that the Code was "a chance" for Catholics "to tie the Ten Commandments in with the newest and most widespread form of entertainment."[198] And it was Lord himself who fiercely denounced the "betrayal" of the Code. As *La Civiltà Cattolica* highlighted in a reportage on the "crusade against immoral cinema in America" in January 1935, the Jesuit was the author of a *j'accuse* pamphlet against Hollywood producers.[199] Published in 1934 and entitled *The Motion Picture Betray America*, it began as follows:

> I accuse the Motion Picture Industry of the United States of the most terrible betrayal of public trust in the history of our country. I charge them with putting the profits of the box office ahead of all considerations of decency, respect for law, or love of a nation's health and happiness. I charge them with betraying the best interests of our people and attacking by the most violent means the morality which is rooted in the Ten Commandments given to Moses and the morality preached by Jesus Christ to the world. And, in company with millions who see the peril and dread it, I call upon Americans to register their disgust with this great betrayal of decency, this treason to the country's best interests, at the only place that the producers themselves know or regard or recognize: The box office.[200]

Cicognani's arrival at the apostolic see of Washington in March 1933 was the prelude to a much more direct involvement of the Holy See in the North-American Church's campaign against

---

198 *Played by Ear. The Autobiography of Daniel A. Lord, S.J.* (Chicago: Loyola University Press, 1956), p. 298.

199 Mario Barbera, "Cinematografo e stampa. 'Legione della decenza'," *La Civiltà Cattolica*, a. 86, vol. 1, n. 2029, January 5, 1935, pp. 10-11.

200 Daniel A. Lord, *The Motion Pictures Betray America* (St. Louis, Queen's Work, 1934). For context, see: Thomas P. Doherty, *Hollywood's Censor: Joseph I. Breen and the Production Code Administration* (New York: Columbia University Press, 2007), pp. 52-60.

immoral cinema. The Apostolic Delegate sought to take matters into his own hands and create direct and continuous contact with the Holy See to a greater extent than his predecessor Pietro Fumasoni Biondi. His speech at the National Conference of Catholic Charities in October 1933 was a clear declaration of aims, and it was considered the first step of the Catholic offensive. "What a massacre of innocent youth is taking place hour by hour," he claimed at the assembly, making a biblical reference. "Catholics are called by God, the Pope, the Bishops, and the priests to a united and vigorous campaign for the purification of the cinema, which has become a deadly menace to morals."[201]

In fact, Cicognani played a leading role not only in the "crusade" against Hollywood, but also, and more generally, in the diplomatic rapprochement of the White House and the Holy See. The foundations of this relationship were laid in the early thirties.[202] The papal representative was well aware that obtaining "moral supremacy" in the debate over cinema would contribute to strengthening and increasing trust in the Church in the United States. This position can be identified between the lines of the report that the prelate sent to Pacelli in July 1934. During Pius XI's pontificate, the Catholics were still among the poorest minorities in America: for this reason, they actively sought out social integration and legitimation by the country's political institutions. Thanks to unprecedented access to the Secret Vatican Archive, scholars have recently illustrated the wide range of factors behind the rapprochement between the Holy See and the United States.[203] The escalation of totalitarian regimes, as

---

201 There are different versions of this speech in various bibliographic references. Here I refer to the version quoted in: Gregory D. Black, *Hollywood Censored: Morality Codes, Catholics, and the Movies* (Cambridge: Cambridge University Press, 1994), p. 162. The Archbishops McNicholas and Quigley's contribution to Cicognani's speech is also examined in the same volume: *ibid.*, pp. 162-163. See also: William Harrison Hays, pp. 450-51.

202 Giulia D'Alessio, "Il dialogo fra Stati Uniti e Santa Sede negli anni Trenta. Tre figure di mediazione: Cicognani, Pacelli, Spellman," in *Gouvernement pontifical sous Pie XI. Pratiques romaines et gestion de l'universel*, pp. 221-35.

203 The specific reference is to Luigi Castagna, *Un ponte oltre l'oceano. Assetti politici e strategie diplomatiche tra Stati Uniti e Santa Sede nella prima metà del '900 (1914-1940)* (Bologna: il Mulino, 2011) and to *Pius XI and America,*

well as Pacelli's diplomatic pragmatism helped to facilitate this process. In fact, the latter played a key role – sealed by his long trip to the United States between October and November 1936 – in favoring America's recognition of the Holy See's political standing within the framework of a steadily growing international crisis. There is no doubt that Franklin D. Roosevelt's appointment as President of the United States in 1932 marked a turning point in the history of diplomatic relations between Washington and the Vatican. From his electoral campaign, Roosevelt publicly expressed appreciation of the *Quadragesimo Anno*, the encyclical by Pius XI that focused on the social doctrine of the Church in the aftermath of the Wall Street crash. Ratti's remedies to the errors and distortions of capitalism were not a far cry from Roosevelt's New Deal politics, which helped America to emerge from the Great Depression. Many American bishops and Catholic leaders, in their fight for social justice, supported the president of the USA's ideas.[204]

The "theoretical foundation" of the episcopal campaign against immoral cinema in the United States complied with Ratti's social doctrine. At the same time, it provided an effective answer to the "need of morals" that both lay and religious branches of American society shared. In this way, this Catholic "battle of morality" found its ideological-religious *raison d'être* in the need to respond to the apostasy from Jesus Christ which immoral cinema conveyed. Indeed, immoral cinema was the degenerate outcome of the capitalism's perversions. After all, the battle was also fought in the name of the models of bourgeois respectability which were the basis of nineteenth-century public morals *tout court*.[205] This complexity probably accounts for the reason why the Catholic model for the moralization of cinema eventually took root in two

Proceedings of the Brown University Conference (Providence, October 2010), ed. by Charles R. Gallagher, David I. Kertzer and Alberto Melloni (Berlin/Munster/Vienna/Zurich/London, LIT Verlag, 2012).

204 Giulia D'Alessio, "Stati Uniti, Chiesa cattolica e questione sociale," in *Diplomazia senza eserciti. Le relazioni internazionali della Chiesa di Pio XI*, pp. 66-73.

205 See George L. Mosse, *Nationalism and Sexuality: Respectability and Abnormal Sexuality in Modern Europe* (New York: Howard Fertig, 1985); see also Id., *The Image of Man: The Creation of Modern Masculinity* (New York: Oxford University Press, 1996).

apparently irreconcilable social systems: Roosevelt's United States and Mussolini's Italy.[206] The eagerness to order a world where phenomena such as industrialization, urbanism and mass society had changed traditional points of reference helped to make a common heritage of ethical and social values desirable.[207]

One of the documents that best informed the ideological core of the US episcopacy's campaign bears witness to this composite approach. In his essay entitled *Priests and the Motion Picture Industry,* published in the *Ecclesiastical Review* in February 1934 – which was widely distributed among North American dioceses – Los Angeles Bishop Cantwell sketches out a connection between the financial crashes of major cinemas and the demoralization of Hollywood films.[208] With a typically pragmatist argument, the bishop notes the common sentiment that was diffuse in American society, explaining the reasons behind the degeneration of the system, and basing his arguments on more than merely apologetic assumptions. In fact, the financial difficulties faced by companies such as Paramount, R.K.O. and Fox Corporation were not entirely due to the crash of Wall Street or to harsh censorship abroad following the advent of sound film (which put about 30% of revenue at risk). It also depended on a parallelism between immoral content and large profits. Cantwell claimed that whenever moral values in modern cinema were at stake, Hollywood always replied with the repugnant motif of financial success.

---

206 See Diane Y. Ghirardo, *Building New Communities: New Deal America and Fascist Italy* (Princeton: Princeton University Press, 1989).

207 In this framework, it is not surprising that – as we have seen – Catholics turned to the models of social organization promoted by the Soviet Union: as Mosse points out, despite concessions as far as sexuality is concerned, the triumph of Stalinism actually signified a return to conventional morality: in this sense, the overturn of bourgeois society implied the very preservation of bourgeois morality. See George L. Mosse, *Nationalism and Sexuality.*

208 John J. Cantwell, "Priests and the Motion Picture Industry," *Ecclesiastical Review*, n. 90, February 1934, 136-146. The essay was also tellingly enclosed with report n. 129/35, that Cicognani sent to the Secretariat of State on June 7, 1935, as one of the "pamphlets that best illustrates the work done by American bishops:" Segreteria di Stato, S.RR.SS., Archivio Storico, AA.EE. SS., Stati Ecclesiastici, IV, Pos. 445, Fasc. 416, ff. 7-15r and 17r Amleto Cicognani's report drafted for Giuseppe Pizzardo, June 7, 1935.

It is a fact, however, that but few immoral films make a real success [...] The greatest success of the season was obtained by the animated cartoon in colours, *The Three Little Pigs*, in which all the moral precepts are respected [...] There are at present a number of fine moral films which are having an extraordinary financial success. On the other hand, we hear from an authoritative source that out of twenty-five indecent films produced this year only two had a real financial success, the others yielding but very moderate profits. We mention this to show that there is no truth in the widely spread contention that indecency means financial success.[209]

Of course, in his attempt to name the "culprits," Cantwell himself was also subject to ideological constraint: his speech contained references to prevailing atheism among the members of film industry[210] as well as to the Judaic plot,[211] both themes that characterize some aspects of the episcopacy's campaign.[212]

Still, the quest for a proposal that would address the widest possible audience was truly at the heart of this process. In this respect, the Bishop of Los Angeles appealed to the federal government in his conclusions. In Cantwell's opinion, the influence of cinema on the young was so great that spending one hour only in a dark theatre, watching a bad story, could nullify years of Church, school and family education. As such, if a "national disaster" was to be prevented, "energetic measures" had to be taken. It is not by chance that *L'Osservatore Romano*, prompted

---

209 *Ibid.*
210 Cantwell reported that 75% of Hollywood's authors were atheists, and therefore did not care about decency and taste. Most of them lead a life of marital infidelity, where religion and moral values were disregarded.
211 As Cantwell wrote in one of the key passages of his article: "Jewish executives are the responsible men in ninety per cent of all the Hollywood studios. If these Jewish executives had any desire to keep the screen free from offensiveness, they could do so. It is not too much to expect that Hollywood should clean house, and that the great race which was the first custodian of the Ten Commandments should be conscious of its religious traditions."
212 On these topics, see: Alexander McGregor, pp. 151-153. On Joseph I. Breen, considered by many to be the ghost writer of Cantwell's article, and his controversial approach to the Jews, see: Thomas P. Doherty, pp. 212-237.

by McNicholas, the chairman of the Episcopal Committee,[213] not only gave great relevance to Cantwell's pamphlet – publishing a long article on July 12, 1934 – but it also underlined that the "holy campaign" had the "authorial support" of the first lady Eleanor Roosevelt, who had praised the episcopacy's actions in a radio broadcast. Similarly, the support of David Philipson, the chief Rabbi of Rockdale Avenue, was also cited in the same pages.[214] In the following months, the ongoing exchange of views between the Secretary of State, the apostolic See of Washington and the episcopacy of the United States testified to Pius XI's growing concern for the outcomes of the campaign of the NorthAmerican Church: it was a sort of triangulation that counted Pizzardo, Cicognani and McNicholas among its main actors. It was Pacelli himself, after all, who reported in his answer to Cicognani's first, detailed account, dated August 1934, that the Pontiff had read the material with "a mixture of interest, bitterness, and hope."[215] The American bishops hoped, as the cardinal wrote, that once the Pope had received more complete information, he would declare "the long-awaited authoritative word <u>in Domino</u>, in the form that he would find most convenient."[216] It was, in other

---

213 Segreteria di Stato, S.RR.SS., Archivio Storico, AA.EE. SS., Stati Ecclesiastici, IV, Pos. 445, Fasc. 415, f. 3r, John T. McNicholas to Giuseppe Pizzardo, June 4, 1934. In his letter, McNicholas requested that a summarised version of Cantwell's pamphlet be published in *L'Osservatore Romano*.

214 "Una grande vittoria dei cattolici degli Stati Uniti nella campagna cinematografica," *L'Osservatore Romano*, July 12, 1934. The article was published in five columns on the second page of the magazine. It was presented as a sort of "fundamental document of the campaign" that American bishops undertook against immoral cinema.

215 ASV, Segreteria di Stato, a. 1934, rubr. 325, n. 6, Eugenio Pacelli to Amleto Cicognani, August 18, 1934: "Interesse misto di amarezza e di speranza."

216 *Ibid.*: "<u>in Domino</u> nella forma che giudicherà opportuna l'attesa autorevole parola." In his letter, the Secretary of State explained: "the account and the enclosed pamphlet confirm the seriousness of this ill and the need to find a remedy; they have been read by his Holiness with a mixture of interest, bitterness [erased "sadness"] and hope; they faithfully reflect the state of affairs, as a trustworthy echo of a broad enough conviction to authorize good hope of success; they provide comforting evidence of the diligence and apostolic zeal of the North-American episcopacy, which, supported illustriously by Your Excellency's great personal interest, has promoted and is leading a campaign to honour the Catholic name. Is it

words, the announcement of what would become the encyclical *Vigilanti Cura*.

9. *The 1935 Inquiry into Cinema*

A landmark in the history of the pontifical document was the international inquiry organized by the Secretariat of State in 1935, with the aim of surveying the Catholics' activities in cinema and the radio throughout world. The initiative was the result of the Church's attempts to confront the new media that we have outlined so far. The Church understood very quickly that gaining full control over the medium would be impossible: the point, therefore, was to assess the concrete possibility, available to the Catholics, to broaden the scope of their actions, to decide on further actions, and, at the same time, to bring the centre of power back to Rome, leaving little or no space for local initiatives. A circular, signed by Pizzardo and sent by the Holy See to all Pontiff's representatives in the world, provides a clear sense of the incredibly intense (and mostly covert) activity that had occupied the Vatican Curia up to that moment. In its brief foreword, the document refers to the Catholics' composite approach to cinema: "it is well known that in many countries, Catholics – so begins the circular – took the lead against immoral cinema, which unfortunately slackens Christianity and corrupts morals. At the same time, they have been trying to exploit such modern inventions, to guarantee a sound Cristian education

---

necessary for me to mention that the Holy Father wishes to follow closely such beneficial action?" ("Rapporto ed opuscolo allegato confermano appieno la gravità del male e l'importanza del rimedio; essi sono stati letti da Sua Santità con interesse misto di amarezza [cancellato "tristezza"] e di speranza; sono apparsi specchio non alterato della triste realtà; eco fedele di uno stato d'animo abbastanza generale per autorizzare buone speranze di successo; e finalmente assai confortanti prove della illuminata solerzia e dello zelo apostolico onde l'Episcopato nord-americano, egregiamente sorretto dalle vigili premure di V. E., ha promosso e persegue una campagna destinata a far onore quanto oltre mai al nome cattolico. Occorre che io aggiunga come il Santo Padre intende seguire da vicino una così benefica azione?")

for the people."[217] Moreover, it claimed that the Holy See had been granted the "opportunity to set up a Central Organization which would coordinate the activities of Catholics, without taking on economic responsibility. It would make their experiences mutually useful and promote further initiatives."[218]

The information system of the Holy See aimed specifically to verify whether the conditions to establish a central coordinating body truly existed: before taking this possibility into account, the circular specified that "knowing what activities Catholics were already promoting in this respect"[219] would be fundamental. The hallmark of centralized organization, as outlined in the circular, undoubtedly resulted from the experiences gained up to that point: the unhappy fates of both Eidophon and OCIC, the positive outcomes of the crusade in the USA and of agreements with the Fascist authorities in Italy, as well as the growing interest in the activities of the IECI (which, not surprisingly, was the basis of one of the questions in the survey). Direct relationships with the IECI were, in fact, at the very heart of the Vatican's inquiry into cinema. The plan to build a central Vatican body that would coordinate all of the Church's initiatives regarding cinema, without resorting to more influential intermediaries (the OCIC in Europe, Jesuits in the USSR and the American episcopacy in Hollywood) was pioneered by Ernesto Cauda. He was among the intellectuals who gravitated round the Genevan body that was in charge of writing a large, multilingual encyclopaedia of

---

217 Segreteria di Stato, S.RR.SS., Archivio Storico, AA.EE. SS., Stati Ecclesiastici, IV, Pos. 445, Fasc. 415, f. 3r, Circolare n. 964/35, signed by Giuseppe Pizzardo, March 25, 1935: "È noto come i cattolici di molti paesi hanno preso delle iniziative per opporsi al Cinema immorale, il quale purtroppo tanto contribuisce all'indebolimento del senso cristiano e alla corruzione dei costumi. In pari tempo essi procurano di dirigere tali moderni ritrovati alla buona e cristiana educazione del popolo." A handwritten note reads: "circular sent to everyone: Nuncios, Internuncios and apostolic deputies, apostolic vicars in Sweden and Norway, and to Rev. Mayes, auxiliary of Westminster."

218 *Ibid.*: "L'opportunità di istituire un Organismo Centrale, il quale, senza assumere responsabilità d'ordine economico, coordini le attività dei cattolici, in modo da rendere reciprocamente utili le loro esperienze, e inoltre promuova possibilmente nuove iniziative."

219 *Ibid.*: "Conoscere quali attività già [fossero] svolte dai cattolici in queste direzioni."

cinema at that time.[220] Cauda himself wrote a memorandum to the State Secretary in July 1934, on the "serious and delicate issue of the approach of Catholic organizations"[221] to cinema. As far as a "direct intervention in production" was concerned, Cauda claimed that, although it was not "to be refused a priori," it would demand "substantial resources:" this problem was thus "not without risks, which could hardly be taken on in a first phase."[222] He was doubtful even about "orienting the production by force," which he defined as "a possible strategy in some countries within certain limits."[223] As Cauda explains,

We should not forget that major production companies (American, English, German and French ones) are unlikely to agree to abandon the current system if they are not compelled to do so for material causes, and the reasons for this are self evident. Pressures on different governments for a stricter censorship and a greater influence on products will produce little more than poor results – especially since those governments that are more likely to collaborate consider cinema to be a significant industrial activity and, at in the best hypothesis, as a means of social and political propaganda, they will supervise filmmaking according to their own principles and aims.[224]

---

220 Later published as Ernesto Cauda, *Dizionario poliglotta della cinematografia. Tedesco, inglese, francese, italiano* (Città di Castello: Edizione Internazionale, 1936).

221 Segreteria di Stato, S.RR.SS., Archivio Storico, AA.EE. SS., Stati Ecclesiastici, IV, Pos. 445, Fasc. 407, ff. 3-8r Memorandum dated July 12, 1934 by engineer Ernesto Cauda: "In ogni suo lato il grave e delicato quesito dell'orientamento e dell'organizzazione cattolica."

222 *Ibid.*: "Intervento diretto nella produzione;" "da escludersi a priori;" "mezzi ingenti;" "non scevro da rischi, difficilmente affrontabili in un primo tempo" (underlined in the text).

223 *Ibid.*: "Una pressione orientatrice alla produzione;" "possibile entro certi limiti e in determinati paesi."

224 *Ibid.*: "Non bisogna dimenticare che la grande produzione (americana, inglese, tedesca e francese) ben difficilmente si piegherà ad abbandonare gli attuali sistemi se non vi sarà costretta da cause d'ordine prevalentemente materiale e ciò per ovvi motivi. Anche la via delle pressioni sui diversi Governi per ottenere un inasprimento della censura e un'azione orientatrice sui prodotti non può portare che a scarsi risultati, dato anche che i Governi meglio disposti considerano il cinema come un importante attività industriale, e nella migliore delle ipotesi, come un mezzo di propaganda politica e sociale, ch'essi si limitano a sorvegliare secondo i propri principi e le

"The creation of a <u>Central Cinema Board or Office</u> at the Holy See that could direct, advise and coordinate the activities of national Catholic Entities and stimulate their development" seemed "<u>indispensable</u>"[225] to Cauda. Such a board – whose tasks clearly resembled those drafted in the circular that Pizzardo sent to all Pontiff's representatives – should be "perfectly competent," but also "completely independent from existing firms and any kinds of other interests, be they direct or indirect."[226]

Pizzardo's March 1935 circular was noticeably influenced by both "Cauda's report" and the complexity of relationships with OCIC. The questionnaire on cinema asked for general information about the existence of a State Production, censorship systems, and actions that aimed to "improve cinema from the moral and religious point of view."[227] The inquiry then investigated the existence of production companies and theatres that showed either "impious and immoral films"[228] or educational ones. Finally, a set of general questions concerned the IECI, in order to retrieve information on its local branches, should they be present. With regard to the actions of the Catholics, the questions concerned their involvement in censorship systems, the existence of a Catholic cinematographic press and of bodies that would federalize catholic movie theatres "to impose the production of good films on production companies."[229]

According to the documentation held in the Vatican archives, the questionnaire was sent to a total of 55 Pontiff's representatives, while the reports received between April and December 1935 amounted to 29 (10 from Europe, 9 from America, 7 from Asia and 3 from Africa). Specifically, only 15 of 34 Nunciatures and

---

proprie finalità."

225 *Ibid.*: "Costituzione, presso la Santa Sede di un <u>Organo od Ufficio Cinematografico Centrale</u> capace di dirigere, consigliare, coordinare le attività dei singoli Enti Cattolici nazionali e di stimolarne lo sviluppo;" "<u>indispensabile</u>" (underlined in the text).

226 *Ibid.*: "specificamente competente;" "indipendente in modo assoluto da ogni legame, diretto o indiretto, colle industrie esistenti e con ogni genere di interessi."

227 Segreteria di Stato, S.RR.SS., Archivio Storico, AA.EE. SS., Stati Ecclesiastici, IV, Pos. 445, Fasc. 407, f. 5rv: "A correggere il cinema dal punto di vista morale e religioso."

228 *Ibid.*: "Pellicole empie e immorali."

229 *Ibid.*: "imporre alle case produttrici la preparazione di buone pellicole."

Internunciatures, and 14 of 21 apostolic delegations responded. Granted the high probability that some items are missing from archive documentation, it is nonetheless worth remembering that the shortage of feedback on the issue of cinema from important nuncios – such as those in Italy (taken for granted in some ways), Belgium, France, Holland and Mexico – did not alter the analytic framework as a whole, the reason being that the State Secretary was already well aware of the situation in these countries **(fig. 1)**.[230]

For their reports, Pontiff's representatives at times used official governmental sources; more often, however, they undertook enquiries through either the local episcopacy or the support of the people who had proved highly sensitive to this issue. In this sense, the enquiry confirmed the Society of Jesus' great sensitivity regarding the new media in many parts of the world, as well as the key role that women in charge of Catholic associations or moral leagues played.[231] What resulted from these reports is a very composite picture, which is not entirely exhaustive, but nevertheless procures several very clear indications.

The "planetary" confirmation of Hollywood's ability films to penetrate all societies is a primary, macroscopic fact: from Central and South Africa to Asia, Pontiff's representatives denounced the "perverting invasion" of American products. The nuncio to Argentina, Filippo Cortesi, speaks of a "flood of immorality spreading across the whole country" without a tailing dam, since the country and "huge, cosmopolitan Buenos Aires" were governed by "ultraliberal laws and institutions."[232] Central

---

230 Responses were submitted from the Nuncios of Czechoslovakia, Venezuela, Austria, Ireland, Guatemala, Costa Rica, Haiti, Bavaria, Germany, Hungary, Portugal, Poland, Argentina, Lithuania, as well as from the apostolic delegations of Persia, The Antilles-Cuba, Turkey, Lebanon, Syria, Egypt, South Africa, Japan, India, the Philippines, Indochina, Canada and Terranova, The Belgian Congo, Unites States and Norway. These are scattered in Segreteria di Stato, S.RR.SS., Archivio Storico, AA.EE. SS., Stati Ecclesiastici, IV, Pos. 445, Fasc. 423, 424, 425.

231 An important role emerged in the reports sent from Egypt, Costarica, The Belgian Congo, Lithuania, and Bolivia. Women's associations were mostly active in Central and South America (Argentina, Venezuela, Cuba, Guatemala, Bolivia).

232 Segreteria di Stato, S.RR.SS., Archivio Storico, AA.EE. SS., Stati Ecclesiastici, IV, Pos. 445, Fasc. 424, ff. 79rv-80r, Filippo Cortesi to Giuseppe Pizzardo, Buenos Aires August 24, 1935: l'"invasione pervertitrice;" "un'alluvione

Fig. 1 - The 1935 Inquiry into Cinema (courtesy Studio Migual).

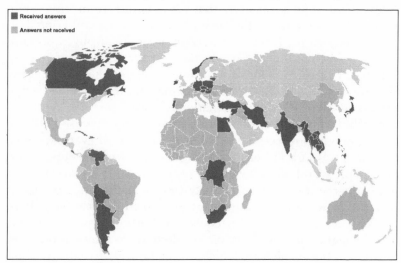

American countries in particular signalled the degeneration of the Hollywood industries' appetite for profit. Nuncio Alberto Levame made this observation: from Guatemala City, he sent news of the situation in Guatemala, as well as in Honduras and El Salvador. From his look-out post, he had the feeling that these three Republics were "tributaries and victims of foreign cinematographic production, especially that of the United States," which had the "tendency to discard [their] old stock in Central America."[233] In addition to other countries in Central America,[234] similar situations were identified in Egypt, India, Syria and Lebanon. The Philippines were an emblematic case in South-East Asia: the country constituted an American protectorate, where,

---

d'immoralità che si estende a tutto il paese;" "grande e cosmopolitica Buenos Aires;" "istituzioni e leggi ultraliberali."

233   Segreteria di Stato, S.RR.SS., Archivio Storico, AA.EE. SS., Stati Ecclesiastici, IV, Pos. 445, Fasc. 423, f. 28r, Alberto Levame to Giuseppe Pizzardo, Guatemala City, June 10, 1935: "tributarie e vittime della produzione cinematografica straniera, e specialmente degli Stati Uniti;" "tendenza a spacciare in Centroamerica [sic] i [loro] fondi di magazzeno [sic]."

234   Confirmation can be found in replies to questionnaires by nuncios and apostolic delegates from Costarica-Nicaragua-Panama, Cuba, and Haiti-Santo Domingo.

as the apostolic deputy observed, "98% of films" were imported from the United States without having to pay customs duties, unlike in other foreign countries.[235]

A second relevant macro-aspect that emerged from the enquiry regarded a widespread denunciation of the scarcity of means available to episcopacies and, more in general, to Catholics, to tackle effectively the "issue of cinema." Almost every Pontiff's representative considered cinema as a threat more than an opportunity. The conditions, causes and intensity of the issue at stake varied, of course, according to the country, as well as to the contexts where Catholics worked. Socio-religious and political conditions, as well as those related to the development of the cinema industry and the status of Catholic organizations, proved to be highly influential factors. Finally, the presence or absence of official relations between the Holy See and a country's government was another relevant aspect, since this could impact the effectiveness of actions by Pontiff's representatives. With regard to this point, it is not surprising that some nuncios reported having approached State representatives with Catholic requests. This happened in countries with a solid Catholic tradition, such as Venezuela, Hungary, Austria and the Philippines, in accordance with the Vatican's perspective – which recommended seeking agreements with governmental authorities, following the Italian example.

In such countries, and particularly in Catholic Europe, the clergy and laymen hoped to impact upon governmental censorship committees which existed almost everywhere.[236] Nevertheless, with the exceptions of Germany, Austria, and, to some extent, Ireland, Pontiff's representatives generally did not believe in the Catholics' ability to influence this issue in a significant way. The response of the nuncio to Hungary

---

235 Segreteria di Stato, S.RR.SS., Archivio Storico, AA.EE. SS., Stati Ecclesiastici, IV, Pos. 445, Fasc. 424, ff. 41-56r, Guglielmo Piani to Giuseppe Pizzardo, Manila, July 12, 1935.

236 The nuncio to Haiti, Giuseppe Fietta, pointed out the existence of preventive censorship, "despite the Bishops' vivid and frequent pressures on the government to obtain it:" Segreteria di Stato, S.RR.SS., Archivio Storico, AA.EE. SS., Stati Ecclesiastici, IV, Pos. 445, Fasc. 424, ff. 56-58r, Giuseppe Fietta to Giuseppe Pizzardo, Port-au-Prince, May 15, 1935.

on the attitude of episcopacy, clergy and catholic Action towards cinema echoed the refrain of many other Pontiff's representatives: Catholics, wrote Angelo Rotta, felt the "great urgency of this issue," while being aware that they were facing "enormous difficulties;" they understood that as long as they were unable "to offer interesting, well-made films to the public, that are irreproachable from a Catholic point of view," it would be impossible to compete with "destructive films." [237]

Of course, it is impractical to put what was happening in Europe on the same level as the situation in Syria and Lebanon, Egypt or Indochina, Nicaragua or the Belgian Congo. Different contexts notwithstanding, most of these responses shared the idea that Catholics faced a very difficult challenge. Catholic infrastructures were particularly poor: among the questionnaires sent back to the Holy See, only the German one identified the presence of a Catholic cinema exhibitors' association that was similar to the Italian CCC.[238] Furthermore, references to relationships with state organizations for educational cinema[239] or to the activities of Catholic institutions were very rare in these reports.[240]

Overall, therefore, the enquiry provided the Holy See with access to a complex and multifaceted scenario: one that confirmed the complexity and far-reaching effects of cinema. It

---

237 Segreteria di Stato, S.RR.SS., Archivio Storico, AA.EE. SS., Stati Ecclesiastici, IV, Pos. 445, Fasc. 423, ff. 79-81rv, Angelo Rotta to Giuseppe Pizzardo, Budapest, June 18, 1935: "la grande importanza di questo problema;" "di essere di fronte a delle difficoltà enormi;" "offrire al pubblico pellicole interessanti, ben preparate e ciò non ostante irreprensibili dal punto di vista cattolico;" "pellicole distruttive."

238 Segreteria di Stato, S.RR.SS., Archivio Storico, AA.EE. SS., Stati Ecclesiastici, IV, Pos. 445, Fasc. 423, ff. 14rv-15rv and f. 16r, Enrico Sibilia to Giuseppe Pizzardo, Vienna, May 5, 1935.

239 State institutions that were involved in the production of films with scientific-educational aims were recorded in Hungary, Germany, Czechoslovakia and South Africa. References to the IECI's activities were reported in Hungary and Poland only.

240 In Bolivia, for example, the actions of the Jesuits in some colleges in La Paz were noted. The country reportedly screened educational films, that would "counterbalance the pernicious influence of cinema in private enterprises:" Segreteria di Stato, S.RR.SS., Archivio Storico, AA.EE. SS., Stati Ecclesiastici, IV, Pos. 445, Fasc. 424, ff. 37rv-38rv-39r, Louis Centoz to Giuseppe Pizzardo, La Paz, June 29, 1935.

also presented the Holy See with precious information regarding the contemporary tendencies in the Catholic word: episcopacies and, more generally, local churches did not correspond to a well-structured organization that could justify a central, coordinating body led by the Roman church, an organization which, indeed, was never created with these characteristics. The outcomes of the enquiry confirmed the need to carry out diplomatic action led by the State Secretariat on the most delicate issues of film policy. At the same time, it underlined the efficiency of the "American model" of the Legion of Decency, which decentralized the Catholic film, instead establishing *ad hoc* organizations under the direct control of episcopacies. Planning centralized coordination from Rome was very difficult, given the extremely diverse situations in different continents as well as the considerable delays in dealing with related problems in each country. Before deploying an executive central office, it was necessary first to equip episcopacies all over the world with directions on how to organize a global answer to the question of cinema.

10. *'Good Americanism' and the Encyclical on Cinema*

On July 3, 1936, the Superior General of the Society of Jesus received a message from the Secretariat of State. Pizzardo fervently thanked Ledóchowski for "supporting the preparation of the encyclical on Cinema by making the most valuable assistants available to this Secretariat"[241]. The Secretary of the Sacred Congregation for Extraordinary Ecclesiastical Affairs made sure to stress to the head of the Jesuits that *Vigilanti Cura* "made the best impression in America. Last night," he explained, "the 'Associated Press' telegraphed it, word for word, praising the nature of the encyclical as modern, convenient... American."[242]

---

241 Segreteria di Stato, S.RR.SS., Archivio Storico, AA.EE. SS., Stati Ecclesiastici, IV, Pos. 445, Fasc. 420, ff. 65-66r, Giuseppe Pizzardo to Włodzimierz Ledóchowski, July 3, 1936: "Tanto favorito la preparazione dell'Enciclica sul Cinematografo, mettendo a disposizione di questa Segreteria validissimi cooperatori."
242 *Ibid.*: "fatto la migliore impressione negli ambienti americani.

That very morning, Pius XI's solemn pronouncement was given
prominence on the front page of the main overseas newspapers;
it was the Pope's only encyclical to be addressed explicitly to
the "Episcopate of the United States of America."[243] Dedicating
its main headline to the encyclical, the authoritative *New York
Times* published the entire text together with an immediate
analysis and some well-informed comments. Arnaldo Cortesi,
the *New York Times* correspondent in Rome, described *Vigilanti
Cura* as "one of the most important, or even the most important
document addressed to America in the annals of the Papacy."
Cortesi also emphasized the core of the document, that is, the
challenge issued to the Hollywood film industry to improve the
moral level of its production.[244] In an interview with the New York
newspaper, Will H. Hays hastened to subscribe to the encyclical's
contents entirely, describing them as the Papal endorsement of
the activities of the PCA. The PCA had been established in June
1934, as a result of the boycott against immoral films led by the
American episcopate, through the Legion of Decency. Managed
by the deeply Catholic Joseph I. Breen, the institution was designed
to ensure that productions faithfully observed the Hays Code.
From the moment of its inauguration, film companies belonging
to the MPPDA were forbidden from distributing films without a
PCA approval in the theatres controlled by the trade association
(that is, most first run cinemas). Violators of the Code could face
a fine of up to 25,000 dollars.[245] Commenting the encyclical, Hays

L'"Associated Press" l'ha telegrafata ieri sera parola per parola dicendo
che l'Enciclica ha tutta una intonazione moderna, pratica... americana."
243 Historical studies have taken only marginal interest in the analysis of
Vigilanti Cura. The most accurate analysis is in Michel Lagrée, pp. 839-
53. See also: Raffaele De Berti, "Dalla *Vigilanti Cura* al film ideale," in
Attraverso lo schermo. Cinema e cultura cattolica in Italia, ed. by Ruggero
Eugeni and Dario E. Viganò (Roma: Ente dello Spettacolo, 2006), II,
Dagli anni Trenta agli anni Sessanta, pp. 79-102.
244 Arnaldo Cortesi, "Pope Orders World Drive to Raise Film Standards;
Urges Boycott Pledges," *New York Times*, July 3, 1936.
245 See: Thomas P. Doherty, *Hollywood's Censor*. On Catholics and the
Production Code Administration see in particular Richard Maltby, pp. 37-
72; Jon Lewis, *Hollywood v. Hard Core. How the Struggle over Censorship Saved
the Modern Film Industry* (New York: New York University Press, 2000);
William B. Johnson, *Miracles & Sacrilege: Roberto Rosselini, the Church, and
Film Censorship in Hollywood* (Toronto: University of Toronto Press, 2008).

quotes, to *The New York Times*, a recent report from the Legion of Decency which "disclosed that since the industry began its own clean-up campaign under Mr. Breen only four productions had been condemned and none of these was produced by a member of the Hays Organization."[246]

Pius XI's encyclical exalted the seemingly striking success achieved by the campaign against Hollywood cinema conducted very decisively by the American Catholic Church over the previous three years. The approval of the American press was by no means a given, predictable response to the encyclical. Indeed, on May 9, the initial reaction of the Vatican to the proclamation of the Fascist Empire, following the conquest of Ethipia, had strengthened the idea of total alignment between the Holy See and the Italian government. The events consequently fed into anti-papal prejudice, which was extensively ingrained in American public opinion. 1935 saw the increasing growth of an antagonistic feeling of the United States towards Italian expansionism in Africa. Two days before *Vigilanti Cura* was announced, this sentiment had intensified: on June 30, the exiled emperor Hailé Selassié's denunciation to the League of Nations that the Italian air force was systematically using poisonous gas provoked outcry and deep resentment towards the Fascists.[247]

From such a perspective, the most articulate twentieth-century papal document on cinema comes across as a series of cautious compromises and strategic silences that are influenced as much by the Vatican leaders' recent experiences with cinema as the geopolitical positioning of the Holy See on an increasingly tense global stage. This hypothesis is confirmed by the documents regarding the encyclical kept in the Vatican Secret Archives: the records attest to the interests that played key roles in the redaction of the text, and reveal the varied discussions, multiple

---

246 "Comment by Will Hays. He Says Catholics Have Approved Most of Recent Films," *New York Times*, July 3, 1936.

247 The *New York Times* gave prominence to Selassié's speech, publishing long extracts of his condemnation: "Summary of the Ethiopian Emperor's Address to the League," July 1, 1936. On American public opinion on Italian expansionism in Ethiopia, see: Lucia Ceci, *Il papa non deve parlare. Chiesa, fascismo e guerra d'Etiopia* (Roma-Bari: Laterza, 2010), pp. 110 and 150-55.

contributions, contrasts and contradictions that accompanied its long drafting process.

The selection of people involved by the Holy See in the redaction of the text –under the attentive direction of Pacelli and Pizzardo in Rome and Cicognani in Washington – suggests how the Pope sought to modulate its themes and objectives. Pizzardo's letter to Ledóchowski on the one hand confirms the consolidated procedure employed in the redaction of the most important papal texts, and on the other highlights the vital role of the Jesuits, too, in drafting *Vigilanti Cura*.[248] Indeed, the first draft of the document was based on a text that Pius XI explicitly commissioned from Daniel A. Lord, one of the main authors of the 1930 Hays Code together with Martin Quigley. Friedrich Muckermann, the 'European' expert on cinema of the Society of Jesus, also played a significant role, albeit secondary. Moreover, a confidential report – a 400-page volume finished in October 1935 – proved very influential: in the text, Monsignor McNicholas, chairman of the Episcopal Committee on Motion Pictures, provided a comprehensive picture of the two-year struggle undertaken by the American Catholics (it included episcopal documents, newspaper and magazine articles, radio messages, reports from Catholic Action etc.).[249] Moreover,

---

248 It is well known, for instance, that the Jesuits were among the main editors of the encyclical on communism *Divini Redemptoris*, and that they occupied a relevant position in the redaction of *Mitt Brennender Sorge*. Together with the American Jesuit John La Farge, they also participated in the unpublished encyclical *Humani generi unitas*. See: Emma Fattorini, *Pio XI, Hitler e Mussolini. La solitudine di un papa* (Torino: Einaudi, 2007), pp. 64-70; David I. Kertzer *The Pope and Mussolini: The Secret History of Pius XI and the Rise of Fascism in Europe* (New York: Random House, 2014) and Georges Passelecq, Bernard Suchecky, *L'Encyclique cachée de Pie XI: une occasion manqueé de l'Église face à l'antisémitisme* (Paris: La Découverte, 1995).

249 The volume entitled *Report of the Episcopal Committee on Motion Pictures* can be found in Segreteria di Stato, S.RR.SS., Archivio Storico, AA.EE. SS., Stati Ecclesiastici, IV, Pos. 445, Fasc. 417. On the cover, the following limitation is specified: "Printed, but not for Publication." Significantly, Pizzardo, a few days after the promulgation of *Vigilanti Cura*, sent a letter to McNicholas in which he expressed his pleasure in having learned that the Pope, through the encyclical, had "approved and integrated a practical solution, ingeniously advocated and realized by Your Excellency,

Pizzardo guaranteed also the participation of the ACI leaders, who contributed to the redaction mainly through its president, Ciriaci, who also coordinated supporting work from CCC functionaries. The balance between these diverse contributions duly mirrors the balance between the themes characterizing the final text. The American episcopate's campaign was adopted and presented as the ideal model for the Catholic world, while the encyclical also discretely considered the action strategy chosen by the Catholics living under authoritarian regimes. Indeed, in terms of practical and organizational recommendations, it presented a course of action that results from a compromise between the American and the European models. Nevertheless, in the text some of the core themes and subjects discussed within religious debates of the previous decade were overshadowed, if not completely eschewed.

On the one hand, the text addresses the issue of production – as we shall see shortly – in only a few lines that are nevertheless quite meaningful; on the other, the absence a very central theme – the attack on Christianity by the soviet cinema – is a lot more glaring. Furthermore, the absence of any mention – even accidental – of the decade-long activities of the OCIC is similarly striking.

Father Muckermann's contributions to the preparations of the project included an important testimony on the OCIC's activity. Consulted by Ledóchowski for the German translation of the encyclical, as well as for a review of the content, the Jesuit – who counted himself among the promoters of the OCIC – suggested that a brief and indirect reference to the activity conducted by the Brussels Office should be included in the text.

Since the Encyclical is addressed to the whole world, it would be appropriate – perhaps on page 13, where the context is suitable – to recall the merits of other nations in at least one sentence: "These departments will conveniently benefit not only from the American experiences, but also from the cinematographic work carried out by Catholics from Belgium, Germany, France, Holland, Luxemburg and other countries, as well as from the outcome of the

---

achieving such positive results:" Segreteria di Stato, S.RR.SS., Archivio Storico, AA.EE. SS., Stati Ecclesiastici, IV, Pos. 445, Fasc. 420, ff. 82-83r.

main international conferences on cinema."[250]

However, in the final version Muckermann's *desiderata* were embraced only in part: direct references to the work of European Catholics and especially to large, international conferences on cinema – which immediately recall the activity of the OCIC – were removed.[251] In fact, the OCIC was the only major Catholic institution that had attempted to address cinema without considering it as merely instrumental. Given its will to become a player in the field of film production, the debates taking place during its international conferences and the intense dialogue with the world of cinema in all its complexity, the OCIC represented the tendency to embrace positive attitudes to cinema, moving beyond purely condamnatory positions. Such a view was so minor within the context of the Church at that time that in September 1935 the head of the OCIC, Brohée, was charged with a *reprimenda* by the Secretariat of State.

Pius XI and his entourage clearly expressed a cinematographic policy that, as Renato Moro has observed, aimed to enable the Church to "enter and master the dynamics of social transformation, bending them so that the influence of the Church

---

250 Segreteria di Stato, S.RR.SS., Archivio Storico, AA.EE. SS., Stati Ecclesiastici, IV, Pos. 445, Fasc. 425, f. 28r, "Desiderata di P. Muckermann:" "Siccome l'Enciclica s'indirizza a tutto il mondo, converrebbe forse alla pagina 13, dove si offre buona occasione, rammentare almeno con una frase anche i meriti di altre nazioni: "Questi uffici approfitteranno opportunamente non solo delle esperienze fatte negli Stati Uniti, ma anche del lavoro nel campo cinematografico esplicato dai cattolici del Belgio, della Germania, della Francia, dell'Olanda, del Lussemburgo e di altri paesi, come pure dei risultati dei grandi congressi internazionali del cinema." The last sentence has been erased with a pencil mark. The model is attached to Włodzimierz Ledóchowski's letter to Giuseppe Pizzardo written on June 23, 1936. In the letter, the Superior General of the Society of Jesus sent the German and Spanish translations of the text, accompanied by a few "minor remarks" (piccole osservazioni" on the Italian version, *Ibid.*, ff. 26rv-27r.

251 The text of the encyclical reads: "These Offices will profit not only from the experiments made in the United States but also from the work which Catholics in other countries have achieved in the motion picture field:" the text taken into account is available on the website of the Holy See <http://w2.vatican.va/content/pius-xi/en/encyclicals/documents/hf_p-xi_enc_29061936_vigilanti-cura.html> [accessed July 24, 2017].

could be guaranteed and strengthened."[252] The way the encyclical addressed the problem was very pragmatic: while criticizing the Hollywood system at the heart of the permanent and perverse bond between cinema and capitalism, the Church ultimately tried to subdue it, in order to control the modern universe of images. From this perspective, the choice of the United States as the addressee of *Vigilanti Cura* reacted to a twofold need on behalf of the Holy See. On the one hand, evidence indicates the Vatican's firm belief that the organizational structures and the methods used during the American episcopate's campaign were key to slowly turning the enormous Hollywood machine (whose extensive power had been unveiled by the Vatican enquiry led in March 1935) from one of the most subtle and pervasive enemies of social re-Christianization into a peaceful partner, or even a strong ally of the Church. On the other hand, as regards the Vatican's geopolitical strategy, the encyclical aimed to legitimate the major role played by the American Catholics within Roosevelt's New Deal, by encouraging American public debate. Cinema was the one field in which the influence of the Church on the New Deal was particularly relevant. Forty years after the publication of the letter *Testem benevolentiae* (1899), in which Leo XIII condemned Americanism, *Vigilanti Cura* can be interpreted, as suggested by Michel Lagrée, "comme une forme de révérence à un nouvel américanisme, cette fois de bon aloi."[253]

Around three months after the promulgation of the encyclical, this 'good Americanism' was sanctioned, at least diplomatically, by the Cardinal Secretary of State and his lengthy visit to the United States. Reinforcing the bond with the White House, which had remained unbroken even during the most critical phases of the Ethiopian crisis,[254] Pacelli arrived in New York on October 9 and embarked on a tour that stoked American public interest. The future Pope hoped to repair the devastating effects of the Italian attack in Africa; in order to ensure some form of alliance with the world's greatest economic and diplomatic power, Pacelli sought to weaken Washington's isolationist policy. It is not possible to know

---

252 Renato Moro, "Il 'modernismo buono'," pp. 714-15.
253 Michel Lagrée, p. 843.
254 Lucia Ceci, *Il papa non deve parlare*, pp. 150-55.

for sure – though it is highly probable – whether cinema was the subject of the confidential meeting with President Roosevelt that took place on 5 November in his Hyde Park residence.[255] During a brief visit to Cincinnati, on another occasion, the Cardinal Secretary of State had the chance to meet Monsignor McNicholas and talk at length with Quigley and Breen, the two most powerful Catholic laypeople in America involved in the 'redemption' programme of the Hollywood system.[256] Under the attentive eye of the American and Vatican press, the Secretary praised the campaign against immoral cinema conducted by the American Church.[257] In perhaps its most important achievement, Pacelli's trip also led to the arrangement of a private audience between the Pope with Will Hays, on November 17. In his memoir, the head of the MPPDA reports that the Cardinal Secretary of State – met on the SS Conte di Savoia as it sailed back to Italy – encouraged this unusual hearing between the representative of the Hollywood majors and the Supreme Pontiff.[258] Hays did not let this chance go to waste: the main aim of his delicate mission to Rome was to persuade Mussolini to withdraw his threat to block the import of American films;[259] ending the mission on a meeting with the leader of the Catholic Church would mean placing an authoritative seal of approval on the Production Code Administration. Hays was quite used to missions across national borders: he had often acted as Hollywood's 'ambassador', as a private plenipotentiary that ensured the export of American products to foreign markets, even by means of boycott threats.[260] His meetings in

---

255 On the confidential nature of the meeting between Roosevelt and Pacelli, see the comment: "Pacelli Lunches with Roosevelt," *New York Times*, November 6, 1936. On the meeting see also: Gerald P. Fogarty, *The Vatican and the American Hierarchy, From 1870 to 1965* (Wilmington: Michael Glazier, 1985, 2nd edn), pp. 246-48.

256 See: Alexander McGregor, pp. 60-61.

257 See: "U.S. Film Campaign praised by Pacelli," *New York Times*, November 20, 1936 and "Fiorente attività cattolica nell'operoso progresso d'una grande Nazione," *L'Osservatore Romano*, November 19, 1936. On the political implications of Pacelli's trip to the United States, see: Leon Hutton, "The Future Pope Comes to America: Cardinal Eugenio Pacelli's Visit to the United States," *U. S. Catholic Historian*, vol. 24, n. 2, 2006, 109-30.

258 William Harrison Hays, pp. 513-14.

259 *Ibid.*, pp. 511-12.

260 Victoria de Grazia, "La sfida dello 'star system'."

Italy had positive results, as reported by the American press. The *New York Times* underlined that during the Vatican meeting "the Pope conveyed to Mr. Hays his approval and appreciation of the progress made by the American films and expressed hope that the progress would continue." In response, Hays "assured him that it was the American producers' intention to see that it did."[261] This report mirrors Hays' own account, in his memoir. The main issue was that Pius XI wanted to establish a strong alliance with MPPDA, so that the most important film productions in the world would conform to Christian moral values. The alliance then provided a second benefit, within the context of the fight against Communist propaganda. Hays agreed with the Pope; however, between his own reasons and those of the Pontiff there was little or no coherence. The ultimate goal of the 'Hollywood religion' was only to guarantee the commercial expansion of American cinema: the Vatican's support of the MPPDA's activity represented an invaluable *passepartout*, providing access to important areas of the international market. The self-censorship strategy adopted by managers also proved to be profitable in the international context: moralizing campaigns faded, and incomes increased once again. Moreover, the moralistic self-regulation strategy also allowed managers to bypass rules much more easily than public censorship would.[262] In his memoir, Hays gave a detailed account of Pius XI's words: "Mr. Hays," he said, "we have asked you to come here in order that we might express to you the appreciation of the Church for the improvement in the moral content of American motion pictures." What the Pope said next struck the American industrialist profoundly ("I have quoted his words scores of times because of their significance"): "You sit at the valve in the conduit through which flows the principal amusement of the great majority of all the people in the world. Your impress is upon the quality of this entertainment and you are very important to us. We are deeply interested, of course, in

---

261 "Pontiff Discusses Movies with Hays," *New York Times*, November 18, 1936. For further reports in the American press, see: "Mr. Hays and the Pope," *Herald Journal*, November 21, 1936; "Will Hays in Accord with Pope on Cinema," *The Evening Independent*, November 18, 1936.

262 For an overview of the effects of PCS on Hollywood's international commercial policy, see: Victoria de Grazia, *Irresistible Empire*.

the success of your efforts." Hays highlighted Pius XI's absolute
certainty that Hollywood would maintain a moralizing policy: "He
said that he had no doubt that the organized American industry
would continue to guard the moral content of the motion pictures,
but that his primary concern was that the people would want to
see the good and would support the good." After these words,
the Pope proceeded to illustrate the great Comintern project,
the aim of which was "taking possession of cinema worldwide."[263]

The issue of film production in Moscow was the subject of the
preparatory discussions of *Vigilanti Cura*: once again, the German
Jesuit Muckermann – who was, together with Father Ledit,
among the most active religious people in the confrontation with
Communism – recommended to no avail the addition of a brief
reference to the dangers connected to the "revolutionary nature"
of the "Bolshevik films imitated everywhere."[264] In this context,
the omission of Muckermann's suggestion does not come as a
surprise: with the aim of an alliance with the Hollywood industry,
a practical and operative agreement was much preferable to
radical condemnations. Defining the guidelines that would
allow Catholics to access the "valve in the conduit" of the world
entertainment industry was a much more promising strategy
than any other plan for Catholic counterpropaganda against
International Soviet film.

The relationship between the American episcopate and Will
Hays as well as the birth of the Production Code Administration
were intently supervised by the Holy See through the apostolic
delegate in Washington. Between August 1934 and April 1936,
Cicognani sent the Vatican a series of detailed reports on the
development of the campaign led by the American ecclesiastical
Hierarchy. Within the American Church, two different ideas on
how to proceed can be outlined: Cardinal Dennis J. Dougherty,
archbishop of Philadelphia, chose a hard-line approach and
opted for an absolute boycott against every cinema in his diocese.
At first, Monsignor John J. Glennon, head of the archdiocese of

---

263 William Harrison Hays, pp. 521-22.
264 Segreteria di Stato, S.RR.SS., Archivio Storico, AA.EE. SS., Stati
      Ecclesiastici, IV, Pos. 445, Fasc. 425, f. 28r, "Desiderata di P. Muckermann:"
      "natura rivoluzionaria;" "pellicole bolscevistiche [sic] che hanno trovato
      dappertutto imitatori."

Saint Louis, followed Dougherty's example; nevertheless, this strategy contradicted the intentions of the Episcopal Committee on Motion Pictures. In November 1934, during the general gathering of NCWC, the seventy-five bishops voted unanimously against the absolute boycott.[265] The archbishop of Philadelphia, who had been elected Cardinal in 1921 by Benedict XV, was in competition with his colleague George Mundelein to be the most influential member of the clergy in the moralizing campaign of the big screen. The latter, archbishop of Chicago, had had a prominent role in putting the Catholic seal on the contents of the Hays Code; moreover, his diocese was given the task of writing the official list that categorized the films inspected by the Legion of Decency.[266] On the other hand, Dougherty, together with Cantwell – the archbishop of Los Angeles – led the group of bishops that presented the course of action of the campaign against Hollywood to Pius XI during the *ad limina* visits in summer 1934. The Pennsylvanian Cardinal also had some influence in the control room of the American press, having managed to intimate that he was among the main ghostwriters of *Vigilanti Cura*, an idea sustained at length by North American newspapers.[267] In November 1934, when the Vatican received the

---

265 Segreteria di Stato, S.RR.SS., Archivio Storico, AA.EE. SS., Stati Ecclesiastici, IV, Pos. 445, Fasc. 416, ff. 31-36r, Amleto Cicognani and Giuseppe Pizzardo, October 28, 1935, report n. 12902/35.

266 *Ibid.* See also: "Il Consiglio di Chicago della 'Legione della Decenza'," *L'Osservatore Romano*, March 10, 1935.

267 The day of the promulgation, the *Prescott Evening Courier* wrote that "the encyclical, entitled 'Vigilent Care' [sic], was believed to have been inspired by Cardinal Dennis Dougherty of Philadelphia, founder of the Legion of Decency who spent a month in Rome and left for the United States a week ago after seeing the Pope on several occasions:" see the article "Movie Censors Set Up by Pope," July 2, 1936. The information is confirmed, for instance, in Arnaldo Cortesi, "Pope Orders World Drive to Raise Film Standards; Urges Boycott Pledges," *New York Times*, July 3, 1936 and "Late Pontiff Created 30 Saints, Chiefly in Later Years of Reign," *Montreal Gazette*, February 10, 1939. Dougherty's crucial contribution to the redaction of the encyclical finds no confirmation in the documentation consulted in the Vatican Secret Archives. Within the American Church, the genesis of *Vigilanti Cura* has been at the heart of an intense debate. The authorship of the document has been attributed to father Lord and Dougherty as well as Quigley and Cicognani. Cfr. William B. Johnson, p. 134.

telegram in which Dougherty asked the Pope to order a "general boycott against every cinema of the United States"[268], the idea was not immediately discarded. The Cardinal maintained a certain pressure in order to gain Papal support for his plan of action,[269] but Pius XI deferred any decision until after the reception of the detailed *Report* promised by the American episcopate: "not enough information has been received on the two tendencies that have arisen in America," the Pope dictated to Pizzardo during the audience of 13 March 1935, "that is, those who would opt for a general boycott to purify Cinema and those who believe that a national boycott is not feasible: thus, a directive on such an important, practical matter cannot be offered."[270] However, before McNicholas' *Report* ultimately arrived, Cicognani had persuaded the Holy See through another one, written in June 1935, of the inconvenience of Dougherty's strict approach. The apostolic delegate did not deny that the strategy proposed by the diocese of Philadelphia had been effective: "such an example of firmness," he wrote in the report, "has been beneficial to the cause, in that it showed to cinema producers that the Church is acting seriously and that, if necessary, the boycott can be extended to every diocese of the United States."[271] In the long run, though, the censorial strategy turned out to have a boomerang effect.

---

268 ASV, Segreteria di Stato, a. 1934, rubr. 325, n. 6, telegram by Amleto Cicognani to Eugenio Pacelli, November 11, 1934: "Apertura boicottaggio generale cinema in tutti gli Stati Uniti."

269 Segreteria di Stato, S.RR.SS., Archivio Storico, AA.EE. SS., Stati Ecclesiastici, IV, Pos. 445, Fasc. 415, f. 46rv, Dennis J. Dougherty to Giuseppe Pizzardo, February 23, 1935.

270 Segreteria di Stato, S.RR.SS., Archivio Storico, AA.EE. SS., Stati Ecclesiastici, IV, Pos. 445, Fasc. 415, ff. 47-50r, Giuseppe Pizzardo to Dennis J. Dougherty, March 16, 1935: "circa le due tendenze manifestatesi in America di quelli cioè che vorrebbero un boicottaggio generale fino a che il Cinema non sia purificato, e degli altri invece che ritengono che un boicottaggio a tutta la Nazione non sia possibile in pratica, non sono giunte qui sufficienti informazioni perché, in cosa di così alta importanza pratica, si possa dare una direttiva."

271 Segreteria di Stato, S.RR.SS., Archivio Storico, AA.EE. SS., Stati Ecclesiastici, IV, Pos. 445, Fasc. 416, ff. 7-15r, Amleto Cicognani to Giuseppe Pizzardo, June 7, 1935, report n. 129/35: "Un tale esempio di fermezza ha giovato anche alla causa generale, nel senso che con esso si è dimostrato ai produttori di cinema che si faceva sul serio, e che,

Such radical measures should have been temporary, especially in the event that the results of the campaign against immoral cinema were as positive as they had been. Its exaggerated extension has limited its effectiveness. At first, the Catholics from Philadelphia responded enthusiastically to the Cardinal's call; later they started to go to cinemas once again without the benefit of knowing which performances were recommended, unlike in those dioceses where a list of immoral films was available. They were aware that an extensive purification of cinema had taken place and they noticed that many movie theatres did not play immoral films anymore. They therefore did not understand why they should not attend such performances, all the more so because they knew that in other dioceses and in the rest of the world no restriction was in place. As a consequence, even the best Catholics and the most pious women did not respect the prohibition and went to the cinema without hesitation.[272]

The initiative of the Episcopal Committee led by McNicholas proved much more effective. The group of prelates opted for a strategic combination of *moral suasion* of public opinion through the Legion of Decency and clandestine pressure on producers: Cicognani reported that "the representatives of 90 per cent of American film producers"[273] attended the second meeting of the Committee held in June 1934. Launched as an experiment in

---

occorrendo, si poteva estendere il boicottaggio a tutte le diocesi degli Stati Uniti."

272 *Ibid.*: "Un provvedimento così radicale avrebbe dovuto avere carattere temporaneo, soprattutto se i risultati della campagna contro il cinema immorale fossero stati buoni; e lo sono stati veramente e largamente. Ora il suo eccessivo prolungarsi ne ha grandemente limitato l'efficacia. I cattolici di Philadelphia, mentre in un primo tempo hanno risposto con slancio e generosità all'appello dell'E.mo Cardinale, poi hanno ripreso a frequentare i cinematografi, senza avere il vantaggio di sapere quali rappresentazioni sono raccomandabili, come avviene in quelle diocesi dove si pubblica la lista dei films morali. Essi hanno constatato e constatano sempre più che è avvenuta una grande purificazione nel cinema; vedono che in moltissimi teatri non si producono più films immorali, e non comprendono quindi perché non li possano frequentare, tanto più che sanno che in tutte le altre diocesi e in tutto il mondo non c'è quella restrizione. So che anche ottimi cattolici e piissime donne non fanno più conto di quella proibizione e si recano al cinema senza scrupolo di sorta."

273 *Ibid.*: "I rappresentanti del 90 per cento dei produttori di films negli Stati Uniti."

the archdiocese of Cincinnati, the Legion of Decency – which, as opposed to the general boycott, expected the believers to sign a pledge of abstention from "indecent performances"[274] – rapidly spread in most American dioceses, and turned out to be very successful. In his report written in June 1935, Cicognani notes that:

> production companies assured that, from 15 July 1934, they would exclusively produce moral films. In fact, we are comforted by the fact that, from that moment, only four or five films were listed in Chicago among the condemned performances. [...] Producers were very surprised by the American public's appreciation for moral films. Before that, they would say they produced salacious films because that was what the audience wanted. Cinema attendance increased, encouraged by the visibility that the Legion of Decency provided for good films, which was much more effective than the publicity financed by the producers themselves – spending around 100 million dollars a year. Today, we can broadly recognize the people's preference for healthy performances.[275]

This was one of the main reasons why the Vatican was convinced that the alliance with Hollywood producers could have a solid future. The economic side of the issue could be reconciled with the moral one. Moreover, Hays was well aware that the moral improvement of films led to increased income. Lord was given the task of describing the planned course of action in the encyclical: in January 1936, Ledóchowski suggested to Pacelli that the American Jesuit could be "useful for the redaction of a letter

---

274 *Ibid.*: "Spettacoli indecenti."
275 *Ibid.*: "Le compagnie produttrici di cinematografi assicurarono che, dal 15 luglio 1934, non avrebbero più prodotto che films morali; e difatti è consolante constatare che, da quella data, solo quattro o cinque films sono state messe tra quelle condannate, nella lista di Chicago. [...] I produttori cinematografici sono rimasti molto sorpresi per il fatto che il pubblico Americano ha mostrato di apprezzare le films morali. E prima, invece, dicevano che essi producevano cose salaci, perché questo voleva il pubblico. La frequenza ai cinema è aumentata, a ciò ha contribuito anche la reclame data dalla Legion of Decency alle pellicole buone, ed ha avuto per i produttori risultati molto più vantaggiosi della reclame che essi finanziavano, spendendovi circa 100 milioni di dollari all'anno. Oggi viene generalmente ammesso che il popolo preferisce spettacoli sani."

on cinema;"[276] the Cardinal Secretary of State responded that the Pope had agreed to give the task to Lord, asking the Jesuit to "prepare all the material that is necessary for the document, so that when he will come to Rome most of the work will already be finished."[277] The most important section of Lord's *Suggested Letter on the Motion Pictures and Catholic Morality*, completed in April, confuted those who believed in the equation of moralized production and lower income; this section was included in the final version of *Vigilanti Cura* almost in its entirety.[278]

11. *Anti-Hollywoodism: Testing Classification Systems*

The issue of 'Hollywoodism' deeply influenced the orientation of the first major papal document on cinema. However, the United Stated, of course, were not the only addressee of the ecclesiastical authority. *Vigilanti Cura* is a summary of Catholic reflection on cinema, and it was destined to become an authoritative source for the whole Catholic universe. On closer inspection, in fact, it is clear that *Vigilanti Cura* aimed to outline a common scheme on the organization of the ecclesiastical apparatuses dealing with cinema, and moreover to promote the double strategy on cinema policy, characterizing therefore the Catholics' attitude towards the moralization of production. The first strategy was applicable in democratic countries and systems based on the separation between State and Church; it mainly consisted in the mobilization of public opinion and targeted lobbying activity. The second

---

276 Segreteria di Stato, S.RR.SS., Archivio Storico, AA.EE. SS., Stati Ecclesiastici, IV, Pos. 445, Fasc. 425, f. 9r, Włodzimierz Ledóchowski to Eugenio Pacelli, January 13, 1936: "Utile per la compaginazione di una lettera sul cinematografo."

277 Segreteria di Stato, S.RR.SS., Archivio Storico, AA.EE. SS., Stati Ecclesiastici, IV, Pos. 445, Fasc. 425, f. 11r, Eugenio Pacelli to Włodzimierz Ledóchowski, January 15, 1936: "preparare tutto il materiale occorrente al noto documento, in modo che quanto [sic] egli verrà a Roma la più gran parte del lavoro sia pronta."

278 Segreteria di Stato, S.RR.SS., Archivio Storico, AA.EE. SS., Stati Ecclesiastici, IV, Pos. 445, Fasc. 418, ff. 42-56r (in particular ff. 44-45r), *Suggested Letter on The Motion Pictures and Catholic Morality* by Daniel A. Lord.

suited authoritarian or 'concordatarian' regimes; it was based on the pursuit of political agreements within power elites. In the context of the encyclical, it was possible to outline the latter approach in no more than an allusive way, which was nonetheless identifiable by the addressees: within the text, the only positive allusion to the work of state censorship committees discretely hinted at the way cinema was controlled in Italy, thanks to the collaboration between the Church and the Fascist government. The text also alluded to alliances built with governments in countries like Germany, Austria, Hungary, the Philippines and Venezuela (to cite only the most representative cases), as shown by the Vatican enquiry on cinema. Thus read the Encyclical:

> And here We record with pleasure that certain Governments, in their anxiety for the influence exercised by the cinema in the moral and educational fields, have, with the aid of upright and honest persons, especially fathers and mothers of families, set up reviewing commissions and have constituted other agencies which have to do with motion picture production in an effort to direct the cinema for inspiration to the national works of great poets and writers.[279]

The two courses of action gave the Holy See the impression of being able to control effectively the modern universe of images. Both strategies allowed them to intervene indirectly on matters related to cinema, thanks to the Catholics' ability to enter both the control room of the Hollywood industry and the censorship systems of the government. However, as a whole, the structure of the papal document on cinema was unbalanced, favouring a strategy that did not address the source of the problem: even the practical recommendations indicated in the encyclical were linked to the indirect control strategies proposed by the Legion of Decency. With regard to formal interventions, bishops were asked not only to chastise the film industry periodically, but also to mobilize Catholic cinema professionals – especially those "who fight in the ranks of Catholic Action," such that they might use

---

279   *Encyclical Letter of Pope Pius XI on The Motion Picture Vigilanti Cura*, June 29, 1936, <http://w2.vatican.va/content/pius-xi/en/encyclicals/documents/ hf_p-xi_enc_29061936_vigilanti-cura.html> [accessed July 24, 2017]. See also: Michel Lagrée, pp. 843-46.

"their influence and authority" for "the promotion of principles of sound morality in the films which they produce or aid in producing." This mobilization also sought to involve average believers, who, as in the case of the American pledge, were asked to repeat every year a ritual "promise to stay away from motion picture plays which are offensive to truth and to Christian morals." As for the modification of the organizational situation, the text envisaged the creation of a decentralized system based on a series of permanent, national offices, established by the episcopates and entrusted to the central organs of Catholic Action. These offices had two aims: first, they were to foster good films and to classify other productions; second, they were to follow the example of Canziani's CUCE, and organize the activity of Catholic movie theatres in a way that would oblige producers to create "motion pictures which conform entirely" to Christian principles.

This arrangement focused mainly on dictating the guidelines to update methods and institutions that controlled film production; however, the strategy also encountered significant difficulties in dealing with the new medium positively. In other words, the attempt on the part of the religious authorities to 'domesticate' modernity in favour of religious objectives, to control the valve in the conduit of the global entertainment industry, did not result in the complete appropriation of its mechanisms nor the acceptance of its rules. At the core of Ratti's proposal was an unresolved ambiguity in that it ultimately betrayed a pessimistic attitude toward the new medium, which came across as more likely to insinuate evil than to lead towards Good. The negative and catastrophic nature of the vocabulary employed in the letter stems precisely from such a vision.

The Vatican Hierarchy was confronted with the issues surrounding the creation of an effective strategy to reconciliation the Church's typically intransigent ideology and a medium which resisted control. In other words, as with any other questions concerning human existence, the Church demanded the full subordination of cinema to religious aims, without specifying how. In the years to come and, in particular, in the forties and fifties in Italy, this absence of direction would engender a series of experiments which often led to negative outcomes. In this sense, uncertainties surrounding the definition of the methods of film classification, even in the text of the encyclical, are revealing. The document stated that, in order to enable the pledge to abstain from immoral films, it would be necessary "that the people be told plainly which films are permitted to all, which are permitted with reservations, and which are harmful or positively bad." At the same time, the document recognized the impossibility to reach a unified and homogeneous global classification, even though every person was subject to "the same moral law."

> Since, however, there is here question of pictures which interest all classes of society, the great and the humble, the learned and the unlettered, the judgment passed upon a film cannot be the same in each case and in all respects. Indeed circumstances, usages, and forms vary from country to country so that it does not seem practical to have a single list for all the world. If, however, films were classified in each country in the manner indicated above, the resultant list would offer in principle the guidance needed.

Thus, national offices were entrusted with the task of classification that, "in order to function organically and with efficiency, must be on national basis and that it must be carried on by a single centre of responsibility."[280] In one of the first drafts of the encyclical, the paragraph concerning national offices was followed by a recognition that the bishops could disregard the national list. As the first draft stated:

> Through their diocesan revision committees, bishops will be able to modify the national list – which, however, must apply norms that are suitable for the entire country – on the basis of stricter criteria, as necessary according to the temprement of the specific region, thus censoring films that are permitted on the national list.[281]

---

280 *Encyclical Letter of Pope Pius XI on The Motion Picture Vigilanti Cura,* June 29, 1936.

281 Segreteria di Stato, S.RR.SS., Archivio Storico, AA.EE. SS., Stati Ecclesiastici, IV, Pos. 445, Fasc. 425, ff. 26-27rv, Włodzimierz Ledóchowski to Giuseppe Pizzardo, June 23, 1936: "I vescovi nella propria diocesi per mezzo delle loro commissioni diocesane di revisione, potranno, sulla stessa lista nazionale – che deve applicare norme adattabili a tutta la nazione – far uso di criteri più severi, come può richiederli l'indole della regione, censurando anche dei film che fossero ammessi nella lista nazionale."

Significantly, Ledóchowski suggested the mitigation of the text, using his personal experience, as well as the American one, as leverage.

It is understandable that every bishop should have the right to censor films in his own diocese, just as he can forbid books that are admitted elsewhere; however, I would like to underline that such a right has inspired feelings of confusion and disorientation in people, and often still does. Father Lord informed me that in America such censorship of films approved by the National Committee led to ambiguities, to the detriment of our authority. I too recall that some time ago in Poland a bishop rightfully forbade a book allowed elsewhere; this decision caused significant damage, since the people hardly understood the differences in judgement and discipline between one diocese and another. Nowadays, considering the ease of fast communication, such differences within the same region would damage the effectiveness of the collective activity of the Episcopate and its national Office. Perhaps, while maintaining a nod to the bishops' rights, it could be perhaps beneficial to mitigate the strength of the claim, using for example 'should serious, local reasons necessitate it', or a similar expression.[282]

Ledóchowski's remark was embraced in the final version of the text (the preamble of the paragraph reads: "Should grave

---

282 *Ibid.*: "È chiaro che ogni Vescovo ha il diritto di censurare films per la sua diocesi, come può proibire libri che altrove non sono proibiti; ma mi permetto di fare osservare che l'uso di tale diritto ha dato spesso e può dare occasione a confusione e disorientamento nel popolo. Il Padre Lord mi riferì che anche negli Stati Uniti tale censura particolare a films che il Comitato Nazionale aveva approvate [sic], diè ansa a spiacevoli confusioni con detrimento dell'autorità. Anch'io mi ricordo che in Polonia tempo fa, avendo un Vescovo proibito per la sua diocesi (com'era suo diritto) un libro permesso altrove, ne nacque un vero e profondo danno nel popolo, il quale difficilmente riesce a capire questa differenza di giudizio e di disciplina tra una diocesi e l'altra. Ora, poi, con l'attuale facilità di comunicazioni, tali differenze in una stessa regione sarebbero generalmente a scapito dell'efficacia dell'azione collettiva dell'Episcopato e dell'Ufficio nazionale da lui costituito. Forse si potrebbe, volendo conservare l'accenno al diritto dei singoli Vescovi, attenuare la portata con una mitigazione, per es. 'qualora gravi ragioni locali lo esigessero' o simili frasi."

reasons really require it"), but it did not influence the relativism in judgement that characterized the classification systems adopted by Catholics in many countries. After all, *Vigilanti Cura* only adapted pre-existing situations, with classification systems that differed at times significantly from country to country. For instance, the Legion of Decency established three categories: A (not disapproved), B (Disapproved for youth with a word of caution even for adults), C (disapproved for all).[283] On the other hand, the Italian CCC included eight categories in its *Segnalazioni cinematografiche* [Cinematographic Warnings], a tortuous method which underwent several modifications through the years: in its first classification (1934-1935), the Italian office distinguished four categories within the group of films approved for parish cinemas, and four categories within the group of films approved for non-parish cinemas only.[284] The American context, which was constantly supervised by the Holy See, is a testament to the difficulty of reaching a satisfactory national and unified classification system. Appointed by the American episcopate in November 1934, the diocese of Chicago, led by Cardinal Mundelein, was the first to compile a list "containing approved films, films featuring questionable scenes and prohibited productions."[285]

283 Segreteria di Stato, S.RR.SS., Archivio Storico, AA.EE. SS., Stati Ecclesiastici, IV, Pos. 445, Fasc. 418, ff. 15-21r, Amleto Cicognani to Eugenio Pacelli, December 6, 1935.

284 In the first volume of *Segnalazioni cinematografiche*, regarding films distributed in Italy in 1934-1935, there were "films approved for Catholic cinemas" divided in A (projections without amendments allowed in oratories, boarding and regular schools), Ac (projections with amendments allowed in oratories, boarding and regular schools), B (projections without amendments allowed in parish cinemas), Bc (projections with amendments allowed in parish cinemas) and "films disapproved for Catholic cinemas" divided in C (projections without amendments allowed for youth in public cinemas), Cc (projections with amendments allowed for youth in public cinemas), D (not recommended for youth) and E (not recommended): cf. Centro Cattolico Cinematografico, *Segnalazioni cinematografiche*, I, *1934-1935*, third ed., Roma, s.d., p. 4. To compare this to the French model, in which six categories were included in the classification system, see: Michel Lagrée, pp. 839-53.

285 Segreteria di Stato, S.RR.SS., Archivio Storico, AA.EE. SS., Stati Ecclesiastici, IV, Pos. 445, Fasc. 416, ff. 7-15r, Amleto Cicognani to Giuseppe Pizzardo, June 7, 1935, report n. 129/35: "Dove fossero contenute le film raccomandate; quelle che avevano delle scene che

Subsequently it became clear that such measures posed several problems, since the majority of films are first screened in New York, where the photographic processing takes place, despite the fact that 90% of of them are produced in the diocese of Los Angeles in Hollywood. Thus, different lists were compiled in Brooklyn, Los Angeles and Detroit. Such differences, however, did not affect the effectiveness of the system also because in each diocese only one list is known, which is published in the diocese's magazine. The Episcopal Committee, while recommending the Chicago list, let each bishop decide autonomously.[286]

Leaving aside the option of declaring the Chicago list the "official list of the Episcopate," so as not to "undermine the authority of the bishops,"[287] a *National Legion of Decency List* was instead compiled. In this way, the direct involvement of the National Catholic Welfare Conference was avoided. On November 15, 1935, the revision committee was moved from Chicago to New York and put into the hands of Cardinal Patrick J. Hayes. It is worth mentioning here the reasons for which the apostolic delegate in Washington had opted for a classification list "presented negatively rather than positively:" "it has been pointed out," Cicognani stated, "that a white list would cause disagreements and discontent on which films should be approved; it is better to publish a black list, that is, a list of immoral and disapproved films. This does not mean that, in each diocese, bishops cannot recommend and praise worthy films; and in any case, the national list, as it is, can be described as

---

lasciavano a desiderare, e quelle condannate del tutto."

286 *Ibid.*: "In seguito poi si vide che il provvedimento presentava delle difficoltà, per il fatto che, mentre il 90 per cento delle films è prodotto in diocesi di Los Angeles ad Hollywood, lo sviluppo fotografico e tecnico delle films è fatto in New York, dove vengono rappresentate prima che altrove. In tale modo vennero fuori liste proprie a Brooklyn, Los Angeles e Detroit. Si sono avute così delle differenze nelle liste, che peraltro non hanno pregiudicato l'efficacia del sistema, anche perché in genere in ogni diocesi è conosciuta una sola lista, pubblicata nel giornale diocesano. Il Comitato Episcopale, pur raccomandando la lista di Chicago, ha preferito lasciare alla decisione dei singoli Vescovi questo dettagli."

287 Segreteria di Stato, S.RR.SS., Archivio Storico, AA.EE. SS., Stati Ecclesiastici, IV, Pos. 445, Fasc. 418, ff. 26rv-27r, memorandum of November 26, 1935 on the activity of the American episcopate: "ufficiale dell'episcopato;" "compromettere troppo l'autorità dei singoli vescovi."

'nearly white'."[288] Nevertheless, the case of American films, subject to large-scale distribution, drew attention to the impossibility to compile, as with books, a "list of prohibited films."[289] Hollywood production manifestly demonstrated that films approved by the American episcopate could be considered inappropriate in other countries, and consequently rejected by the Catholic board of control. In this sense, Pizzardo's confidential letter to Cicognani is quite emblematic; in it, Pizzardo enquired after the possibility of films that had already been approved by the Legion of Decency undergoing further inspection, in view of their exportation to Italy. The letter also hints at how much progress the 'cinema concordat' between the Church and the Fascist government had made by the beginning of 1937.

In order to avoid the disapproval, on the part of bishops, of the films the American studios want to import in Italy, a chief administrative official of the General Film Office could indicate them in advance to the CCC, so as to have a precautionary evaluation. However, the CCC is in a difficult position, because many films that have already been <u>universally approved by the Legion of Decency</u> in America are not suitable for the Italian sensitivity, and would trigger the disapproval of the Episcopate. On the other hand, the claims of the Episcopate cannot be accepted by the General Film Office, as it would be easy to entrench oneself in the approvals that were already formulated by the Legion of Decency. Thus, the films

---

288 Segreteria di Stato, S.RR.SS., Archivio Storico, AA.EE. SS., Stati Ecclesiastici, IV, Pos. 445, Fasc. 418, ff. 15-21r, Amleto Cicognani to Eugenio Pacelli, December 6, 1935: "esposta in modo negativo più che positivo;" "si è constatato che si va incontro a discussioni e dissensi col mettere innanzi una lista bianca, e cioè di approvazione delle tali e tali films [sic], meglio riesce pubblicare la lista nera, vale a dire di disapprovazione delle films immorali e non raccomandabili. Ciò peraltro non toglie che i Vescovi nelle singole diocesi non possano indicare e lodare certe films che lo meritino; e del resto la lista nazionale, così com'è indicata, potrebbe dirsi più propriamente 'quasi bianca'."

289 Unwilling to abolish it, Pius XI attemped to revive the *Index librorum prohibitorum*, and published, from 1929, the Italian edition: see, in particular, Luisa Mangoni, "I Patti Lateranensi e la cultura cattolica" in *La Chiesa cattolica e il totalitarismo*, ed. by Vincenzo Ferrone (Firenze: Olschki 2004), pp. 93-196. On the general history on the Index, abolished only in 1966 by Paul VI within the picture of the council renovation, see: Hubert Wolf, *Storia dell'Indice. Il Vaticano e i libri proibiti* (Roma: Donzelli, 2006).

approved by the Legion of Decency must be re-examined by an audience with a Latin or Italian sensibility. The CCC could then signal those films to the General Film Office. The issue can be formulated as follows: is it possible to organize in such a private way a second unofficial, yet confidential and informal examination? Or at least is it possible to find a person in New York who can indicate to the CCC a list of films that would not be received favourably in Italy?[290]

During the preparatory debate on *Vigilanti Cura,* the semantic limitations of the Italian word "decenza," generally used to translate the English word "*decency,*" were stressed: one of the comments on the first Italian translation of Lord's *Suggested Letter* underlines the fact that the word did not fully correspond "to the philosophical thought of the natural and Christian ethics."[291] It was suggested that "decency" could

---

290 Segreteria di Stato, S.RR.SS., Archivio Storico, AA.EE. SS., Stati Ecclesiastici, IV, Pos. 445, Fasc. 427, ff. 4-5r, Giuseppe Pizzardo to Amleto Cicognani, January 19, 1937, underlined in the text: "Per evitare che i films che le Case Americane vorrebbero importare in Italia provochino la disapprovazione dei Vescovi, un alto funzionario della Direzione Generale per la Cinematografia in Italia sarebbe disposto a segnalarli preventivamente al Centro Cattolico Cinematografico allo scopo di averne un giudizio preventivo. Il Centro Cattolico Cinematografico però si trova in grande imbarazzo perché vari Films, già approvati per tutti dalla Legion of decency in America non sono adatti alla sensibilità italiana, e susciterebbero la disapprovazione dell'Episcopato. D'altra parte i reclami dell'Episcopato stesso non potrebbero essere accolti dalla predetta Direzione Generale perché sarebbe facile trincerarsi nella approvazione già data dalla Legion of Decency. Si è quindi nella necessità che i Films approvati dalla Legion of decency siano rivisti da chi ha la sensibilità latina o italiana. Il Centro Cattolico Cinematografico, segnalerebbe tali films alla Direzione Generale per la Cinematografia. La questione quindi si presenta così: è possibile costituire così privatamente una seconda revisione non ufficiale, ma confidenziale, amichevole? O almeno è possibile trovare a New York persona che possa segnalare al Centro Cattolico Cinematografico quei films che pensa non saranno ben accolti in Italia?"

291 Segreteria di Stato, S.RR.SS., Archivio Storico, AA.EE. SS., Stati Ecclesiastici, IV, Pos. 445, Fasc. 425, f. 45r, note without date nor signature located in the volume dedicated to the redaction of *Vigilanti Cura*: "In tutto al pensiero filosofico dell'etica naturale e cristiana."

be translated with the word "decoro" [decorum] or "dignità morale" [moral dignity], as understood by Cicero when he writes: 'in omni re videndum est quatenus: vocant id graeci "Prepon" nos dicamus sane decorum'." This entailed "a much wider and inclusive meaning than 'decenza', which seemed to exclude only obscene and lecherous representations."[292]

12. *The Forms and Limits of Moralized Cinema*

Defining a unitary classification method that would allowed the Catholics to protect decency by indicating "evil motion pictures" was not the only issue at hand. Religious authorities had to face the challenge of defining the standards of film content which conformed to the rules of "Christian and natural ethics." The encyclical includes only a brief depiction of the nature of "good motions:" "they are able to arouse noble ideals of life, to communicate valuable conceptions, to impart a better knowledge of the history and the beauties of the Fatherland and of other countries, to present truth and virtue under attractive forms, to create, or at least to favour understanding among nations, social classes, and races, to champion the cause of justice, to give new life to the claims of virtue, and to contribute positively to the genesis of a just social order in the world."[293] This pedagogic programme was not in itself dissimilar to the one developed during the same period by élites of lay sensibility, such as the IECI.[294]

How could the Catholics make cinema – as, clearly, the core of the modern entertainment industry – into an "effectual instrument for the education and the elevation of mankind"? And how could the assumption that cinema encouraged the identification of the audience and its passive amazement be reconciled with the

---

292 *Ibid.*: "un senso molto più largo e comprensivo che non quello di 'decenza', che sembra escludere solo l'oscenità o licenziosità della rappresentazione."

293 *Encyclical Letter of Pope Pius XI on The Motion Picture Vigilanti Cura*, June 29, 1936.

294 On the same topic, see also Michel Lagrée's enlightening contributions in "L'encyclique Vigilanti Cura sur le cinéma (1936)," pp. 847-48.

possibility that it could, at the same time, induce viewers to analyse and elaborate the stream of images consciously? The encyclical failed to answer these questions. Similarly, it is evident that the section dedicated to the possibility of a Catholic film production was affected by the clamorous failure of Eidophon, and by the rejection of the OCIC's responsibility for production and distribution. The Soviet model, as understood by Ledit, conceived of cinema at simultaneously as a "creator of pure propaganda," as "a technically successful creation" and as a "means to educate the masses." This combination was not the easiest path to take. *Vigilanti Cura* reads:

> The problem of the production of moral films would be solved radically if it were possible for us to have production wholly inspired by the principles of Christian morality. We can never sufficiently praise all those who have dedicated themselves or who are to dedicate themselves to the noble cause of raising the standard of the motion picture to meet the needs of education and the requirements of the Christian conscience. For this purpose, they must make full use of the technical ability of experts and not permit the waste of effort and of money by the employment of amateurs. But since We know how difficult it is to organize such an industry, especially because of considerations of a financial nature, and since on the other hand it is necessary to influence the production of all films so that they may contain nothing harmful from a religious, moral, or social viewpoint, Pastors of souls must exercise their vigilance over films wherever they may be produced and offered to Christian peoples.[295]

The letter thus acknowledges the difficulty in embracing the necessary capitalistic mechanisms to ensure an autonomous Catholic presence within the film industry. However, the encyclical contained very few observations on what exactly characterized a cinema that was "wholly inspired by the principles of Christian morality." The complete exclusion of the most influential figures of the OCIC from the preparatory procedure of the document, in the name of 'good Americanism' and of the needs related an intended centralization of Rome, deprived the Pope of kinds of

---

295 *Encyclical Letter of Pope Pius XI on The Motion Picture Vigilanti Cura,* June 29, 1936.

contributions which would probably have enabled him to develop a discourse that was not exclusively limited to moral issues. Such contributions would have opened the discussion to more specific considerations on creation processes of the filmic text, on film aesthetics, and on the statute of cinema as a new art form. Among the members of the Belgian institution, there were people who had experienced the phenomenon from within, who had spoken at length with producers, actors and directors; people who were willing to listen to and engage with artistic and literary avant-gardes.[296] In one of his first articles written as executive director of OCIC, Joseph Reymond clearly specified the attitude that should have characterized the activity of the new institution:

> We do not want [...] as someone, luckily with few followers, has insinuated in a more or less superficial way, to turn every theatre into a grim temple, and every screen into a boring teacher of morality. The Church has always rejected members who want to deprive flowers from their colours and perfumes. We are not demanding that the silver screen become a permanent *moralizer.* We are aware that everything must be achieved at the right time and place. Instead, we believe that the so-called *moralizing* film should be banished from public cinemas, since we know that a film can moralize solely through productions that do not look *moralizing* [...]; yet, by means of such films, faith and morality should be preserved. Healthy joy, healthy emotion. Catholics do not have the right to ask for anything more, and nobody will find such a request unusual.[297]

The contents of this passage clash with the essential aspirations of *Vigilanti Cura*. In spite of its efforts to understand cinema as a complex phenomenon, the Roman curia remained distant from the world of cinema, which it observed with stark snobbery. In this sense, the absolute candour of Cicognani's claim does not seem surprising: during the campaign led by the Legion of Decency, he plainly admitted to Pizzardo that he could not "personally guarantee" the validity of the results of episcopal action since

---

296 Robert Molhant, *Les catholiques et le cinéma.*
297 Joseph Reymond, "I cattolici e il cinema," *Rivista internazionale del Cinema Educatore*, a. I, n. 2, August 1929, pp. 185-91, italicized in the text.

"he had never visited a cinema."[298] Yet, the soon-to-be Cardinal Secretary of State under Pope John XXIII was the backbone of the activities of the American Church or, as Pizzardo defined him, the main "host and thruster" of the attempts to "heal Cinema."[299]

Within this picture, it is necessary to underline how the efforts of the American episcopate through the Legion of Decency – solemnly blessed by Pius XI – did not really decrease Hollywood's ability to enchant global audiences. Cicognani, McNichols and the other forerunners of the 'holy crusade' against 'Hollywoodism' did not emphasize the results of their campaign: the immediate radical modification of American cinema that took place from 1934 is an incontrovertible fact. Nevertheless, the concrete outcomes were destined to prove less important in the long term: the lack of a deep understanding of cinema, of its language and its mythopoeic mechanisms prevented the religious authority from identifying, in their complexity, the expedients used by the Hollywood industry to seduce the audience, while rigorously following the strict guidelines provided by Production Code Administration. As opposed to the witch hunt that characterized McCarthyism during the fifties, the campaign led by the episcopate was not perceived as an attack on creative freedom:[300] indeed, even if cinema followed the rules imposed by Catholic moralizers, it still conveyed values and desires that were very distant from "natural and Christian ethics."[301] The seemingly easy integration to a new, moralized climate can be explained in terms of the directors' and producers' ability to conform to the Hays Code instead of transgressing it. To this end, they used the

---

298 Segreteria di Stato, S.RR.SS., Archivio Storico, AA.EE. SS., Stati Ecclesiastici, IV, Pos. 445, Fasc. 416, ff. 5rv-6r, Amleto Cicognani to Giuseppe Pizzardo, June 7, 1935: "attestare per esperienza personale;" "non avendo mai visitato un cinema."

299 Segreteria di Stato, S.RR.SS., Archivio Storico, AA.EE. SS., Stati Ecclesiastici, IV, Pos. 445, Fasc. 427, ff. 4-5r, Giuseppe Pizzardo to Amleto Cicognani, January 19, 1937: "l'animatore e il propulsore;" "tentativi di risanare il Cinematografo."

300 On "cinema McCarthyism" see: Giuliana Muscio, "Cinema e guerra fredda (1946-1956)," in *Storia del cinema mondiale*, ed. by Gian Piero Brunetta (Torino: Einaudi, 2000), 2/II, *Gli Stati Uniti*, pp. 1437-61.

301 Segreteria di Stato, S.RR.SS, Archivio Storico, AA.EE. SS., Stati Ecclesiastici, IV, Pos. 445, Fasc. 425, f. 45r: "etica naturale e cristiana."

resources of cinematographic language wisely in order to nourish the alluring power of cinema: thus, it became fundamental to pry the polysemy of images and to choose evocative locations, as well as actors gifted with sex appeal, to achieve the goal of putting "sex in brackets" ("sesso tra parentesi"), without diminishing the sensuality of films. Moreover, the ways in which sexual content was represented in the '30s and '40s also conformed to the typical, unwritten codes of respectability, tastefulness and decorum: thus, while some forms of manifest sexuality were prohibited, in time the ban created a vast array of alluring erotic meanings and signals.[302] Such a tendency entailed a shift in perspective on intimately-sensualized Hollywood glamour: as Gundle has rightly noted, "directors, screenwriters, cinematographers and costumers could not be explicit, so they evoked sex through the atmosphere, allusions and transpositions."[303]

---

302 See: David Forgacs, "Sex in the Cinema," pp. 144-71.
303 Stephen Gundle, "L'età d'oro dello Star System," in *Storia del cinema mondiale*, 2/II, pp. 714-15.

BETWEEN SEXUAL AND DEVOTIONAL EXCITEMENT
BY TOMASO SUBINI

1. *Towards a Definition of Religious Cinema*

"What is a religious film?"[1] asked André Ruszkowski in *Religion and the Film*, a booklet that originated in a lecture held on February 23, 1950 at University College Dublin and one of the first serious attempts to provide a definition of religious cinema. Ruszkowski was General Secretary for International Affairs of the Office Catholique International du Cinéma [International Catholic Office for Cinema, hereafter OCIC], and General Secretary for *Revue Internationale du Cinéma*, therefore one of the leading figures engaged in the field of mass communication within international Catholicism. Ruzskowski's main aims in dealing with the question were the apostolate and propaganda: "Modern means of communication make possible the world-wide circulation of what before could only be a local manifestation. The cinema, the radio, and television, give Catholics an opportunity which they have never had before of showing the whole of mankind a way of living."[2] Such a statement did not imply that artistic cinema was best suited for this aim: "Very few people – perhaps one in a thousand ordinary filmgoers – were capable of understanding the significance of the very beautiful and cleverly taken pictures of Drayer. All the rest remained completely indifferent, or even bored. What can be the religious influence of such a production in the circumstances, even though it remains one of the 'classics' of the history of film art?"[3] Furthermore, Ruszkowski's reflection was

---

1   André Ruszkowski, *Religion and the Film* (Dublin: National Film Institute of Ireland, 1950), p. 4.
2   *Ibid.*, p. 9.
3   *Ibid.*, p. 8.

characterized by a particular awareness of the dynamics shaping the relation between the text and its viewer: "It is quite clear that the effects of a religious film upon public opinion depends to a very large degree on the public itself. This must always be borne in mind by those who hope to use the cinema as a powerful means of apostolate."[4] On the one hand, Ruszkowski found Rossellini's cinema to be paradigmatic of a filmic text open to a high degree of interpretive cooperation from the viewer, stating that "the same film [by Rossellini] may produce very different reactions in different audiences."[5] On the other hand, he acknowledged that there were texts, such as those produced by Nazi propaganda, that were "presented in such a convincing [...] manner that it was practically impossible for the individual spectator to interpret them in a spirit other than that intended by the sponsors."[6]

The second part of Ruszkowski's essay addressed the main problems faced by religious cinema. Ruszkowski's argument revolved around three main types of film: films about saints, films about Jesus, and films dealing with the representation of miracles. At stake in all three cases was the very possibility of representing the sacred aspects which the stories relate. For example, one of the issues considered was the responsibility of the actors impersonating a figure shrouded in sanctity:

> All his private life should be dominated by the sense of this responsibility. One remembers the terrifying words of Christ about those who have scandalized the innocents. How many millions of modern innocents have been scandalized, losing their faith in the true character of the saintly figures they admired on the screen, when they learned afterwards of the public scandals, broken marriages, and others offences against divine and human laws committed by those who had personified these figures? The question is even more grave when it is Our Lord's life which is represented.[7]

---

4   *Ibid.*, p. 9.
5   *Ibid.*, p. 4.
6   *Ibid.*, p. 7.
7   *Ibid.*, p. 12.

Ruszkowki's essay finally provided the following definition of religious cinema:

> When I speak of a 'religious film' I have in mind, not just a 'film about religion,' but a film whose significance and message has a bearing on the impact of God on human life. Where you can't find God, there is no religion; and to find God you must look for Him, unless by an exceptional privilege He chooses you for an undeserved revelation. I insist on this point, because it explains why even the best religious film cannot automatically bring about conviction, unless there is some co-operation on the part of the spectator. But a film may help us in our search for God, and a religious film might be described as a film which makes us aware of the Divine presence, and reminds us of the real purpose of our life on earth – the saving of our soul. In this sense, any film may be a religious film, if both those who make it and those who see it co-operate in giving it such a meaning.[8]

Theoretically speaking, this was clearly a weak definition, since, given certain conditions, any film could be defined as religious.

Half a century later, the same conceptual difficulty still characterizes scholarship in so-called "Religion and Film Studies," a discipline which has emerged within the field of Anglophone Religious Studies and which has given life to its own scientific societies,[9] journals,[10] and book series.[11] Surveying this field of

---

8   *Ibid.*, p. 4.

9   See, for example, the International Society for Media, Religion, and Culture's conferences.

10   See, for instance, *The Journal of Religion and Film*, published by the University of Nebraska, Omaha: http://www.unomaha.edu/jrf/.

11   For example, *Routledge Studies in Religion and Film* by Robert Johnston and Jolyon Mitchell. Recently, a similar vein has begun to be established in Italian academia. However, it has not been decided (and might never be, due to the interdisciplinary nature of the research) whether studies of religion and film should be based in departments carrying out research in film studies or those working on Christianity and the history of religions. The issue is by no means secondary, since it concerns the epistemological status of a discipline, the aims that it pursues as such, and the ways in which the respective disciplines carry out their research. Thus, at stake is the very possibility for scholars coming from different research backgrounds to investigate religious film jointly, without masking their background but rather sharing knowledge and skills. In Italy, the most

study in her 2007 work, *Religion and Film: An Introduction,* Melanie Wright underlined the widespread lack of competence in film analysis by scholars mainly coming from Religious Studies. In particular, Wright complained about the arbitrariness in the choice of analysed movies, thus prompting a very direct question: what are the distinctive features of a religious film? Does a film's qualification as religious depend on somehow objective criteria, or is it just the consequence of the specific approach that some scholars take, tending to see religious aspects everywhere, especially where others see no trace of them?[12]

The difficulty that scholars encounter when trying to agree on a definition of "religious film" – that is, on the very subject of Religion and Film Studies – mostly originates with the problems characterizing the dialogue between "religion" and "cinema," which many scholars take for granted. While some scholars maintain that cinema performs the same function as religion in secular societies (producing new myths[13]), others think that cinema should be studied insofar as it provides insights into the cultural perspective of a given religion, thus confirming its centrality in modern society, in-keeping with the spirit of the age. In the former case, consistent with religious cultural studies,

---

fruitful occasion of interdisciplinary dialogue on this question has been offered by the seminar series organized by the Department of History, Cultures, and Religions at Rome Sapienza University. See *Cinema e religioni* edited by Sergio Botta and Emanuela Prinzivalli (Roma: Carocci, 2010). Sandra Isetta and Marcello Marin instead use cinema for religious discourse, without considering the specificity of the medium. See *Il volto e gli sguardi: Bibbia, letteratura, cinema,* ed. by Sandra Isetta (Bologna: EDB, 2010) and *Auctores Nostri,* 10 (2012), ed. by Marcello Marin and Vincenzo Lomiento. Additionally, David Zordan's work represents a key Italian point of reference for scholars working within Religion and Film Studies. See, for example his monograph, *La Bibbia a Hollywood. Retorica religiosa e cinema di consumo* (Bologna: EDB, 2007).

12   Melanie Wright, *Religion and Film: An Introduction* (London: J.B. Tauris, 2007).

13   This was also Pius XII's impression. The Pope's concerns emerged in a speech he gave in 1943: "It has been said that the modern man's church, in big cities, is the cinema. It can appear and it is a paradox of very bad taste; but you very well know that there is some tragic truth in it, as well as disappointments and dangers." See *Acta Apostolicae Sedis,* vol. XXXV, 1943, p. 107.

religious facts are part of the problem under analysis, while in the latter case they are just the starting point of the analysis, and thus, its rationale. While they differ radically, the culturalist and the confessional approaches often coexist within the field of Religion and Film Studies without being problematized, since they are both inspired by the same dialogue between religion and cinema. As Davide Zordan, the most competent Italian Religion and Film scholar, has remarked, "the reason why the metaphor of a bilateral dialogue between religion and cinema is not sufficient to qualify the various approaches within Religion and Film Studies is that three poles should be considered instead of two: competence on cinema, competence on religion, and a culturalist sense, which, however hard to pin down and identify, demands particular competency and cannot be taken for granted, just as the first two competencies. In other words, religion and cinema as such do not necessarily dialogue: in fact, they are 'dialogued' by a third element – the public, society, culture."[14]

Over the last few years, Wright's book has initiated a discussion about the weak disciplinarity of Religion and Film Studies, a field that has nonetheless grown remarkably, as evidenced by two companions published in 2009: *The Routledge Companion to Religion and Film*[15] and *The Continuum Companion to Religion and Film.*[16] Issued by major academic publishers, the two volumes united several scholars who contributed to this field of study. At the same time, the two companions met consumer demand

---

14 Davide Zordan, "Il cinema italiano nella prospettiva dei Religion and Film Studies," unpublished paper read on May 28, 2014 on occasion of a workshop of the PRIN research project on "Catholics and Cinema" coordinated by Milan Statale University: "il motivo per cui la metafora del dialogo bilaterale tra religione e cinema non è sufficiente a qualificare gli approcci dei *religion and film studies* è che in realtà i poli da mettere in relazione sono tre e non due: la competenza sul cinema, la competenza sulla religione e la sensibilità culturalista, che, per quanto difficile da isolare e identificare, esige a sua volta competenze proprie e non può essere data per scontata, esattamente come le altre due. In altre parole la religione e il cinema come tali non dialogano tra loro, sono 'dialogati' per così dire da un terzo, che è il pubblico, la società, la cultura."

15 *The Routledge Companion to Religion and Film,* ed. by John Lyden (London: Routledge, 2009).

16 *The Continuum Companion to Religion and Film,* ed. by William Blizek (London: Continuum, 2009).

generated by the increase in courses on religion and cinema in US universities and throughout the Anglophone world more generally. Zordan writes that

> the two companions are an implicit and indirect response less to Wright's critiques than to the risk, evoked by Wright, that the discipline might disappear even before it even begins, because of the lack of a sound methodological framework and of a clearly identifiable object of study. The editors of the two companions counter such a warning by stating that the discipline does exist, that it is taught, that academic handbooks, rich in details and explanations, are being written and published, and that there is a well-established group of scholars who work together and who have become authoritative enough to set the guidelines for current and future research.[17]

Yet, Wright's main question – what is a religious film? – remains unanswered. Blizek's handbook, for example, begins with this statement: "There are different kinds of movies in which religion and film scholars may be interested, from Hollywood blockbusters to foreign films, from documentaries to short films. Religion and religious themes can be found in different kinds of movies and this fact is one reason for the wide interest in religion and film studies."[18] While Wright was calling for an assessment of the disciplinary and methodological boundaries of the field of study, Blizek maintains that its success depends on its very indeterminacy, that is, on the fact that any film is potentially relevant for Religion and Film Studies, any film will ring a bell to

---

17   Davide Zordan: "I due manuali rappresentano una risposta implicita e indiretta non tanto alle critiche mosse da Wright, quanto al rischio, paventato dalla studiosa, che la disciplina possa scomparire prima ancora di imporsi, per mancanza di un impianto metodologico adeguato e di un oggetto chiaramente identificabile. Contro questo monito allarmistico viene fatta valere l'evidenza che la disciplina esiste, che viene insegnata, che si compongono manuali accademici ricchi di chiarimenti e descrizioni del campo di indagine, che c'è un gruppo consolidato di studiosi che si relazionano e hanno guadagnato sul campo l'autorevolezza necessaria per proporre dei percorsi da seguire."

18   William Blizek, "Religion and the Movies," in *The Continuum Companion to Religion and Film*, p. 19.

an ear attuned to religious discourse. Still the question remains: what is a religious film?

Given the difficulty of defining religious cinema at a theoretical level, it is convenient to move to an empirical level, to outline an objective description of religious film as it was conceived in a given period and within a given context – in our case, Italy during the post-war period.

This is possible by referring to the lists of religious movies drafted during the fifties and sixties by one of the most important offices to which *Vigilanti Cura* entrusted control of cinema on behalf of the Church: the Italian Centro Cattolico Cinematografico [Catholic Cinematographic Centre, hereafter CCC]. The drafting of such lists was prompted by provisions contained in the circular on parish cinemas, issued on May 23, 1950 by the Direzione Generale per la Cinematografia [hereafter General Film Office] and signed by Giulio Andreotti. According to these provisions, parish cinemas were institutionally dedicated to screening religious movies, which allowed them to overcome the legal limitations that differentiated parish from commercial movie theatres: "in the towns or districts that already have a commercial cinema, advertising activity is to be limited to the exhibition of photographs and bills and to the distribution of flyers advertising the show, within the perimeter of the parish premises. Such limitation does not apply to the advertising of religious films."[19] The decision as to what was meant by "religious film" was left to parish cinemas themselves, which had some discretionary power until the mid-fifties, when they were forced to publish their lists of religious movies.

Such lists resulted from a conflict between two interest groups. The Associazione Cattolica Esercenti Cinema [Catholic Exhibitors' Association, hereafter ACEC] sought to overcome the legal restrictions on its activity and therefore promoted a broad as well as unofficial definition of "religious film" to be shown

---

19 Giulio Andreotti, *Disciplina delle sale parrocchiali*, May 23, 1950, ACEC Archive (DB: ACEC 89): "nei Comuni o Frazioni dove già esistono cinema industriali la pubblicità deve essere limitata soltanto all'esposizione delle fotografie e degli affissi e alla distribuzione di avvisi annuncianti lo spettacolo, nel perimetro degli edifici parrocchiali. Tale limitazione non si riferisce alla propaganda dei film a carattere religioso."

in their theatres. On the contrary, the Associazione Nazionale Esercenti Cinema [Commercial Exhibitors' Association, hereafter ANEC], which viewed parish cinemas as dangerous competition, requested official and unequivocal lists of religious movies, seeking to circumscribe the advertisement of parish cinemas. In this way, the ANEC forced the CCC (to which the ACEC deferred on such a delicate matter) to take an official stance on the religious content of the films they intended to screen.

"An initial list of films that the Ecclesiastical Consultant of the CCC considers to have a 'religious character'"[20] was issued

---

20   Albino Galletto, letter to Francesco Dalla Zuanna, May 20, 1955, ACEC Archive (DB: ACEC 3): "un primo elenco di film che il Consulente Ecclesiastico del Centro Cattolico Cinematografico considera 'a carattere religioso'." Founded in 1934, the CCC became a section of the Ente dello Spettacolo, established in 1946 at the same time as the issuing of the new ACI's statute, which changed its structure enhancing its verticality. At the top of the organizational structure was the Central Committee, composed of four branches: "Unione uomini" [the Men's Branch of Catholic Action], "Unione donne" [the Women's Branch of Catholic Action], "Gioventù maschile" [the Young Men of Catholic Action], and "Gioventù femminile" [the Young Women of Catholic Action]. This main structure had several side associations, each performing a specific function, such as the Ente dello Spettacolo, which reported to the Central Committee and was led (like the four branches) by a lay President and an Ecclesiastical Consultant. Before the foundation of the Ente dello Spettacolo, we find evidence of "Centri dello Spettacolo" [Entertainment Centres] or, alternatively, "Segretariato dello Spettacolo" [Secretariat for Entertainment]. The first Ecclesiastical Consultant for the Centri dello Spettacolo was Luigi Civardi, who was replaced in 1945 by Ferdinando Prosperini. After an extenuating confrontation with President Luigi Gedda, Prosperini was invited (read: forced) to resign from his position in 1947, handing it over to Albino Galletto. Circumstances were extenuating at least for Prosperini, since Gedda did not bother to answer the letters that Prosperini sent him on a regular basis to voice his complaints. Prosperini's policies, which remained mostly programmatic and were only implemented in a few, largely second-rate events, were antithetical to Gedda's. Prosperini wished to restore the centrality of the Centro Cattolico Radiofonico [Catholic Radio Centre] and the Centro Cattolico Teatrale [Catholic Theatre Centre], putting them on the same level as the CCC. On the contrary, Gedda was only interested in the CCC's activities. In fact, Prosperini thought that complying with *Vigilanti Cura* and in-keeping with film policies adopted in other Catholic countries, the CCC had to limit its task to reviewing films – that is, to guaranteeing their morality. Perhaps risking too much, Gedda had instead pushed

in 1955, featuring 52 titles.[21] This list was progressively updated in subsequent years until, as far as we could gather, 1967, when it eventually included 24 new titles.[22] According to the CCC, the complete list of religious films consisted of 76 titles **(fig. 2)**.

Fig. 2 – The list of films that the Ecclesiastical Consultant of the CCC considers to have a "religious character."

1919	*Giuda* (Febo Mari)
1923	*The Ten Commandments* (Cecil B. DeMille)
1925	*Ben-Hur* (Fred Niblo)
1935	*Golgotha* (Julien Duvivier)
1935	*The Crusades* (Cecil B. DeMille)
1936	*Conquistatori d'anime* (Renzo Chiosso, Felice Minotti)
1936	*Don Bosco* (Goffredo Alessandrini)

the CCC towards production, employing his best people and investing a considerable amount of money in the production of films that could compete with commercial movies. Gedda was President of the Ente dello Spettacolo from its foundation until 1952, when became General President of the ACI and consequently handed over leadership to Ildo Avetta. Galletto was Ecclesiastical Consultant to the Ente dello Spettacolo until September 1960, when his role was taken over by Francesco Angelicchio.

21 CCC, *Primo elenco di film considerati dal CCC a carattere religioso* [*Initial list of films with religious character according to the CCC*], May 18, 1955, ACEC Archive (DB: ACEC 2).

22 Albino Galletto, letter to Francesco Dalla Zuanna, November 7, 1955, ACEC Archive (DB: ACEC 4); Albino Galletto, letter to Francesco Dalla Zuanna, June 13, 1956, ACEC Archive (DB: ACEC 5); Albino Galletto, letter to Francesco Dalla Zuanna, March 12, 1956, ACEC Archive (DB: ACEC 6); Albino Galletto, letter to Francesco Dalla Zuanna, January 8, 1958, ACEC Archive (DB: ACEC 7); Albino Galletto, letter to Francesco Dalla Zuanna, March 11,1959, ACEC Archive (DB: ACEC 8); Francesco Angelicchio, letter to Francesco Dalla Zuanna, November 22, 1960, ACEC Archive (DB: ACEC 9); Francesco Angelicchio, letter to Francesco Dalla Zuanna, November 7, 1961, ACEC Archive (DB: ACEC 10); Francesco Angelicchio, letter to Francesco Dalla Zuanna, Novemebr 30, 1965, ACEC Archive (DB: ACEC 11); Francesco Angelicchio, letter to Francesco Dalla Zuanna, February 17, 1966, ACEC Archive (DB: ACEC 12); Francesco Angelicchio, letter to Francesco Dalla Zuanna, February 28, 1967, ACEC Archive (DB: ACEC 14). An updated list, dating to 1983, is available in the ACEC archive (DB: ACEC 1), though it was never made official.

1936	*L'appel du silence* (Léon Poirier)
1939	*Abuna Messias* (Goffredo Alessandrini)
1941	*Creo en Dios* (Fernando De Fuentes)
1942	*Pastor Angelicus* (Romolo Marcellini)
1942	*Sancta Maria* (Pier Luigi Faraldo, Edgar Neville)
1943	*Les anges du péché* (Robert Bresson)
1943	*Rita da Cascia* (Antonio Leonviola)
1943	*The Song of Bernadette* (Henry King)
1944	*Going My Way* (Leo McCarey)
1944	*The Keys of the Kingdom* (John Malcolm Stahl)
1945	*La porta del cielo* (Vittorio De Sica)
1945	*The Bells of St. Mary's* (Leo McCarey)
1946	*María Magdalena, pecadora de Magdala* (Miguel Contreras Torres)
1946	*Saint Francois d'Assise* (Alberto Cout)
1946	*Un giorno nella vita* (Alessandro Blasetti)
1947	*Caterina da Siena* (Oreste Palella)
1947	*Monsieur Vincent* (Maurice Cloche)
1947	*The Fugitive* (John Ford)
1948	*Guerra alla guerra* (Giorgio Simonelli, Diego Fabbri)
1948	*Joan of Arc* (Victor Fleming)
1948	*L'ultima cena* (Luigi Giachino)
1948	*La mies es mucha* (José Luis Saenz de Heredia)
1949	*Antonio di Padova* (Pietro Francisci)
1949	*Cielo sulla palude* (Augusto Genina)
1949	*Come to the Stable* (Henry Koster)
1949	*La passione secondo San Matteo* (Ernst Marischka)
1949	*Le sorcier du ciel* (Marcel Blistène)
1949	*Un gregge chiama* (Mario Milani)
1949	*El Capitán de Loyola* (José Diaz Morales)
1950	*Anno Santo 1950* (Giorgio Walter Chili)
1950	*Francesco giullare di Dio* (Roberto Rossellini)
1950	*Guilty of Treason* (Felix Feist)

1950	*Mater Dei* (Emilio Cordero)
1951	*Das Tor zum Frieden* (Wolfgang Liebeneiner)
1951	*Dieu a besoin des hommes* (Jean Delannoy)
1951	*Journal d'un curé de campagne* (Robert Bresson)
1951	*La señora de Fatima* (Rafael Gil)
1951	*The First Legion* (Douglas Sirk)
1952	*Don Camillo* (Julien Duvivier)
1952	*Gli uomini non guardano il cielo* (Umberto Scarpelli)
1952	*Procès au Vatican* (André Haguet)
1952	*The Miracle of Our Lady of Fatima* (John Brahm)
1953	*The Robe* (Henry Koster)
1953	*I Was a Parish Priest* (*La guerra de Dios*, Rafael Gil)
1954	*Giovanna d'Arco al rogo* (Roberto Rossellini)
1954	*Il figlio dell'Uomo* (Virgilio Sabel)
1954	*Le défroqué* (Léo Joannon)
1954	*Judas' Kiss* (*El beso de Judas*, Rafael Gil)
1955	*Marcelino pan y vino* (Ladislao Vajda)
1955	*Un missionnaire* (Maurice Cloche)
1956	*Biruma no tategoto* (Kon Ichikawa)
1956	*Il più grande mistero d'amore* (Pier Giuseppe Franci)
1956	*Il suo più grande amore* (Antonio Leonviola)
1958	*El hereje* (Francisco De Bordja Moro)
1958	*La redenzione* (Vincenzo Lucci Chiarissi)
1959	*La luce sul monte* (Mario Costa)
1959	*Molokay la isla maldita* (Luis Lucia)
1960	*Les dialogues des Carmélites* (Philippe Agostini, Raymond Leopold Burckberger)
1961	*Francis of Assisi* (Michael Curtiz)
1961	*King of Kings* (Nicholas Ray)
1961	*La tragica notte di Assisi* (Raffaello Pacini)
1963	*Giacobbe l'uomo che lottò con Dio* (Marcello Baldi)
1964	*El padrecito* (Miguel Melitón Delgado)
1964	*Il Vangelo secondo Matteo* (Pier Paolo Pasolini)

1964	*Saul e David* (Marcello Baldi)
1965	*E venne un uomo* (Ermanno Olmi)
1965	*I grandi condottieri* (Marcello Baldi, Francisco Pérez Dolz)
1965	*The Greatest Story Ever Told* (George Stevens)
1966	*The Bible: in the Beginning* (John Huston)

I suggest that the films contained in the list should be classified on the basis of the different ways in which they represent the sacred. However, before addressing taxonomical issues, we need to deal with a preliminary question: can (filmic) images represent the sacred?

2. *Can (Filmic) Images Represent the Sacred?*

Historically, Christianity's relationship with images has never been consistent, characterized, as it was, by great leaps forward and dramatic backpedaling. Hans Belting thus summarizes the factors that determined early Christians' resistance to images:

> We should always keep in mind that in the beginning, the Christian religion did not allow for any concession in its total rejection of the religious image, especially the image demanding veneration. The religious community did not approach a cult image but assembled around the altar, or *mensa*, where sacrifice addressed an invisible God. The church did not house a divine image, as the cella of the pagan temple had done, since such images were vigorously opposed as idols [...] the final acceptance of cult images by the Church seems to be an unexpected change from very early and very important convictions. The Church, to be sure, resisted this change for a long time but, in the end, admitted images [...] as the object of worship. The new attitude was backed by a theory that, in retrospect, justified the worship of images within the context of the theological debate over Christ's dual nature.[23]

---

23   Hans Belting, *Bild und Kult. Eine Geschichte des Bildes vor dem Zeitalter der Kunst* (München: C.H. Beck, 1990), translated into English as *Likeness and Presence. A History of the Image before the Era of Art* (Chicago and London: The University of Chicago Press, 1994), p. 144.

Belting is explicitly skeptical about this justification (which was initially presented in the 6th century, and became a doctrine in the 7th century as a consequence of the iconoclastic crisis): "We should [...] not be taken in by a doctrine that, in an attitude of self-defence, merely sublimates existing practices with icons and retrospectively lends them a theoretical sanction."[24] The Church's central power, therefore, was eventually "forced" to accept and justify a state of affairs that it had resisted for as long as possible. The practice of icon veneration was not endorsed by the "official Church," which, in fact, feared that the veneration of images could have a centrifugal effect. The cult of images (like that of relics) often went hand in hand with an anti-institutional attitude: a cult image was locally rooted (it had a local origin) and often served to voice local claims. Furthermore, it offered a direct connection to the divine, which was of course perceived by the Church to be dangerous, since it presented itself as the only legitimate institutional mediator. Icons, therefore, eluded the very way in which the Church administered the sacred – that is, the Eucharist. Belting suggests that the Church's decision to use icons was inspired by its increasing awareness of their power, that was better exploited than countered. Still, this process of appropriation has always been fraught with doubts and resistance.[25]

The Holy See's film policy rests on the same tensions that have characterized the relation between the Church and images through the centuries, first and foremost regarding the legitimacy of sacred images. In brief, it could be said that while "by making the icon-imprint something similar to a relic and by linking memory to a formal similarity [...] Byzantium gave artistic representation the significance of a *res sacrata* provided with theological value [...], which was close to sacramental value," the Western world – albeit with many uncertainties – eventually "broke the strong link between art and the 'sacred' or, more

---

24   *Ibid.*
25   On the relation between the Church and images see also: Daniele Menozzi, *La Chiesa e le immagini. I testi fondamentali sulle arti figurative dalle origini ai nostri giorni* (Cinisello Balsamo: San Paolo, 1995) and François Boespflug, *Dieu et ses images. Une histoire de l'Éternel dans l'art* (Montrouge: Bayard, 2008).

precisely, it lay new foundations for it, distinguishing between 'presentation' and 'presentification'."[26] Such a distinction, which became clear once and for all with the "foundation of Eucharistic realism, which stated the substantial (and not figural) truth of Christ's body and blood in the bread and wine consecrated on the altar," established that "the real presence of God [...] was ensured and circumscribed in the commemoration." On the contrary, dramatic and artistic representation could at most aspire to a "commemorative 'presentation'"[27] or, even more simply, to a visual presentation of doctrine for educational aims. Starting with these premises and seeking to design a film policy that would enable the Catholic world to become involved in film production, three strategies were devised.

a) The first, promoted directly by the Holy See, limited the aim of religious film to the cult of the living Pontiff. The advantage of such a choice lay in the fact that the sacral dimension did not have to be presentified using filmic language, but it could more simply be exhibited. The role of cinema is thus limited, in a theologically correct way, in that the sacral element concerned still belongs to the present. Believers, in fact, would have direct access to it (in traditional ways such as pilgrimages to the Holy See, Jubilees, and private audiences). In this way, cinema does not exceed its mundane role, that is, "to excite devotion and attachment to the Vicar of Jesus Christ in believers"[28] (as Giuseppe Pizzardo wrote), through filmed evidence of the present. The best example of film belonging to this line of production is *Pastor Angelicus*. When, during the electoral campaign for the 1948 elections, the film

---

26   Carla Bino, *Il dramma e l'immagine. Teorie cristiane della rappresentazione (II–XI sec.)* (Firenze: Le Lettere, 2015), p. 10.

27   *Ibid.*, p. 11.

28   Giuseppe Pizzardo, letter to Camillo Serafini, October 13, 1936, Secretariat of State, Section for Relations with States, Historical Archive, Sacred Congregation for Extraordinary Ecclesiastical Affairs, Ecclesiastical States, position 445, folder 426, sheet 14r, quoted in Gianluca della Maggiore, *La Chiesa e il cinema nell'Italia fascista. Riconquiste cattoliche, progetti totalitari, prospettive globali (1922-1945)*, PhD dissertation in History and social-philosophical sciences, Rome "Tor Vergata" University, academic year 2013-2014, p. 199: "eccitare la devozione e l'attaccamento dei fedeli al Vicario di Gesù Cristo."

was screened using vans in the villages of southern Italy where the parish still did not have any movie theatres, it was perceived and defined by both the clergy and the local population as "the Pope's cinema."[29] The semantic shift signalled that devotion to what is shown in the text (the Pope) was eventually transferred onto the text itself, which, according to documents of the time (as we will see shortly), local population regarded in the same deferential way as the one they had with sacred objects.

b) The second strategy was even more circumspect, since it gave up on the representation of "strong" religious content and instead promoted films that could be considered Catholic because of their implied values rather than for their explicit content. Thus, they were able to pass unobserved within secular production, according to a "Trojan horse" kind of logic. This line of production had no devotional aim, but rather was used for informational and educational purposes.

c) Browsing the lists of religious films issued by the CCC, we can observe that, besides the two aforementioned types of religious movies, a third emerged, albeit it was not always tolerated by the Holy See. Together with documentaries on the Pope (*Pastor Angelicus*) and with fiction movies inspired by the principles of Christian morals (*Un giorno nella vita*), we also find films dedicated to the representation of Jesus' and the saints' lives. It is the most numerous category, but also the most problematic one. While the theory is very clear ("presentation" is allowed, "presentification" is not), the practice is erratic and difficult to control from above. Therefore, in this third type of religious cinema, where are the borders between images that attempt to popularize religious content, images that sustain a given cult, and images that become objects of that cult? While both documentaries on the Pope and fictional movies generically inspired by Christian morals can be unequivocally located on the side of "presentation," Christological and hagiographical biopics loom dangerously towards "presentification." An extreme example of this can be found in

---

29   Rocco Pellettieri, letter to Giuseppe Lazzati, March 10, 1948, ISACEM Archive, PG VI, envelope 54 (DB: ISACEM 7): "il cinema del Papa."

the popular devotion shown for the actress Ines Orsini, who played Maria Goretti in *Cielo sulla palude*. In this case, the reality of the sacred (the real sanctity of Maria Goretti) was mistaken not only for the "representation of the sacred" (the film), but also for the tool of that representation (the actress).[30] This is the reason why one of the most important problems for films of this kind was finding actors who were suitable for sacred roles.[31] Rossellini attempted to solve this problem in *Francesco giullare di Dio* by making real friars act. Once he had obtained the permission from the Order of Friars Minor, he selected a group of novices whom he entrusted with the task of playing the roles of Francis and his first fellows. If he had limited himself to offering a factual "presentation," through documentary, of what it actually meant to be a Franciscan friar in 1950, he would have avoided the ambiguous position in which he inevitably found himself. The problem was that he used real friars, but still he made them act. Such contradiction was promptly noted by the Servite Friar Camillo De Piaz, who, interviewed about the film, said: "Another element that I can hardly tolerate is the fact that real Franciscan friars were involved as actors, because it is immoral – with the exception of documentaries or films related to them – that they should recite for the public what they want and have to be in their real lives."[32]

All three cases inevitably question the autonomy of the media language used to convey the message. The representation of saints in film rested on a century-old tradition of literary hagiography, which was subsequently taken over by the twentieth-century media system. The debate within the Catholic world about the radio's hagiographic potential provides us with useful evidence: "As widely demonstrated by experience, with rare exceptions, there is proof that the illustration of any figure of

---

30   Martina Giacomini, "Una santa senza volto. La storia di Maria Goretti nell'illustrazione fotografica," in *Santi in posa. L'influenza della fotografia nell'immaginario religioso,* ed. by Tommaso Caliò (Roma: Viella, in print).

31   Hence Pier Paolo Pasolini's desecrating idea to characterize as communist the actor playing Jesus in *La ricotta*. See Tomaso Subini, *Pier Paolo Paolini. La ricotta* (Torino: Lindau, 2009).

32   Antonio Pitta, Ettore Capriolo, "Sacerdoti: Dio ha bisogno degli uomini," interview to Camillo De Piaz, p. 354.

a saint almost always fatally leads the writer to encroach on the territory of homily and sermon, which, on the radio means to make 'sacristy art' that triggers the listener's cry of protest. The device is becoming popular in households because it is essentially considered a means of entertainment and fun. Therefore it is always important to entertain. Always: even with an obituary."[33] The autonomy of the media language to which the religious message is entrusted demands a readjustment (often together with some compromise) of a traditional hagiographic language which moves from the inclusion of a love plot (see for example Arnaldo di Sassorosso's affair with Misia of Leros in Antamoro's 1927 *Frate Francesco*, which inspired Johannes Jørgensen's fury)[34] to the narrative roughness of recent TV fictions.[35]

---

33   Relazione del Centro Radiofonico Cattolico, 1941, ISACEM Archive, PG XV, envelope 6, folder 2 (DB: ISACEM 846): "Come l'esperienza ci ha ampiamente dimostrato e, fatte rare eccezioni, le prove hanno documentato, l'illustrazione della figura di un santo qualunque esso sia, conduce quasi fatalmente lo scrittore nell'ondeggiamento dell'omelia o nell'enfasi della predica che, alla radio [...] si risolvono in arte di sacrestia che provoca le beccate da parte degli ascoltatori. [...] l'apparecchio nelle abitazioni si popolarizza perché è considerato essenzialmente un mezzo di divertimento e di trattenimento. [...] Occorre, quindi, intrattenere divertendo. Sempre: anche con un necrologio."

34   See Tommaso Caliò, "Il ritorno di San Francesco. Il culto francescano nell'Italia fascista," in *San Francesco d'Italia. Santità e identità nazionale*, ed. by Tommaso Caliò and Roberto Rusconi (Roma: Viella, 2011), p. 59. Jørgensen acted as advisor for the film.

35   Thus read a comment to *Fatima*, one of the first hagiographies produced by Lux Vide, broadcasted by Mediaset in 1997: "Television is becoming increasingly populated by priests and nuns, prayers and miracles. Yet faith has nothing to do with it. Nothing. To dispel all doubts, one had only to watch Fatima's miracle on Canale 5. When the Blessed Virgin Mary appears to the kids, she looks exactly like Mr Clean: the same colours, the same effects, the same magic. The same spiritual intensity: for this kind of television there is no difference between the Immaculate Virgin and the genius of bleaching" (Gualtiero Peirce, "Un Dio c'è ma la fede non c'entra," *la Repubblica*, December 10, 1997).

3. What Was the Purpose of Films on St. Francis?

Christological and hagiographical biopics represent the most numerous category as well as the most problematic one, and therefore deserve to be investigated in depth and with particular attention. In view of their quantitative and qualitative relevance, I will focus on films dedicated to the figure of St. Francis of Assisi, and below I refer to two cases in particular: Roberto Rossellini's *Francesco giullare di Dio* and Michelangelo Antonioni's *Frate Francesco*.

The first (partial) attempt at a comparative approach to the representation of St. Francis in cinema dates back to 1972.[36] Since then, the issue has been the subject of several – not always remarkable – contributions, which have focused on the aesthetic quality of the films; on their more or less assumed religiosity, that is, on their ability to convey St. Francis' religious message; on their more or less assumed historicity, that is, on their ability to stick to the historical portrait of Friar Francis provided by historians; and, finally, on their location in a precise context, and thus their ability to witness the transformations of Francis' image through the centuries.[37] In this section, I intend to explore the corpus of films dedicated to the Saint by considering their usage uniquely as tools for the apostolate: my aim is to understand how this type of religious film was considered by the ecclesiastical hierarchy (with particular reference, obviously, to the Franciscan Family's hierarchy).

This corpus, adding up to almost twenty films, covers the entire chronology of film history: it features, among others, Giulio Antamoro's 1927 *Frate Francesco*, produced on occasion of the 700th anniversary of Francis' death; Roberto Rossellini's 1950 *Francesco giullare di Dio*, which was also made for an occasion, the 1950 Jubilee; the corny *Fratello Sole, Sorella Luna*, directed in 1972 by Franco Zeffirelli; and, more recently, *Francesco* by

---

36   Enrico Baragli, "Una favola bella. 'Fratello Sole, Sorella Luna' di Franco Zeffirelli," *La Civiltà Cattolica*, a. 123, vol. 3, n. 2930, July 15, 1972, pp. 126-43.

37   See Tomaso Subini, "San Francesco e il cinema," in *Francesco plurale*, ed. by Alvaro Cacciotti and Maria Melli (Milano: Edizioni Biblioteca Francescana, 2015).

Liliana Cavani, which starred Mickey Rourke and was released
in 1989. It includes Hollywood movies (such as Michael Curtiz's
1961 *Francis of Assisi,* produced by Twentieth Century Fox) and
auteur films (including Pier Paolo Pasolini's lyrical and political
foray into the Franciscan universe in 1966, in *Uccellacci e uccellini*);
early cinema (such as Enrico Guazzoni's 1911 *Francesco il poverello
d'Assisi*) as well as contemporary TV productions. It also includes
screenplays and the preparatory materials for projects that were
never produced but that are nevertheless relevant, especially
for the personalities involved, such as Guido Gozzano, Alberto
Savinio, Augusto Genina, and Michelangelo Antonioni.

The reasons for such a proliferation of narratives lies in the
fascination exerted by the figure of Francis through the centuries
and well into the twentieth century, when cinema and, later,
television reshaped in their own specific languages the image
that by then had become well established in literature, music and
art.[38] This fascination, however, was ambivalent, and functioned
on both religious and fictional levels. Francis radically changed
the approach to the Christian conduct of life with a reform that
still has a huge attractive potential; at the same time, however, his
life can also be read as a compelling narrative full of adventures,
coups de théâtre, and exciting encounters, not to speak of betrayals,
misunderstandings, and conflicts.

Two facts, however, deserve particular attention:

1. No relation can be established between the films and the
number of people who choose to enter the Franciscan Family.
The complex factors regulating the fluctuations in the number
of friars (and therefore in the number of novices) do not seem to
relate in any way to the distribution of one of the films dedicated
to Francis **(fig. 3)**. My survey was carried out exclusively using
data concerning the Order of Friars Minor, published in *Acta
Ordinis Fratrum Minorum.* This question clearly demands further
investigation, since that report considers the total number of
friars at the global level, though films were not always distributed
worldwide. However, it does provide some significant information,

---

38   See Sandra Migliore, *Mistica povertà* (Roma: Istituto Storico dei
     Cappuccini, 2001).

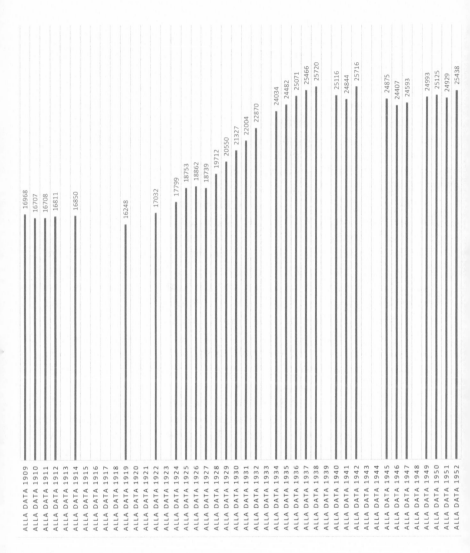

Fig. 3 – Total number of Friars (Source: Acta Ordinis Fratrum Minorum).

ALLA DATA 1953	25848
ALLA DATA 1954	26061
ALLA DATA 1955	26151
ALLA DATA 1956	26320
ALLA DATA 1957	26330
ALLA DATA 1958	26162
ALLA DATA 1959	26511
ALLA DATA 1960	26871
ALLA DATA 1961	26961
ALLA DATA 1962	27136
ALLA DATA 1963	27140
ALLA DATA 1964	27009
ALLA DATA 1965	26940
ALLA DATA 1966	26666
ALLA DATA 1967	26275
ALLA DATA 1968	25653
ALLA DATA 1969	25071
ALLA DATA 1970	24413
ALLA DATA 1971	23821
ALLA DATA 1972	23337
ALLA DATA 1973	22987
ALLA DATA 1974	22286
ALLA DATA 1975	22128
ALLA DATA 1976	21799
ALLA DATA 1977	21611
ALLA DATA 1978	21333
ALLA DATA 1979	21119
ALLA DATA 1980	20337
ALLA DATA 1981	20130
ALLA DATA 1982	20150
ALLA DATA 1983	19973
ALLA DATA 1984	20180
ALLA DATA 1985	20040
ALLA DATA 1986	19726
ALLA DATA 1987	19595
ALLA DATA 1988	19251
ALLA DATA 1989	19214
ALLA DATA 1990	19038
ALLA DATA 1991	18738
ALLA DATA 1992	18557
ALLA DATA 1993	18204
ALLA DATA 1994	18067
ALLA DATA 1995	17992

in allowing us to consider movie production and the internal apostolate as two separate entities.

2. Scrutiny of the *Messaggero di Sant'Antonio,* a high-circulation Franciscan magazine, sheds light on a further relevant fact. While cinema (in particular religious cinema) gets much attention, discourse on films about Francis is almost absent. The only film reviewed was *Fratello Sole, Sorella Luna,*[39] the success of which (at least in Italy) was such that it could not be overlooked.

Therefore, if films dedicated to Francis did not directly relate to an increase in the number of novices – and, in fact, they represented a cause of embarrassment for the Catholic critics of the *Messaggero di Sant'Antonio* – then what purpose did they serve? A possible answer is that more than the needs of the Franciscan Family, they met the needs of the public.

Let us now turn to the relevance of religious fiction within Italian TV production. Starting, unsurprisingly, with Liliana Cavani's 1966 *Francesco d'Assisi,* religious fiction has secured a predominant position in the field of Italian TV production over the last fifty years. The list prepared by the Osservatorio sulla Fiction Italiana, run by Milly Buonanno,[40] shows that 7 of the 10 most successful series in the decade 1996-2006 had a religious subject **(fig. 4)**: their average audience had the same ratings as a World Cup Final.

Some scholars consider the need for religious fiction, which has witnessed remarkable growth since the 2000 Jubilee, as a typical phenomenon of New Age postmodernity.[41] Yet, this very phenomenon had been observed and harshly criticized as early as 1965 by a refined Catholic intellectual, in the context of an internal survey (with limited access) on the Catholics' activities in social communication: "In certain cases such as *Marcelino pan y vino* or *The Song of Bernadette,* the public has been moved by

39   Enzo Natta, "Fratello Sole Sorella Luna," *Il Messaggero di Sant'Antonio,* April 1972, pp. 18-23.
40   *La bella stagione. La fiction italiana, l'Italia nella fiction,* ed. by Milly Buonanno (Roma: Rai-ERI, 2007), p. 95.
41   Gianluca della Maggiore, *La fiction agiografica televisiva,* in *L'Italia e i santi. Agiografie, riti e devozioni nella costruzione dell'identità nazionale,* ed. by Tommaso Caliò and Daniele Menozzi (Roma: Istituto della Enciclopedia Italiana, 2017), pp. 661-681.

sentiment: a boy, a girl, good people fighting villains, goodness finally triumphing and evil defeated by a sensation voicing some kind of 'Here come our men!' rather than some implicit doctrine. Now, we'd rather see 'our men' coming in a less ostentatious way and bringing some Gospel with them."[42] *Marcelino pan y vino*'s format would eventually prevail, gaining efficacy and catering to an increasingly wide public. That such a kind of religious fiction could become one of the main attractions for the Italian spectator was finally confirmed in 1977 by Zeffirelli's *Gesù di Nazareth*.

Fig. 4 - The 10 most successful series in Italy in the decade 1996-2006.

N.	Titolo	Stagione	Rete	Formato	Ascolto medio
1	*Papa Giovanni*	2001-2002	Rai Uno	miniserie	13.180.000
2	*Padre Pio tra cielo e terra*	2000-2001	Rai Uno	miniserie	13.123.000
3	*Karol. Un uomo diventato Papa*	2004-2005	Canale 5	miniserie	12.832.000
4	*Perlasca*	2001-2002	Rai Uno	miniserie	12.205.000
5	*Padre Pio*	1999-2000	Canale 5	miniserie	11.660.000
6	*Giovanni Paolo II*	2005-2006	Rai Uno	miniserie	11.329.000
7	*Il maresciallo Rocca 2*	1997-1998	Rai Uno	serie	11.261.000
8	*Paolo Borsellino*	2004-2005	Canale 5	miniserie	10.834.000
9	*Jesus*	1999-2000	Rai Uno	miniserie	10.806.000
10	*Madre Teresa*	2003-2004	Rai Uno	miniserie	10.600.000

42 Carlo Alianello, *Osservazioni al "progetto di schema dell'Istruzione Pastorale,"* enclosed to Francesco Angelicchio, letter to Nazareno Taddei, March 15, 1965, ANT (DB: ANT 1249): "In certi casi, come ad esempio *Marcellino pane e vino* o [...] *Bernadette*, il pubblico s'è lasciato commuovere dal sentimento: un bambino, una ragazza, i buoni in lotta contro i cattivi, dove però la bontà riporta il suo trionfo e la malvagità è sconfitta da un sentimento diciamo da "arrivano i nostri" piuttosto che dalla dottrina implicita. Ora bisognerebbe che "i nostri" arrivassero portando senza troppa ostentazione un po' di Vangelo."

While the success of films dedicated to the figure of St. Francis of Assisi made producers very happy, it also represented cause for embarrassment for the General Ministers of the Franciscan Family – perhaps understandably, since discourse surrounding the films enjoyed wide circulation and therefore eluded central control. While in the thirteenth century Franciscans could still try to impose their official portrait of the Saint by forbidding the circulation of alternative reconstructions (even though, as history has shown, this was not always successful), nowadays, it is clear that this is no longer possible.

As we have seen, one factor that is inextricably related to religious cinema in general and to hagiographic films in particular, emerges as particularly problematic: the existence of a flourishing market. I will consider the role of this factor in the aforementioned case studies, Rossellini's *Francesco giullare di Dio* and Antonioni's *Frate Francesco*, which will illuminate the contradictions of hagiographic cinema.

4. *"Famous Directors Are to Be Feared"*

The two case studies that I have selected are paradigmatic. Neither Rossellini nor Antonioni chose to deal with the figure of St. Francis for religious reasons. They did so because they felt the lure of a burgeoning marketplace.

I have already studied *Francesco giullare di Dio* extensively elsewhere.[43] I will therefore limit myself to providing the main historical framework here. As for Antonioni, a comparative reading of some heretofore scattered and unknown documents preserved in three different archives – the Archivio Storico della Provincia di Cristo Re dei frati Minori dell'Emilia Romagna, the Archivio Michelangelo Antonioni of Ferrara's city council, and Roberto Roversi's private archive – has made the investigation of the (failed) production of *Frate Francesco* possible.

---

43   Tomaso Subini, *La doppia vita di "Francesco giullare di Dio."* *Giulio Andreotti, Félix Morlion e Roberto Rossellini* (Milano: Libraccio, 2013, second augmented edition).

Rossellini started working on *Francesco giullare di Dio* in the immediate aftermath of the victory of the DC at the general election in 1948. Eager to side with the winner, Rossellini knew that gaining favor with republican institutions as the DC's film director meant that his films would win state prizes and be shown in parish cinemas. However, while Rossellini profit from *Francesco giullare di Dio*, it is also true that, by staking his own artistic sensibility, he found the way to produce a film bearing his signature. In so doing, he saw the film develop along unexpected lines.

The production was supervised by a host of religious advisors, who focused almost exclusively on the figure of Francis. It is perhaps also for this reason that Rossellini and his screenwriter Federico Fellini ultimately focused their attention on two side-figures, John the Simple and Juniper, whom they certainly felt closer to their sensibility. The two friars, champions of humility, ended up occupying the centre stage, even if the title of the film was such that everyone expected the Saint to be its main protagonist.

The combination of these two elements – Rossellini's very limited intervention into the figure of Saint Francis, constrained as a conventional and devotional holy image by religious advisors, and the great affinity felt by both Rossellini and Fellini for humble and simple characters – shifted the focus of the film from Francis to the friars John the Simple and Juniper. And these two characters caused critics to write that the film fuelled "the suspicion that Francis' fellows were nothing more than a company of idiots;"[44] John, in particular, being "completely dumb," "has us believing that Francis, with his sermons, was only able to attract insane people that he met on the road."[45] Enrico D'Alessandro's review, written for the Catholic daily newspaper of the Milan diocese, summarizes the gist of such criticism very well. After a long diatribe against John the Simple's character, D'Alessandro serves him the final blow with the following rhetorical question:

44   Fabrizio Dentice, "'Girotondo' di Max Ophüls nella deliziosa Vienna ottocentesca," *Il Giornale d'Italia*, August 29, 1950.
45   Renzo Renzi, "Festival di Venezia," *Hollywood*, a. VI, n. 261, September 16, 1950, p. 9.

"If we stick to Rossellini's representation, how could we ever trust such a friar to preach around the world?!"[46]

While the film depicts Francis by drawing on traditional narratives that made him a Saint (for example, the episode in which he speaks to birds), it is also true that, in the economy of the text, his figure is eventually perceived to be subordinate to John the Simple and Juniper, two characters whose features are outlined by drawing on alternative sources. This was so much the case that the hagiographic image of "Saint Francis superstar"[47] is questioned by foregrounding another aspect, the spirit of evangelical simplicity. This, despite being one of the essential prerogatives of the Franciscan movement, had been side-lined in the evolution of the order, for the very reason expressed in D'Alessandro's rhetorical question. The film therefore involuntarily represented the dilemma that had always been at the core of the Franciscan Family's history: should friars possess books, study Latin, attend university, and occupy key positions within Church hierarchies, or should they instead remain at the margins of society? In 1950, Juniper and John still embodied this open question. Although religious advisors supervised the director's work, cinema proved to be a too complex machine, outside of the Order's control.

Antonioni's project was prompted by Father Ernesto Caroli, one of the founders and organizers of Bononia's Antoniano. In the unpublished article, *Come ho conosciuto Michelangelo Antonioni* [*How I met Michelangelo Antonioni*], Caroli himself reports the planning of the project. In 1979, Caroli met Antonioni and invited him to produce a movie for the 800th anniversary of Francis' birth. Antonioni was reluctant to accept the invitation, but Caroli succeeded in overcoming his reticence. The exchange around Antonioni's final reply reads as follows:

"Let's make this film," Antonioni went on, "but I have to tell

---

46   Enrico D'Alessandro, "San Francesco sbagliato e un film soltanto per Ingrid," *L'Italia*, August 27, 1950.

47   See André Vauchez, *François d'Assise. Entre histoire et mémoire* (Paris: Arthème Fayard, 2009); Ital. tr. *Francesco d'Assisi. Tra storia e memoria* (Torino: Einaudi, 2010); Engl. tr. *Francis of Assisi. The Life and Afterlife of a Medieval Saint* (New Haven/London: Yale University Press).

you something that is not very Franciscan, which causes some embarrassment. In order to prepare a treatment, I'll need collaborators and, I regret to say, money."

"How much?"

"Around fifty million, but you can discuss later this with my producer."[48]

Fifty million liras was quite a lot of money for a Franciscan friar: in fact, Caroli despaired about being able to raise it, until a friend of his, an entrepreneur and devotee of St. Francis, decided to help him and wrote him a check. The money was transferred in May 1980. After visiting, under the friars' guidance, Assisi's Basilica – to be inspired by Giotto's paintings – and having received a long reading list from Caroli, Antonioni delivered a first draft of the screenplay in September, which he then handed to Roberto Roversi and Tonino Guerra, "both devotees of the hammer and sickle" (as a concerned Caroli could not help noticing).[49]

Caroli maintains that the film was not produced because of the stroke Antonioni suffered in 1985. Dates, however, tell a different story. The deal was struck in 1980 and the screenplay was written the following year. Five years past from the initial deal to the stroke; something else must have deterred Antonioni.

First of all, let us consider Antonioni's intentions. Just before he started shooting *Identificazione di una donna*, he was asked by an interviewer about his next film and answered with a list: a science-fiction film to be shot in the Soviet Union, a new film to be shot in the United States, the adaptation of *Il nome della rosa*, and finally, he declared, with a note of incredulity, "there is even a *St. Francis* in the air."[50] This project hardly seemed

48   Ernesto Caroli, *Come ho conosciuto Michelangelo Antonioni, s.d.*, AFMER, Section VI, Carte di Padre Ernesto Caroli (the papers are still being ordered and classified) (DB: AFMER 1): "– Facciamo questo film – riprese Antonioni – ma ora debbo farle, con un certo imbarazzo, un discorso che non è proprio francescano. Occorre fare un trattamento, ho bisogno di collaboratori e, purtroppo, occorrono anche denari./Quanto? – dissi senza aggiungere altro./– Una cinquantina di milioni, ma di questo parlerà poi col mio produttore."

49   DB: AFMER 1: "entrambi devoti di falce e martello."

50   Dario Zanelli, "Un'attrice da amare," *Il Resto del Carlino*, February 10, 1981.

consistent with the author's self-declared identity as an atheist. Yet, parallel to *Frate Francesco*, Antonioni was working on another film concerning religion, *Patire o morire* (a film dealing with an architect who approaches the world of cloistures with curiosity), which was abandoned, for unknown reasons, at a more advanced stage of production. Crucial for both projects was Antonioni's relationship with a Clarisse nun named Chiara Augusta Lainati. Caroli's papers provide evidence of the important role played by Lainati: she was the one who put Caroli in touch with Antonioni, and it was she (not Caroli) who provided Antonioni with guidance when he was writing the screenplay.[51]

Reading the few letters exchanged between the two, held in the Antonioni archive in Ferrara, a friendship clearly emerges, and advice on religious matters often ends up concerning spiritual matters. Lainati does not hide her wish that Antonioni would convert: "I sense that God is just waiting for your prayer, together with ours, to show you his greatness and his power over people and things...Shall your prayer be a deep thirst from the heart, a desire for that Infinity of Joy and of Love that He is, after which our poor human soul is always searching for."[52] In particular, a long letter from Lainati dated 1983 deals with issues raised by Antonioni regarding sin, celibacy, and cloisture – which caused some revisions to the screenplay of *Patire o morire*.[53] By the time she wrote that letter, the Francis project had apparently been

---

51   Lainati acted as official advisor, as witnessed by the fifty thousand lira payment that she received for her services. Receipt of the payment to Augusta Lainati, December 6, 1980, AFMER, Section VI, Carte di Padre Ernesto Caroli (the papers are still being ordered and classified) (DB: AFMER 5).

52   Augusta Lainati, letter to Michelangelo Antonioni, January 20, 1979, Fondo Michelangelo Antonioni, Gallerie d'Arte Moderna e Contemporanea di Ferrara, envelope 9B/4, file 337: "Chissà che il Signore non stia proprio aspettando anche la tua preghiera, insieme alla nostra, per farti vedere la sua grandezza e la sua potenza sopra persone e cose... Che la tua preghiera sia una sete profonda del cuore, un desiderio di quell'Infinito di Gioia e di Amore che Lui è, e di cui il nostro povero cuore umano va sempre in cerca."

53   Augusta Lainati, letter to Michelangelo Antonioni, March 18, 1983, Fondo Michelangelo Antonioni, Gallerie d'Arte Moderna e Contemporanea di Ferrara, envelope 9B/4, file 334.

shelved. Any interest Antonioni ever had in religion had shifted, by then, to *Patire o morire*.[54]

Antonioni's *Frate Francesco* was due to be funded by a consortium of broadcasting companies headed by the Radiotelevisione Italiana [hereafter RAI] (this would also be the case with Cavani's *Francesco*, which took over the project along with some of its features a couple of years later). It is highly probable that someone at RAI might have had some reservations about the project, as we seem to gather from this letter written by Antonioni to Sergio Zavoli: "At this point I'd like to know whether the RAI really intends to produce the film. It's already 1982, Francis' commemorative year, so there's no time left to waste."[55] The reservations at RAI, of course, did not concern the film on Francis generally but Antonioni's film on Francis in particular (as would become evident with the company's engagement in Cavani's

---

54   The meaning of the title is made explicit in this passage of the screenplay: "If an enclosed nun falls prey to the sin of sensuality, she is punished. In the past, the punishment was the same as that for apostasy: life imprisonment. No more. [...] However, a rule remains, according to which an enclosed who has been accused cannot defend herself, even if she is innocent. Another rule is that no nun should use coloured clothes or coloured bed sheets. And she should not possess anything. Should the prioress notice that a sister has become attached to an object, she will have to take it away from her. It is forbidden to touch, even innocently, a fellow nun or to enter her cell. [...] And silence is another rule. Either suffer or die: these must be our wishes, as Saint Thérèse recommended." / "Se [...] una claustrale cade nel peccato di sensualità, viene punita. Nei tempi passati, come per chi si rendeva colpevole di apostasia, era il carcere a vita. Oggi non più. [...] Rimane però la regola che la claustrale accusata non può difendersi, anche se innocente. Un'altra regola è che nessuna usi nel vestito o nel letto cose di colore. O abbia cose proprie. La Priora quando vedrà una sorella affezionata a un oggetto, procuri di levarglielo. È proibito toccare, anche innocentemente, una compagna o entrare nella sua cella. [...] E il silenzio è un'altra delle regole. O morire o patire, ecco quali devono essere i nostri desideri, raccomandava Santa Teresa" (excerpt from the screenplay for *Patire o morire*, Fondo Michelangelo Antonioni, Gallerie d'Arte Moderna e Contemporanea di Ferrara, envelope 9B/4, file 334).

55   Michelangelo Antonioni, letter to Sergio Zavoli, January 6, 1982, Fondo Michelangelo Antonioni, Gallerie d'Arte Moderna e Contemporanea di Ferrara, envelope 9A/1, file 9: "A questo punto vorrei sapere se la RAI è veramente intenzionata a fare il film o no. Siamo già nell'ottantadue, l'anno commemorativo di Francesco, non c'è un minuto da perdere."

project few years later). An ANSA dispatch from September 1982 describes Antonioni's "polemic with RAI about St. Francis:" "I have a deal with RAI," Antonioni states "but, since its bureaucracy is very complex, things have been dragging on too long, and I can't really wait anymore."[56]

In fact, not only RAI had reservations about the project. Even more vocal in their dissent were Franciscan Friars. In March 1980, Caroli received a letter from a friend, the provincial secretary of Capuchins in Genoa, who outlined very passionate and extensively detailed advice: "If you are seriously considering the production of that film, I would be very pleased if you would seek the advice of Architect Ricchetti in Genoa, since he is very skilled and prepared in this field. He worked in television for ten years and we have already commissioned him for six films [...]. If you are really thinking of producing the film, well, I think we would save much money if you commissioned it from our architect. Really, he is very skilled, well-prepared, he has very good taste and...we wouldn't need to involve too many people."[57] In the very same way, Caroli received a greeting card from a friar living in the monastery of San Pietro in Montorio, with a newspaper cutting enclosed, reporting that Antonioni was running as an "independent candidate in the Italian Communist Party's list"[58] for the city council elections in Spello. This was the friar's comment: "I wonder how the true spirit of St. Francis can be expressed by someone who follows Marxist ideals [...] Shouldn't we turn to some younger director, or at least someone

---

56   Editorial, "Antonioni (polemico con la Rai per 'San Francesco') va a girare il suo secondo film USA," *Il Corriere della Sera*, September 3, 1982.

57   Guido Alberto Bonacina, letter to Ernesto Caroli, March 4, 1980, AFMER, Section VI, Carte di Padre Ernesto Caroli (the papers are still being ordered and classified) (DB: AFMER 2): "Se realmente pensa alla realizzazione di detto FILM avrei piacere se potesse interpellare anche l'Arch. RICCHETTI di Genova, perché è molto capace e competente in materia. Egli ha lavorato dieci anni per la TV e noi gli abbiamo già fatto eseguire sei film. [...] Se si pensa di realizzare il film penso sarebbe un grandissimo risparmio se desse l'incarico a detto Architetto. Ripeto, è molto capace, competente, ha molto gusto e... non ci sarebbe bisogno di mobilitare tanta gente."

58   Editorial, "In lizza anche Antonioni," *Il Messaggero*, April 18, 1980.

closer to our ideals?"[59] However, the piece of advice that probably made Caroli reflect the most came from a Minister General: "Dear Father Ernesto, I have received the article on Antonioni's proposal, which I'm enclosing to this letter... well, if this is his agenda, we can't be happy or even confident. Famous directors are to be feared, since they manipulate the subject according to their taste. St. Francis needs no propaganda of this kind."[60] The enclosed article contained a preview of Antonioni's screenplay, which, it is said, focused on "episodes with church members committing crimes, and he has lingered on the looting of Pope Innocent's corpse, left completely naked on the altar of Foligno cathedral, where he was exhibited for one night."[61]

In fact, the criteria governing the writing process, made explicit by Antonioni himself in a one-page introduction to the screenplay, seems to question deeply the image that the Franciscan Family had handed down for centuries. Antonioni wrote that he sought to "break away from the legendary figure and to accommodate it in the real world. Breaking free from the myth of Francis as 'God's jester' to discover the man within him. We have therefore avoided dealing with his miracles [...] and, where this was not possible, as with the stigmata, we have tried to insert realistic elements that would downplay such aspects of the event."[62] Furthermore, Antonioni explained that

---

59 Zaccaria Bertoldi [?], letter to Ernesto Caroli, April 29, 1980, AFMER, Section VI, Carte di Padre Ernesto Caroli (the papers are still being ordered and classified) (DB: AFMER 3): "Non so cosa possa esprimere dello spirito autentico di S. Francesco, in un film, uno che ha come ideale il marxismo. [...] Non sarebbe meglio uno più giovane e più vicino ai nostri ideali?"

60 Vitale Bommarco, letter to Ernesto Caroli, October 13, 1981, AFMER, Section VI, Carte di Padre Ernesto Caroli (the papers are still being ordered and classified) (DB: AFMER 6): "Caro P. Ernesto, mi è stato trasmesso l'accluso articolo sulle ipotesi di Antonioni... e se esiste questa "scaletta" non possiamo certo restare molto contenti e tranquilli. Dei registi famosi bisogna aver paura per la manipolazione del soggetto ai loro gusti. S. Francesco non ha bisogno di questa propaganda."

61 Editorial, "Santo 'laico' il Francesco di Antonioni," *Il Giornale d'Italia*, October 6, 1981.

62 Michelangelo Antonioni, *San Francesco*, Fondo Michelangelo Antonioni, Gallerie d'Arte Moderna e Contemporanea di Ferrara, envelope 8B/18, file 79: "disancorare la figura di Francesco dalla leggenda e calarla nella

he meant to "tackle the discourse dialectically,"[63] which meant that he intended to historicize the relation between Francis and his Order, in the wake of recent historiography: "in drafting this text [...] we have relied on the advice of Raul Manselli, professor of Medieval History at the University of Rome and author of the most exhaustive biography of Francis available."[64] In short, Antonioni's *Frate Francesco* had all the features of an innovative and unsettling film.

From these two case studies, we can grasp an idea of the Franciscan hierarchy's stance towards hagiographic cinema, which is characterized by a positive attitude towards catechistical and documentary films but strong suspicion about fiction films, especially when signed by a famous film director. Both films entrusted to Rossellini and Antonioni turned out to be mistakes. In the former case, the Order paid a high price in terms of symbolic capital, since it ended up jeopardizing the traditional image of "Saint Francis superstar," even running the risk of associating Francis' figure with Rossellini's *gallismi matrimoniali*.[65] As for the costs of the latter film (which was never produced), we might note that fifty million liras in 1979 is roughly equivalent to 150,000 euro, a considerable sum, which Caroli was supposed to receive at the beginning of production: "Should the film not be produced due to circumstances beyond the producer's control, Father Ernesto Caroli will become owner of the treatment as equivalent to the sum paid."[66] Right from the start, the idea that

---

realtà. Sfuggire al mito di Francesco "giullare di Dio" e cercare in lui l'uomo. Si è quindi evitato l'aspetto miracolistico della sua attività [...] e dove non è stato possibile, come nel caso delle stimmate, si è cercato di inserire elementi realistici che attenuassero quell'aspetto dell'evento."

63   *Ibid.*: "un'impostazione dialettica del discorso."

64   *Ibid.*: "Nella stesura del presente testo [...] ci siamo avvalsi della consulenza del Prof. Raoul Manselli, docente di Storia medievale all'Università di Roma e autore di quella che forse può essere considerata come la più esauriente e importante biografia di Francesco."

65   Nazareno Fabbretti, "I cattolici e la censura. La legge non fa miracoli," *Humanitas*, a. XVII, n. 5, May, 1962, p. 436. Fabbretti referred to Rossellini carefree attitude towards marital infidelity.

66   Ernesto Caroli, Mauro Berardi, contract, May 18, 1980, AFMER, Section VI, Carte di Padre Ernesto Caroli (the papers are still being ordered and classified) (DB: AFMER 4): "al momento in cui avrà inizio la lavorazione del film. Qualora, per ragioni di forza maggiore, non si dovesse realizzare

the film would not be produced was a possible scenario. While Caroli was determined to carry out the project, Antonioni was hesitant, at times insisting for the film to be completed, at others delaying its production to focus on other projects. RAI, too, was reluctant to invest in what appeared dangerous ideological mixture. However, the most reluctant party was the Franciscan Family, from the rank and file to the highest authorities, who were reasonably suspicious of famous directors. One wonders indeed if Caroli himself, at a certain point, thought that he should have opted for the documentary by Ricchetti instead of a film by Antonioni.

5. *Religious Cinema vs Obscene Cinema*

The history of the relationship between Catholics and cinema has been marked by an original sin. In fact, when the Church began to engage with the cinema, at first it did so not to spread its message (which would happen at a later stage), but to counter the actions of other agents within the field of communication. For Catholics, film images were particularly treacherous because of their direct impact on the spectator's senses. In 1935, Giuseppe Dalla Torre (who was then editor in chief of *L'Osservatore Romano* and would later become president of Universalia Film) wrote an emblematic article entitled "Il più immane pericolo" ["The greatest danger"]. In it, he underlined that the menace of cinema rested on "the instant speed with which it reaches the senses, without leaving further room for reflecting, reasoning and counteracting."[67]

Cinema had a power that the Church wanted to harness, if not at least to control. As Dario Viganò has shown, "the relationship between the Church and the cinema developed along lines that were already traced"[68] by the Milan diocese in the first decades

---

il film in parola, il P. Ernesto Caroli, quale corrispettivo della somma versata, diventerà proprietario del Trattamento."

67   Giuseppe Dalla Torre, "Il più immane pericolo," *L'illustrazione Vaticana*, n. 6, 1935; see also Editorial, "L'immane pericolo per gli uomini di domani," *L'Osservatore Romano*, March 17, 1935.

68   Dario E. Viganò, *Un cinema ogni campanile. Chiesa e cinema nella diocesi di*

of the twentieth century: on the one hand there was fear of an instrument that could have such a considerable impact on the senses and on the other, the desire to control it and "bend it to precise pastoral needs."[69] On the one hand we find religious cinema (in its three different versions: "the Pope's cinema," "cinema inspired by Christian morals" and "Christological and hagiographic biopics"), while on the other we find immoral and obscene films.

Catholics addressed the latter through two different formulations of the notion of obscenity. The first relied on a broad definition, that was not necessarily associated to the representation of sexuality, but concerned an ethics of the gaze. This was perceived as a crucial need in "modern cinema:"[70] for example, the tracking shot in *Kapò* (Gillo Pontecorvo, 1960) was considered obscene in terms of it being not ethical.[71] However, such formulation of the notion held mostly outside of Italy. Unlike French Catholics (i.e. Amedée Ayfre, André Bazin, Eric Rohmer, Jacques Rivette), Italian Catholics thought that an ethical gaze was first and foremost a chaste gaze. In fact, they preferred the term "pornographic" to the term "obscene."

While Italian Catholics endowed the term "pornographic" with the same meaning that it had in secular culture (that is, a pornographic image was one that represented sexual intercourse with the aim of arousing the viewer), they implemented it in a

---

Milano (Milano: Il Castoro, 1997), p. 20.

69   Dario E. Viganò, "Il progetto cattolico sul cinema: i pionieri," in *Un secolo di cinema a Milano*, ed. by Raffaele De Berti (Milano: Il Castoro, 1996), p. 139.

70   This relies on a periodization on which most film scholars agree, which distinguishes three main periods: the cinema of the origins (1895-1915); classical cinema (from the mid-tens to the fifties); modern cinema (from the fifties onwards). See Francesco Casetti, *La forma cinema nella sua evoluzione storica*, in Aa. Vv., *Enciclopedia del Cinema*, I, Istituto dell'Enciclopedia Italiana, Roma, 2003, pp. 40-61.

71   The tracking shot in *Kapò*, through which Pontecorvo frames the corpse of Emmanuelle Riva's character, who has committed suicide, has become an emblem of the exploitation of film techniques in favour of aestheticism, of misplaced formalism. This reading was first suggested in a review by Jacques Rivette, who defined such camera use as obscene in relation to the film's subject (Jacques Rivette, "De l'abjection," *Cahiers du cinéma*, n. 120, June 1961).

broad way, considering *La dolce vita* a pornographic film. Among the many letters of protest sent to the Archbishop of Milan, Giovanni Battista Montini (later Paul VI), one, written by a priest, summarized as follows the content of the film: "Concubinage, profuse free love, male and female homosexuality, morbid scenes, a monstrous makeup of a supposed miracle by the Holy Virgin, an excessively possessive girl attempting suicide, a suicide preceded by a double parricide (a sequence of bewildering realism), the bacchanalia of an emotion-seeking diva, who later eccentrically visits St. Peter dressed in clerical-prelate fashion, a father supinely pleased with his son's debaucherous lifestyle, and conversely the son for his father's romantic adventure, a long nocturnal orgy described in detail, with a lady who performs a striptease on a whim, all of this accompanied by indecent gestures and words, a challenge to the last remains of decency, the complete loss of human dignity."[72]

For Italian Catholics, religious and obscene (i.e. pornographic) images were at two ends of a spectrum and their opposition can be scaled down to the fundamental conflict between the soul and body. They do, nonetheless, share a clear, pragmatic vocation. All images are made to be used, but religious and pornographic ones in particular. It is not by chance that David Freedberg's work on the power of images revolves, albeit not exclusively, around the effects of sexual arousal and mystical ascesis that are produced by images.[73]

---

72 Father B.B., letter to Battista Montini, February 1960, ASDMI, Montini papers, first series, box 257, folder 17, sheet 47: "Concubinaggio, amore libero a piene mani, omosessualità maschile e femminile, scene di morbosità, una mostruosa montatura di un presunto miracolo della Madonna, un tentativo di suicidio di una ragazza troppo possessiva, un suicidio preceduto da un doppio parricidio (sequenza di un realismo veramente sconcertante), i baccanali di una diva in cerca di emozioni, la stessa che visita San Pietro eccentricamente vestita su moda clerico prelatizia, la supina compiacenza di un padre per la vita dissipata del figlio e del figlio per l'avventura galante del padre, una lunga orgia notturna descritta minutamente, con uno spogliarello di una signora che lo fa per un capriccio, il tutto accompagnato da gesti e da parole anche sconce, di sfida all'ultimo residuo di pudore, e di perdita completa della dignità umana."
73 David Freedberg, *The Power of Images. Studies in the History and Theory of Response* (Chicago: University of Chicago Press, 1989; second edition

The cinematographic versions of these two types of images were subjected to clearly defined rules of consumption, in clearly defined places: parish cinemas on the one hand, and 'red-light' movie theatres on the other. These places were as specific as the images exhibited inside them. The red-light movie theatre is a place where one consumes sexual experiences that are favoured by the darkness and the sensual arousal caused by the images on the screen. The parish cinema generates a sense of belonging to a religious community, and thus favours the experience of spiritual ascesis. However, parish theatres and red-light theatres polarize two different modes of the consumption of film images, which were already present, albeit in a more nuanced and moderate way, in 'normal' theatres. These modes of consumption defined the focus of Catholics film policy, which on one hand proactively supported religious movies, and on the other countered immoral films, and, more specifically obscene (thus pornographic) ones.

During the forties and the fifties, these two trends coexisted and maintained an equilibrium. Later on, the acceleration of the break-down of taboos related to obscenity – which, in Italy, was like a rupture in a dam – resulted in the pre-eminence of prohibitive actions.

6. *The Clergy in the Cinematographic Apostolate*

Between the forties and the seventies in Italy, cinema played a key role in negotiating the conflict between religious (traditionalist and intransigent) and secular (modern and progressive) cultures. However, this took place despite the intentions of the clergy in charge of cinematographic institutions within the Catholic world. Documents preserved in ecclesiastical archives reveal these intentions, confirming furthermore the historiographic thesis of "modernization without modernity."[74] According to this interpretive model, the Church did not

1991).

74 Daniele Menozzi, "Cristianesimo e modernità," in *Le religioni e il mondo moderno*, ed. by Giovanni Filoramo, I, *Cristianesimo*, ed. by Daniele Menozzi (Torino: Einaudi, 2008), p. XXXV.

consider cinema a beneficial instrument of modern culture that could spread good values, but instead it exploited the medium as means of achieving its own goals – which were usually opposed to the principles of modernity. Indeed, the Church actively fostered dialogue only with certain aspects of "modernization," and not with "modernity" as a whole, "under the vigilant eye of the hierarchy, the only authority entitled to make sure that the desired modernization would not turn into modernism, that is, in the insidious infiltration into the Church structure of those modern values that had to be uncompromisingly opposed."[75] The alternative interpretive model – which defines Catholic media policy as a "tempered modernization"[76] – outlines the Church's attitude towards cinema as a process of gradual opening, that was tempered (and therefore slowed down) by doubts and reservations regarding some aspects of the medium's modernity, but at the same time progressive, that is, focused on affirming belief in the possible positive use of cinema *qua* means of social communication. The "tempered modernization" model, however, does not seem to account for the moments that counteract this trend, when the so-called 'progressive' line seems to fall apart. By framing the Church's relation to modernity through functionalist perspective, the "modernization without modernity" model (also defined as "selective modernity")[77] can account for the interchange between opening and closure, which emerges clearly from the archival documents collected for this volume. In other words, the Church refused modernity entirely, and took from modernization only what could prove useful to achieve its ultimately very traditional goals.

---

75   *Ibid.*
76   The definition has been used by Francesco Casetti and Elena Mosconi, "Il cinema e i modelli di vita," in *Chiesa, cultura e educazione tra le due guerre*, ed. by Luciano Pazzaglia (Brescia: La Scuola, 2003), p. 148, and subsequently by Mariagrazia Fanchi, "The 'Ideal Film'. On the Transformation of the Italian Catholic Film and Media Policy in the 1950s and the 1960s," in *Moralizing Cinema. Film, Catholicism and Power*, ed. by Daniel Biltereyst and Daniela Treveri Gennari (New York/London: Routledge, 2015), pp. 224-25.
77   Renato Moro, "Il 'modernismo buono'. La modernizzazione cattolica tra fascismo e postfascismo come problema storiografico," *Storia Contemporanea*, a. XIX, n. 4, 1988, pp. 713-16.

In particular, the documents shed light on the activity of the clergymen who specialized in the cinematographic apostolate – that is, on those who were in charge of ecclesiastical media offices, and those who held the licenses for parish cinemas. The Italian documents provide only a partial picture: they would need to be integrated with others that are preserved at the Vatican archive (which is classified post-1939). However, they have already generated huge advances in our understanding of a phenomenon (the use of social communication tools) which acquired increasing importance for the Church, from Pius XI onwards.

Albino Galletto (the Ecclesiastical Consultant to the Ente dello Spettacolo between 1947 and 1960) was a typical representative of the high-ranking clergy, who received and carried out the orders of the top-most levels of the hierarchy. His effort to bring cinema back to a subaltern position, serving the aims of the ecclesiastical institution, developed in two directions: on the one hand, he promoted and implemented (as much as he feasibly could) strict censorship policies; on the other, he worked towards the construction of a cinema that sought to communicate the Church's religious message. Galletto, therefore, was active in countering the effects of the "sexual excitement" connected to obscene images and to exploit the effects of "devotional excitement" that were central to certain attempts at Catholic film production. As already seen, these two lines of action were only apparently antithetical, since in reality they were two results of the same policy.

First, the documents clearly trace out the intereference of ecclesiastical representatives in Italian cinematic institutions (from State censorship to the Venice Film Festival). This occurred with growing intensity from 1948 to 1958, when the DC, in order to maintain control of the Ministry of Public Education, was forced to surrender Entertainment to the Socialist-Democrats, thus ending a decade of absolute monopoly and, in fact, initiating a phase of negotiations which later characterized Centre-Left governments. This compromise led to a redefinition of the Catholics' influence, to the extent that, in 1965, the CEI president Giuseppe Siri wrote to Floris Ammannati – the latter having reported to the former the ongoing political negotiations concerning the 'allocations' of the main cinematographic institutions controlled by the State – "I have read through the 'attachments' and see that your remarks are on the mark. A clear fact does indeed emerge: until four years ago the Catholics could choose honestly, today they no longer can, they suffer setbacks and sometimes are thrown a bone to gnaw upon."[78] Though the sixties heralded change, in the previous decade the Catholics' power on cinematic institutions was massive. For example, the documents reveal that until 1958 the State's censorship board unofficially hosted representatives of the CCC, whose role was, we can presume, far from passive. We also know that, following an agreement with Andreotti, these representatives could not be priests, since in those years they still wore cassocks, and would therefore be conspicuous. However, when it came to particularly controversial films, government-nominated members would join representatives of CCC, and not the other way around; that is, censorship acts would be signed in a small room in Via della Conciliazione, where the CCC had its see, in the presence of the Ecclesiastical Consultant. Evidence of this can be found in a letter from Giovanni De Tomasi (an official at the General Film Office) to Andreotti: "The movie *A Streetcar Named Desire* had been sitting on our desk for months. [...] Last week I realized [...] the matter had to be settled: [...] therefore I agreed to meet with Monsignor Galletto, with whom we watched the film in the utmost secrecy, in the CCC's room to which I myself had taken the film, in a taxi."[79]

In post-war Italy some members of the clergy, like Galletto, specialized   almost   exclusively   in   the   cinematographic

---

78   Giuseppe Siri, letter to Floris Ammannati, December 30, 1965, ACEC Archive (DB: ACEC 495): "Ho considerato gli 'allegati' ed ho visto che fai considerazioni assai pertinenti. Certo, un fatto emerge: fino a quattro anni innanzi i cattolici potevano onestamente decidere, oggi non lo possono più, debbono subire e qualche volta riescono ad ottenere qualche osso."

79   Giovanni De Tomasi, letter to Giulio Andreotti, February 25, 1954, Giulio Andreotti Archive at the ASILS, series "Cinema," envelope 1072 (DB: ASILS 6): "Da parecchi mesi giaceva in attesa di revisione il film *Un tram che si chiama desiderio*. [...] Nella scorsa settimana ho ritenuto [...] dover risolvere questo problema: [...] mi sono messo d'accordo con Monsignor Galletto col quale abbiamo visionato la pellicola con estrema riservatezza, nella sala del CCC ove l'avevo io stesso portata con un taxi."

apostolate. This gave the Church the opportunity to improve the clericalization process of Catholic cinematographic institutions, which developed in parallel to Catholic's awareness of the sector's importance. The case of the Società Cattolica Assistenza Esercizi Cinema [hereafter SCAEC], which was active in the diocese of Milan, is emblematic: a joint-stock company, the SCAEC was established in 1952 to support and above all control the activity of parish cinemas. The SCAEC's capital was provided by a group close to the ACI. The SCAEC worked efficiently until 1956, when Montini decided that five priests would join the board of directors. This was the first of a series of measures that would bring the society under the direct control of the diocesan clergy, which eventually, in 1959, bought all the shares.[80]

The clericalization of cinema institutions gained momentum at the beginning of the sixties. This happened for two reasons. After a long apprenticeship in the secular world, the clergy felt ready to take direct responsibility for the Catholics' action in cinema. It *could* do so because it had finally acquired the right skills. It *had to do* so because the situation had become critical, due to the crucial role played by social communication media in the transformations that Italian society was experiencing in the years of the economic boom. The clericalization process can be seen as complete by the mid-sixties when, by having the Ente dello Spettacolo transferred from ACI to the CEI, Giuseppe Siri (then CEI president) brought one of the activities that was traditionally entrusted to Catholic laymen back under the bishops' control.

In 1963, the CEI's Commissione per le Attività Ricreative [Commission for recreational activities] advised Siri to found a National Office at the CEI, which would be tasked with managing issues related to social communication.[81] Siri wrote that he "fully agree[d] on the necessity for a National Office under Vatican leadership, and that he wanted it too."[82] He stressed the need to "ensure the Office would be located at the Ente dello

---

80   Dario E. Viganò, *Un cinema ogni campanile*, pp. 88, 112.
81   Giuseppe Amici, letter to Giuseppe Siri, April 3, 1963, CEI Archive (DB:
      ACEI 93).
82   Giuseppe Siri, letter to Giuseppe Amici, April 4, 1963, CEI Archive (DB:
      ACEI 94): "pienamente d'accordo nel ravvisare le necessità di un Ufficio
      Nazionale […] alle dipendenze della Gerarchia e nel volerlo."

Spettacolo."[83] The Office, therefore, was not to be a new body mediating between the Ente and the CEI, but the same body as before, only, with a new legal status. In Siri's reply, concerns about "conciliar concessions" reveal his aims, as does his insistence on the need to find trustworthy theologians to lead the new Office:

> His Excellency knows very well that in this moment of undoubtedly rich transformations, which are as necessary as they are inevitable albeit essentially contingent, too many people seem to believe in a substantial transformation of the human and moral order. This produces concessions, which appear to be guided by panic or even mental alienation. The study of a great number of magazines published in recent months provides revealing insight. Therefore I believe that we must be very prudent in choosing people [to lead the new Office] who will know how to stick to sacred Doctrine, rather than to evanescent shadows, in matters of moral theology and more.[84]

These events were the cause of much concern for Albino Galletto, who remarked that the status of the new Ente dello Spettacolo appeared to be a "complete substitution of everything that previously existed under Pontifical direction."[85] On May 11, 1963, writing to Giuseppe Amici about a meeting with Galletto, Siri specified: "I haven't told him of the origin and the aim of this Scheme [...] I told him instead that the various institutions would maintain their structure, and that our action served only

---

83 DB: ACEI 94: "ottenere che la Sede dell'Ufficio progettato sia presso l'Ente dello Spettacolo."

84 DB: ACEI 94: "È ben noto a Vostra Eccellenza come questo momento che è indubbiamente ricco di mutazioni necessarie quanto alla inevitabilità, ma contingenti quanto alla essenza, presenta troppa gente che dà la impressione di credere a mutazioni sostanziali nello stesso ordine umano e in quello morale. Ne seguono cedimenti che rassomigliano al panico o addirittura alla alienazione mentale. Uno spoglio di molte riviste di questi ultimi sei mesi contiene e offre una documentazione rivelatrice. Credo pertanto che si debba dare molto importanza alla scelta dei nominativi, i quali in fatto di Teologia morale e non solo in quella, sappiano stare alla sacra Dottrina e non alle ombre evanescenti."

85 Giuseppe Siri [?], letter to Giuseppe Amici, May 11, 1963, CEI Archive (DB: ACEI 96): "una sostituzione di tutto ciò che esiste secondo le direttive Pontificie."

to coordinate better their pastoral work."[86] Why would he vague on the real aims of the operation? Perhaps because it came across as not in-keeping with the conciliar climate. While the Council was redesigning the role of laymen within the Church, Siri's CEI appropriated one of the activities that had traditionally been entrusted to laymen, and placed it under the hierarchy's control.

The CEI's action was doubtless initiated under the provisions of par. 21 of the *Inter Mirifica* conciliar decree. However, Siri's and Galletto's comments lead us to think that much more was at stake. Confirmation of this can be found in a document drafted in April 1963, entitled *Appunti per contribuire a un chiarimento* (*Notes to assist a clarification*), that sought to settle the dispute between ACI and the CEI. The document clearly shows that a crucial question for ecclesiastical policies was up for discussion. Who should manage cinema: laymen or the clergy? The document reads: "the categorization of films, which represents the CCC's primary and most delicate task, has become the exclusive responsibility of a priest [...]. Besides categorization, the priest responsible for the National Office performs, in the diverse context of cinema, both pastoral and apostolic activities, within a 'hierarchical apostolate' that ACI should support, and not *viceversa*."[87] Cinema had become too important to be left to ACI's laymen. The Ente dello Spettacolo paid for this, entering into a phase of structural crisis that led it to a slow decline. The document continues, "All in all, it clearly appears that the Ente dello Spettacolo's activities have become crucial for the orientation of believers and [...] it cannot therefore be considered merely a specialized branch under ACI's control. And this is not to mention the ACEC, which, being an

---

86   DB: ACEI 96: "Io non gli ho detto dell'origine e dello scopo di questa
      Schema [...] e gli ho invece detto che i vari Enti ed Istituti dovevano
      rimanere con la loro fisionomia e che si trattava soltanto di una base per
      un lavoro pastorale coordinato."

87   *Appunti per contribuire ad un chiarimento*, April 4, 1963, ACEC Archive (DB:
      ACEC 39): "l'opera di classificazione dei films, costituente l'impegno
      precipuo e più delicato pertinente al Centro Cattolico Cinematografico,
      è affidata per ovvie ragioni alla esclusiva responsabilità di un Sacerdote
      [...]. Oltre alle classificazioni, il sacerdote responsabile dell'Ufficio
      nazionale svolge nei vari ambiti cinematografici un'azione di ordine
      pastorale ed apostolico, di quell''apostolato gerarchico' a cui l'Azione
      Cattolica è chiamata a collaborare, e non viceversa."

association of priests cannot – in view of both its function and its nature – be placed on the same level as the 'organizations adhering to ACI'."[88]

7. The Answers to an Internal, Confidential Questionnaire

Supported and controlled by the clergy, the Catholics' increasing engagement in the cinematographic apostolate became manifest during the sixties thanks to a handful of institutional initiatives, such as the XXXV Settimana Sociale dei Cattolici (35th Catholic Social Week) dedicated to audiovisual media; the establishment of the Scuola Superiore di Giornalismo e Mezzi Audiovisivi (Advanced School for Journalism and Audiovisual Media) at the Università Cattolica del Sacro Cuore in Milan; and, above all, to the wide diffusion of the aforementioned *Inter Mirifica*. However, Vatican II only made statements on principles, whereas it was the duty of the Pontifical Commission for Social Communications to draft a Pastoral Instruction, setting out practical guidelines. To this end, the Pontifical Commission circulated a lengthy questionnaire among the Catholic institutions involved in the field of social communication. For example, in Italy it was sent, among others, to the Centro San Fedele in Milan and to the ACEC. The answers to the questionnaire can be read in two reports elaborated by the CEI,[89] which scrupulously avoid

---

88 DB: ACEC 39: "In definitiva appare chiaramente che l'attività dell'Ente dello Spettacolo ha assunto una dimensione ed una portata di netto orientamento per i fedeli per i settori di pertinenza [...] non può perciò considerarsi una semplice branca di specializzazione a servizio dell'Azione Cattolica. Si tace poi della ACEC, che essendo una associazione composta di Sacerdoti non può per natura o per funzione essere posta sul piano delle 'opere aderenti all'ACI'."

89 The first 47-page working document was used during a meeting that took place on March 8, 1965, which was presided by Andrea Pangrazio and united all of the Catholic cinema organizations, from the managers of the Ente dello Spettacolo to the organizers of the Settimane di Assisi [ACEC Archive (DB: ACEC 1003)]; a second document of just six pages provides a final summary that was sent to the Pontifical Commission, enclosed in a letter by Francesco Angelicchio dated May 26, 1965 and entitled *Risposta della Commissione Episcopale Italiana per le Comunicazioni Sociali al questionario proposto dalla Pontificia Commissione circa l'Istruzione*

mentioning the author of the answers – who were presumably members of the clergy, for the most part. The two documents are of great interest, since they give us an insiders' perspective in a very direct language, that is a far cry from the stilted words of official Vatican documents.

First and foremost, the answers to the questionnaire depict the "sizeable gap," as one of the consulted priests puts it, "between the criteria underlying the main pontifical and conciliar documents and the mentality that inspires many ecclesiastical practices nowadays. On the one hand, indeed, such instruments are appreciated as gifts from the Lord [...] yet on the other, cinema and the likes are considered only as creating the danger of sin."[90] The remainder of the answer polemically addresses a series of limitations to the clergy's activities, the persistence of which demonstrates that cinema never stopped inspiring fear:

> Certain questions arise in particular: a) is it really necessary to ask the permission of the Holy See's Secretariat or the Pontifical Commission for Social Communications for a priest to attend the Venice Film Festival? Or for a priest, or even simply a religious man, even if he is fully engaged in the sector, to attend public exhibitions in Rome? b) how are we to consider the measures taken by the Roman Synod (forbidding the clergy and religious men from attending parish cinemas [...]), since the clergy and religious men are excluded from any movie exhibition, yet tempted to attend them all the same invoking a compromise of conscience? [...] e) is the categorical statement by the Sacred Congregation of Religious to the Superiors General (August 6, 1957) really sustainable? i.e. "There is no reason that justifies the introduction of televisions into communities dedicated to the contemplative life of both men and women; radios will be tolerated with the exclusive aim of allowing priests and nuns to listen to the Pope's word"?[91]

Pastorale [ACEC Archive (DB: ACEC 43)].

90   DB: ACEC 1003: "grande divario tra i criteri informatori dei grandi documenti pontifici e del Concilio, e la mentalità alla quale si ispira molta prassi ecclesiastica odierna. Da una parte, infatti, si dice di apprezzare questi strumenti come doni di Dio [...] dall'altra si mostra di giudicare cinema e simili soltanto come pericolo di peccato."
91   DB: ACEC 1003: "In particolare ci si domanda: a) se proprio occorra arrivare alla Segreteria di S.S., o alla Pontificia Commissione per le Comunicazioni Sociali, perché un sacerdote o un religioso possa

However, for the respondents to the questionnaire, the biggest restriction, which moreover reveals the most significant contradictions of three decades of film policy, was the one pointed out in a circular letter by the Seminary Congregation in June 1964. The letter set the following rule: "The Rector will not allow seminarists to attend film and TV exhibitions too often, which means not more than twice a month."[92]

The "no more than twice a month" rule created difficulties first and foremost for those clergymen who had based their apostolate in the field of cinema, for example managing a parish cinema. The ACEC General Secretary (which in fact was an association of priests) interpreted the spirit of the rule as follows: "It seems to me that, from now on, we can say that the ACEC intends to provide Seminaries with classes and materials for a cinematographic education, intended not so much to see films (which are of course important, but only as examples and not

---

recarsi alla Mostra di Venezia; oppure, perché a Roma, un sacerdote o religioso, anche se tutto applicato a questo settore, possa recarsi a spettacoli pubblici; b) come si debba giudicare quanto, in merito, è stato disposto dal Sinodo Romano (proibizione, per il clero e per i religiosi, di frequentare anche i cinema parrocchiali [...]), sicché clero e religiosi si trovano tagliati fuori da qualsiasi spettacolo cinematografico, o tentati di andarvi giocando sul compromesso di coscienza; [...] e) se sia del tutto sostenibile l'affermazione categorica della Congregazione dei Religiosi ai Superiori generali (6 agosto 1957): 'Non esiste alcun motivo che giustifichi la introduzione di apparecchi televisivi nelle comunità di vita contemplativa sia di uomini che di donne; un apparecchio radio potrà tollerarsi all'unico scopo di permettere ai religiosi di udire la parola del Papa'." The text licensed by Congregation for Institutes of Consecrated Life and Societies of Apostolic Life on August 6, 1957 was published in Francesco Tinello, *La televisione nelle comunità religiose e negli istituti di educazione* (Città del Vaticano: Tipografia Poliglotta Vaticana, 1958; second edition 1959, pp. 100-03). On the reception of television in the Italian Catholic world, see Giorgio Vecchio, "L'arrivo della televisione in Italia: diffidenze e illusioni dei cattolici," in *Democrazia e cultura religiosa*, ed. by Camillo Brezzi, Carlo Felice Casula, Agostino Giovagnoli and Andrea Riccardi (Bologna: Il Mulino, 2002), pp. 401-22; and Mariagrazia Fanchi, "Specchio di virtù. Il mondo cattolico e l'arrivo della televisione," in *Televisione. Storia, Immaginario, Memoria*, ed. by Damiano Garofalo and Vanessa Roghi (Soveria Mannelli: Rubbettino, 2015), pp. 35-48.

92   DB: ACEC 1003: "Il Rettore non permetterà che i seminaristi assistano troppo frequentemente a spettacoli cinematografici e televisivi, e ciò mai più di due volte al mese."

as an update [on contemporary production]) but rather to gain theoretical training."[93] The compromise by which ACEC tried to protect its activity within a seemingly hostile ecclesial context can be summarized as follows: the encouragement of theory (thus books about cinema), and the discouragement of practice (thus seeing or screening films, with the exception of one or two movies per month, and only when really necessary to provide examples of what is explained in the books).

Despite the *Inter Mirifica*, contact with audiovisual images was considered potentially dangerous, creating therefore a need to impose limitations. The contradiction between, on the one side, official statements that originated from debates with Catholic cinematographic cultural associations (i.e. FIC, the Italian Federation of Cineforums), Catholic critics (i.e. Mario Verdone or Gian Luigi Rondi) and Catholic scholars (i.e. Mario Apollonio or Gianfranco Bettettini) and, on the other, a kind of practice that often diverged from official statements, is testified by those priests consulted through the questionnaire.

It should also be recalled that, while Vatican II theoretically revised the laity's role, the Church's governance ultimately remained in the hands of the clergy. Even a markedly mundane context such as that of cinema is under strict clerical control.[94] This is indicated by several responses by the priests consulted through the questionnaire: "The laity's role is very important and invaluable, but only when it works in accordance with established principles and criteria."[95] Another reads: "I would hand over to

---

93   Silvano Battisti, letter to Francesco Dalla Zuanna, July 30, 1964, ACEC Archive (DB: ACEC 86): "A me sembra fin d'ora che si possa dire che l'ACEC intende fare un servizio ai Seminari preparando corsi di lezioni e sussidi per la formazione cinematografica intesa non tanto e non soltanto come visione di film (anche questa, certo, ma più a titolo di esemplificazione che di aggiornamento) quanto come preparazione teorica."

94   The only exception to this rule is Gedda, whose decision-making power, thanks to his personal relationship with Pius XII matched the one of the ecclesiastical consultants assigned to the Ente dello Spettacolo, in fact, in certain cases it was greater.

95   DB: ACEC 1003: "Il ruolo dei laici è importantissimo e forse insostituibile, ma a condizione che agiscano in armonia con i principi ed i criteri che sono stati fissati."

the laity anything which is not a prerogative of the clergy, but only once they have been adequately instructed [...]. Without denying to priests what the laity is allowed."[96]

Among the few laymen who responded to the questionnaire was Carlo Alianello. Not surprisingly, there is no trace of his answers in the CEI's report. However, they were also sent to Taddei for information, by Angelicchio, allowing us to read them today. Alianello explained his point of view as a Catholic writer and layman, stressing the existence of a radical "mistrust," which was reciprocal, "of the clergy towards laymen and of the laity towards the clergy."[97] The clergy's attitude was described in the following terms: "In general the lay author's language is not approved, because he speaks just like the masses and moreover adjusts to their understanding of everyday life. A new and detestable language, where there is little or no unction, where sacred things are too often mixed with profane ones, and the respect of the Sixth Commandment seems at risk at any moment. But most of all the clergy complain about the fact that the Gospel reaches the people by mouth of laymen, and not consecrated men."[98] Alianello's analysis was ruthless:

> All methods have been attempted to prevent the lay intellectual from taking any responsibility or concrete action in those things – incidental things, indeed, but things considered necessary by the Council and due to the incredible rush of our times – that make up the very instruments of communication. It all began with the congregation of friars acting as journalists, publishers, writers,

---

96   DB: ACEC 1003: "Darei ai laici tutto ciò che essi possono compiere e che non è riservato al clero, una volta che siano [...] sufficientemente istruiti [...]. Senza negare ai sacerdoti ciò che i laici possono."

97   DB: ACEC 1003: "diffidenza [...] del clero verso i laici e del laicato contro il clero."

98   Carlo Alianello, *Osservazioni al "progetto di schema dell'Istruzione Pastorale,"* allegato a Francesco Angelicchio, letter to Nazareno Taddei, March 15, 1965, ANT (DB: ANT 1249): "In genere non s'approva il linguaggio dell'autore laico perché parla come parlano le masse e si adegua a loro anche nel modo di intendere le cose d'ogni giorno. Un linguaggio nuovo, detestabile, dove non c'è unzione, punto o poca, dove le cose sacre sono troppo spesso mescolate alle profane e l'equilibrio sul sesto comandamento pare azzardato. Ma assai più gli dispiace che la buona novella giunga agli uomini per bocca di laici non consacrati."

producers and directors. The idea itself would not be so bad, were it not founded on a totally absurd premise, which, however, is still alive and well, that is, that the status of being a priest alone makes that person a writer, a journalist, a film director and, who knows, even a painter or a musician; one is not born a poet, but rather becomes one when he enters a convent or a seminary.[99]

Finally, he appears to hint at his personal experience when writing that:

> The clergy, be it secular or regular, save for some rare and praise worthy exceptions, never allows people to think independently, which could be dangerous, not even to express the most orthodox thoughts in one's own words. [...] It is a staircase: at the top people give orders for which they do not need to account to anyone, save those who are even further up, on a higher, unreachable level. They certainly will not listen to the lamentations of a layman whose bread is snatched from his hands! And this happens for a reason which is irrelevant for many people, but crucial for the convent. A superior, one of those men ranked on the midway landing of the staircase, only has to decide, one day, that a certain article, a certain column or a certain film is too expensive, he has only to say that some high prelate has voiced his discontent [...] and the collaboration with the layman will cease.[100]

---

99   DB: ANT 1249: "Son stati già provati tutti i metodi per tener lontano l'intellettuale laico da ogni responsabilità e da ogni intervento concreto in quelle cose, accessorie per quanto si voglia, ma che il Concilio e la vertiginosa corsa dei tempi riconoscono necessarie, le quali formano giusto gli strumenti di comunicazione. S'è cominciato con le congregazioni di frati giornalisti, editori, scrittori, produttori e registi. La idea in sé non sarebbe malvagia se non fosse fondata su un presupposto del tutto assurdo, ma ancora vivo e vegeto: che basti lo stato sacerdotale [...] per ritrovarsi d'un tratto scrittori, giornalisti, registi e magari pittori e musici, ché poeta non si nasce, ma ci si diventa entrando in convento o in seminario."

100 DB: ANT 1249: "Il clero, sia secolare che regolare, tranne qualche rara e lodevole eccezione, non ti lascia quasi mai la libertà di pensare di testa tua, il che potrebbe essere pericoloso, ma neppure di esprimere un certo ortodossissimo pensiero con le parole tue. [...] È una scala in cima alla quale c'è chi dà ordini di cui non deve dare conto a nessuno, se non a chi sta ancora più in alto, su un piano superiore, inarrivabile. Figuriamoci se darà retta ai lai d'un laico che si vede d'un tratto strappare il pane di mano! E questo può accadere per una ragione futile agli occhi del mondo,

Apparently, things had not changed much since 1936, when Giuseppe Pizzardo, the mastermind behind the Holy See's film policy in the years of *Vigilanti Cura*, wrote of *L'Osservatore Romano*'s film criticism: "Neither Scattolini nor Meneghini are qualified enough. We need a priest."[101] In 1965 that same priest was asked to answer to the questionnaire. Thirty years had passed, during which he had gained relevant experience in the field of cinema, broadening the scope of his activity and taking on tasks that were traditionally carried out by laymen: his decision-making power was wielded in several institutional contexts, ranging from the censorship office to the cinema exhibitors' association, from cultural cinematographic associations to the editorial board of specialist magazines, and even in the field of film production, as an advisor but also with more relevant roles, such as screenwriter or film director. Nonetheless – or perhaps for this very reason – the Italian clergy still considered cinema a dangerous occasion for sin, at least in what we gather from the questionnaire. If the clergy complained about the limitations imposed on its activities by the leaders, however, it also confirmed (as we will see) the basic reasons for this caution. This is the contradiction at the core of Catholic intervention in the field of cinema.

8. *Cinema in the Background of the Post-Tridentine Penitential Model*

While official Catholic discourses tried to frame the moral issues relating to cinema within a broader reflection on the medium, which also took into account its positive functions, with the aim to present the Church as in dialogue with modernity, internal debates and circular letters addressed exclusively to the clergy

---

importantissima per il convento. Basta infatti che qualche superiore, uno di quelli che stanno scaglionati nei vari pianerottoli della scala, decida un giorno che per quell'articolo o per quella rubrica, oppure per quel film si spende troppo, che qualche altissimo prelato abbia fatto conoscere a mezza bocca il suo scontento [...] perché la collaborazione del laico cessi."

101 Note by Giuseppe Pizzardo, *s.d.* (presumably 1936), Secretariat of State, S. RR. SS., Historical Archive, AA. EE. SS., Ecclesiastical States, IV, position 445, folder 425, sheet 55r, cit. in Gianluca della Maggiore, *La Chiesa e il cinema nell'Italia fascista*: "Né lo Scattolini né il Meneghini sono sufficientemente preparati. Occorrerebbe un Sacerdote."

were characterized by doubt and fear as well as the awareness that cinema is often an occasion for sin.

Before focusing on the answers to the moral question gathered by the aforementioned questionnaire, we must clarify the intended meaning of the expression 'occasion for sin'. For if the moral question is central to the Catholics' reflections on cinema, this is the very point on which we must concentrate, in trying to adopt the mindset that produced those reflections. That strain of thought was deeply rooted in the Counter-Reformation, which enjoyed a major revival during the Pontificate of Pius XII, for example through the creation of models of sanctity inspired by purity, such as Maria Goretti.[102]

Catholic morals (unlike Lutheran morals) are willfull: they consist in single acts of will and revolve around the individual's responsibility for sin. Faced with the necessity to retaliate to protestant heresy, Catholic theology theorized that the subject had to be made highly responsible, since his/her salvation did not depend exclusively on faith but also on the goodness of his/ her deeds, that is, on his/her ability to fight off temptation. For Catholicism, "sin consists in any single *deed* for which the subject, internally and freely, complies with a bad purpose against which he has been warned and, even if only in his wish or with a *movement of the soul*, breaks divine law."[103] In the penitential model elaborated by the Counter-Reformation, which remained valid still in the Church of Pius XII, guilt is primarily connected to internal deeds of conscience rather than to realized actions, and sin is seen as an offence secretly caused to God rather than damage to a fellow creature. The stress therefore falls not on empirical sins but on

---

102 The promotion of the cult of Maria Goretti began in 1935 with the cause for her beatification. At the same time, the authors of catholic handbooks and treatises paid much attention to the issues of chastity and purity, in connection and competition with the fascist moral campaign. See Francesco Piva, "Educare alla 'purezza': i dilemmi della Gioventù cattolica nel secondo dopoguerra," in *Chiesa, laicità e vita civile*, ed. by Lucia Ceci and Laura Demofonti (Roma: Carocci, 2005); Bruno Wanrooij, *Storia del pudore. La questione sessuale in Italia 1860-1940* (Venezia: Marsilio, 1990).

103 Pino Lucà Trombetta, *La confessione della lussuria. Definizione e controllo del piacere nel cattolicesimo* (Genova: costa & nolan, 1991); second edition *La confessione della lussuria. Sessualità, erotismo e potere nel cattolicesimo* (Genova: costa & nolan, 2005), p. 20.

inner ones (that is, sins committed in the mind). Penitential literature (concerning the Christian sacrament of penance) divides inner sins into three different forms, depending on whether the evil thought refers to something in the future, the present or the past. When will complies with a bad action in the future, we speak of 'desire'; when will is pleased for evil committed in the past, we speak of 'being pleasured'; whereas internal sin committed in the present is defined 'morose delectation', which consists in being morose, that is, dwelling on the contemplation of evil instead of immediately rejecting the malicious thought.

As Pino Lucà Trombetta explains: "In principle, internal sins concern all the precepts of the Decalogue: one can desire or take pleasure in theft, murder, in lies etc. However, authors of penitential treatises admit that, in confessions, the major part of those sins concerns the desires of flesh and lust."[104] While, according to Catholic doctrine on lust, the objective and external level is regulated by the premise that sexuality is legitimate only within the bond of marriage, the subjective and internal one (where cinema has a greater impact, since it deals with the imagination) develops around desires, pleasures and delectations.

In the postwar period, lust received increasing attention from Catholicism, concomitantly with an alarming decay in sexual habits (caused by the War and, later, the economic boom) to which the Catholic world responded with a massive campaign for purity – one of the key areas for the re-Christianization of Italian society. Cinema became a main focus for this campaign, in both the reports of the Secretariat for Morality (one of the ACI's technical offices) and confessional handbooks. While in the twenties the latter included prohibitions concerning balls and books,[105] and no mention was made of cinema, from the thirties onwards, and in particular in the forties and fifties, confessors were explicitly invited to consider cinema, within the category of "occasions for sin,"[106] during their investigation of lust.

---

104 *Ibid.*, p. 26.
105 See for example Sebastiano Uccello, *Manuale del confessore: compilato secondo il nuovo cod. di D. C.* (Vicenza: Società anonima tipografica, 1924).
106 See for example Gerolamo Luzi, *La condotta dei confessori riguardo al 6° comandamento* (Torino: Lice/Berruti, 1943; second edition 1946; third edition 1953).

The possible sin committed in a movie theatre is first and foremost disobedience to ecclesiastical authority – that, through the *Segnalazioni Cinematografiche* (Cinematographic Warnings), had distinguished licit from illicit films and warned believers of the danger in attending an occasion for sin. This form of sin moreover has the features of internal sin, since it can take the shape of desire, pleasure and delectation. As this implies, it would be misguided to assume that the clergy's main preoccupation was with the public's behavior inside the movie theatre itself. Such preoccupations did exist, especially in the first half of the twentieth century, as is testified, for example, by the first article on cinema published in *La Civiltà Cattolica*.[107] Yet, when in 1960, the organizers of the "Giornata per la moralizzazione del cinema" [Day of moralization of the cinema] voiced a complaint about the "so frequently vulgar and immoral behavior in movie theatres, where particularly delicate scenes come with a quiver of excitement and the darkness favours strange encounters,"[108] they were clearly referring to commercial movie theatres, which had to be moralized in same way as parish cinemas. In fact, the latter were under such strict control that it is very difficult to imagine sexual encounters taking place in them during the fifties. Indeed, parish cinemas were literally under the surveillance of the ecclesiastical authority. In 1966, the Verona branch of the ACEC organized a symposium on the "preservation of morality in movie theatres:"[109] parish cinemas had finally achieved moralization – a good result that necessitated preservation. The symposium was attended by "all managers and watchman of Catholic cinemas of the diocese."[110] The document leads us to believe that it was not unusual for the cinema manager (the priest and license-holder) to be assisted by a "watchman," whose task was the surveillance of behavior inside the theatres.

If the issue at stake was not the public's behavior inside the movie theatre (which had been substantially regulated through

---

107 See the Editorial, "Cinematografo e moralità pubblica," *La Civiltà Cattolica*, a. 65, vol. 4, n. 1546, November 21, 1914, p. 435.

108 A.G., "La promessa cinematografica," *Verona Fedele*, a. XVI, n. 3, January 15, 1961 (DB: PER 271).

109 Giacomo Gentilin, leaflet, 1966, ACEC Archive (DB: ACEC 107).

110 DB: ACEC 107.

the creation of a network of moralized parish cinema), why should the cinema represent a cause of growing concern? In the fifties, once the ACEC had placed parish cinemas under the jurisdiction of bishops, why was cinema still considered as an occasion for sin? Why would priests need a special license even to enter parish cinemas? The answer is, evidently, that the sin occasioned by the cinema was internal rather that external. There is no need to emphasise that the latter is more difficult to control than the former.

As we have seen, not only did the post-Tridentine penitential model persecute forms of sin that originated in committed acts (which, of course, can occur in the dark room of the theatre, even though this was not very frequent, especially in closely supervised parish theatres) but it also considered equally critical those minor sensations that preceded actual sexual consummation, or preparing it, or remaining in a state of imagined sex. The cinema was therefore an occasion for sin "because of the weakness of human nature, which does not easily resist lust."[111]

Considering these premises, let us now turn to the answers to the questionnaire, and how they tackle the issue of morality. This can be summed up in the following answer: "Moral habit consists of raising awareness of the ethical relevance of the phenomenon and on the responsibilities we each have [...]. It consists, therefore, in [...] acknowledging the moral judgements of the Church and in financially supporting Catholic initiatives. This can be achieved through catechesis."[112] Although such a formulation might strike us as lapidary, the statement gets right to the heart of the question: first, the need to acknowledge the righteousness of the moral judgments expressed by the *Segnalazioni Cinematografiche*, thus averting the risk of sinning by attending the exhibition of immoral films; and second, the need to support good cinema by purchasing a ticket.

---

111 Pino Lucà Trombetta, p. 48.
112 DB: ACEC 1003: "L'abitudine morale è la sensibilizzazione sulla portata etica del fenomeno e sulle responsabilità relative a ciascuno [...]. Consiste in pratica nell'apprezzare [...] i giudizi morali della Chiesa e nell'appoggiare con il denaro le iniziative cattoliche. Si ottiene mediante catechesi."

The moral discourse produced by the answers to the questionnaire depict cinema as an "occasion for sin" in view of the viewer's passivity: "We must teach, we must train people not to remain passive when watching a film [...] they should reflect, judge, that is, take active part in it."[113] We must not commit the mistake of considering such passivity on an intellectual level: people were certainly not invited to develop their individual critical opinion. In fact, behaving morally meant trusting the sentences expressed by the *Segnalazioni Cinematografiche*, which actually implies complete passivity, leaving no space at all for autonomy judgment. The passivity mentioned in the statement is of another kind, and it concerns the constitutional 'weakness of human nature' that we mentioned earlier.

A 1953 internal circular, addressed to the managers of Salesian movie theatres, further underlines that film projections must be "guided" with a "method [...] following the scheme of the so-called 'Cineforum'."[114] In fact, this method was far more radical in applying the principles that inspired the inventor of Cineforums (Félix Morlion), given that, it even requested "warnings during the show"[115] to guide the audience: "even during the show, the viewer should be reminded of the main points discussed before the screening by means of brief hints, so that he will not passively endure the film (which is one of the greatest dangers of cinema) and he will actively judge with the full faculty of his intelligence."[116] Setting this discourse against the background of the Catholic penitential model, it is clear that the opposition at play is not between an active (that is, critical) intelligence and a passive one (that is, predisposed to assimilating the ideology of the text). For if the only question at stake was interpretation –

---

113 DB: ACEC 1003: "Occorre insegnare, abituare, a non essere passivi davanti allo spettacolo [...] ma riflettere e giudicare quindi partecipare."
114 Secondo Manione, confidential circular letter, July 24, 1953, ACEC Archive (DB: ACEC 98): "metodo [...] ricalcato su quello in uso nei cosiddetti 'Cineforum'."
115 DB: ACEC 98: "richiami durante la stessa proiezione."
116 DB: ACEC 98: "anche durante la proiezione, si ricordino, con brevissimi cenni gli spunti presentati all'inizio, in maniera da aiutare i partecipanti a non subire passivamente lo spettacolo (che è uno dei pericoli più gravi del cinema), ma a giudicarlo attivamente e ad essere padroni della propria intelligenza."

that is, the necessity to resist influence from the hostile ideology of the text – a brief introduction and keen conclusive remarks would suffice (as Morlion taught). But in this case the stakes are much higher, since the real problem is the conflict between the intellect and the senses, where the latter are always ready to take the lead. Comments during the film screening aimed to avert this danger and to break "the spell of the cinema" (as *Vigilanti Cura* defines it), or, to say it in the terminology of moral theology, to avoid "morose delectation."

The debate on the dialectic between the active and passive viewers, starting from these same premises, developed in the secular context, too. Evidence of this can be found in Silvio Alovisio's studies of cinema and cognitive science at the beginning of the twentieth century. As a conception of the medium based on the opposition between a disembodied subject and an external reality was progressively replaced by one centred on the embodiment of perception, a new complex of fears emerged, this time related to the body: "exposed to often overpowering currents, to sensorial stimuli [...], potential victim to the dangers of suggestion and immoderate excitement."[117] The images that turned out to have a particularly strong impact on the viewer's body were, of course, representations of sexuality: "Any boy who starts going to the cinema inevitably becomes a masturbator,"[118] stated psychiatrist Guglielmo Mondio in his 1925 study on the nervous diseases caused by the cinema. Secular and Catholic culture responded to this common fear that cinema might appeal to uncontrollable instincts in two different ways, as we shall see shortly.

For Catholics, then, what was the marker of maturity, that is, what was the difference in age between the boy risked becoming a masturbator and the adult man who could control his own instincts? The answer to this question was provided by the "Pro

---

117 Silvio Alovisio, "L'immagine prima della coscienza. Cinema e sensazione nella riflessione scientifica del primo Novecento," in *Cinema e sensazione*, ed. by Paolo Bertetto (Milano: Mimesis, 2015), p. 69.

118 Guglielmo Mondio, "Il cinematografo nell'etiologia di malattie nervose e mentali soprattutto dell'età giovanile," *Il Manicomio*, n. 38, 1925; in Silvio Alovisio, *L'occhio sensibile. Cinema e scienze della mente nell'Italia del primo Novecento* (Torino: Kaplan, 2013), pp. 207-208.

famiglia" association, which in 1961 organized an exhibition of film posters in Trento, in order to expose their immorality: "More than five thousand visitors [...] in seven days. [...] The hot [...] material exhibited has attracted the attention of parents and educators who [...], coming from all over the country, stopped in front of such topical documents. [...] Admission to the exhibition, as is well known, is reserved to parents or teachers (with no age limit), and strictly forbidden to people under 24."[119] In other words, at age 23 one was not considered mature enough to visit an exhibition of cinema posters, unless that person had already procreated.

9. *Consciousness and the Pre-Reflexive Reaction to Cinema*

The theoretical and critical work of Jesuit Nazareno Taddei, one of the shrewdest and most influential scholars within the Italian ecclesiastical context, illustrates very clearly the modes in which the post-Tridentine penitential model merged into Catholic studies on cinema. Taddei's analyses took their cue from his observations of cinema's huge potential to influence the audience. Taddei was well aware that individual freedom could be jeopardized by an uneducated use of the mass media. His method of film analysis – which he considered an antidote to unawareness, that is, a tool that could make the viewer aware of the difference between reality and representation – was doomed, initially, "to clash with the perspectives that implicitly denied the existence of an objective truth, and with the hermeneutics based on the conception of the 'open text' and the consequent variety of possible meanings."[120] However, Taddei's methodology, and indeed that of his students, has recently been reconsidered thanks to the discovery of mirror neurons.[121]

---

119 Editorial, *L'Adige*, January 22, 1961 (DB: PER 259).
120 Massimo   Pampaloni,   "Nazareno   Taddei: un   pioniere   della comunicazione," *La Civiltà Cattolica*, vol. 4, n. 3995, December 10, 2016, p. 496.
121 See Luigi Zaffagnini, "Nazareno Taddei: missione e ricerca," *Edav*, n. 441, June 2016, pp. 3-8.

In classical cognitivism, intersubjectivity took shape entirely within the linguistic-inferential mechanism of the so-called Theory of Mind:[122] here, the notion of intersubjectivity refers to the intellect's explicit acknowledgment of other people's desires, beliefs, and intentions. Conversely, direct access to the meaning of other people's behavior and experiences, which is enabled by mirror neurons, occurs regardless of such attribution and is more instinctual than intellectual. Vittorio Gallese has suggested that such direct access could be defined "embodied simulation," a phenomenon in which the observation of a conspecific individual's actions induces in the brain of the beholder the activation of the same nervous circuits that underpin the execution of that actions. In other words, embodied simulation produces an automatic simulation, 'as though' an actual execution was taking place.

The same cortical sites that become active in first-hand experiences of emotions and sensations are also active when we perceive the expression of emotion and sensations in other people's bodies. Gallese has demonstrated, for instance, how mirroring occurs in tactile sensations: the same area of the parietal lobe is activated both when a part of my body is touched, and also when I see someone else being touched in the same spot. Through an automatic and pre-linguistic mechanism of motor simulation, the beholder is granted access to direct comprehension of someone else's motorial intentions 'from within'. This occurs if other person is alive, and in the presence of the beholder, but also when he/she is imagined: the mechanism of embodied simulation is the same.

Cinema has likely boosted the potential impact of the dynamics of embodied simulation inscribed in imaginative processes,[123] thanks to a series of factors depending on the corporeality of the viewer who is at the same time relaxed[124] and hyperstimulated. Precisely this condition (being relaxed and hyperstimulated) is

---

122 The Theory of Mind is the ability to attribute mental states to oneself and to others.

123 Vittorio Gallese, Michele Guerra, *Lo schermo empatico. Cinema e neuroscienze* (Milano: Raffaello Cortina, 2015).

124 And also his/her psychology, since the viewer, aware of finding him/herself in a protected situation (such as at the cinema) can let down his/her guard.

that which moral theology considers as an occasion for sin. This is the reason why it is necessary to intervene during the film's screening with comments (as recommended by the internal circular addressed to the managers of Salesian movie theatres, mentioned above): to interrupt sensorial suggestionability through the reactivation of consciousness.

In the embodied simulation activated by a film, the empathic comprehension of the other occurs automatically and pre-reflexively. According to this hypothesis, a human being can experience first hand action, emotion and intention that is also experienced by someone else. It follows that immoral cinema therefore leads the viewer to behold immoral actions, to experience them automatically and pre-reflexively. What are the implications then for moral theology? Since the viewer's reaction is automatic and pre-reflexive, and moral discourse implies that sin is intentional, at worst the viewer can be accused only of having exposed him/herself to risk: the sin consists in buying the ticket, since the reactions the movie might trigger are automatic, and reach beyond the moral control of the viewer's consciousness. They depend by the proverbial weaknesses of the flesh. This is why it is so important to follow the warnings expressed by *Segnalazioni Cinematografiche.*

The two theoretical models that we have considered so far (the post-Tridentine penitential model and the neurofilmological one) reach the same conclusions: when immoral, cinema represents an occasion that (at least theoretically) leads to sin due to a reaction that mainly eludes conscious control. It should be noted, then, that what is at stake here is the match between two models, both of which do not historically determine the viewer. The accusation of reductionism that one might level to neurofilmology might as well be levelled to Catholic theology, too, since the latter founds its arguments on revelation, with an inexorable top-down movement. Still, historical studies of Catholic culture must necessarily consider a broad notion of the "model Catholic" which is superimposed onto the "real Catholic," even when the latter appears historically disparate to the former – as in the second half of the twentieth century as far as sexual morals were concerned. One of the reasons why Catholic film policies failed is precisely this: the unbridgeable gap between the model viewer, imagined by theologians, and the real viewer, who would attend commercial movie theatres, and not only parish cinemas, and who would see films deemed immoral and obscene by *Segnalazioni Cinematografiche* without feeling like a sinner. More generally, therefore, the real reason for this failure was the Catholics' inability to intervene proactively in the complex historical processes that governed the formation of the audience, aside from defensive policies that were destined to deteriorate and become out-dated. Still, the current interest of Catholic film studies in recent discoveries in neurofilmology is easy to understand, since the discipline seems to legitimize many of the fears and the resulting practices (including censorship) that secular culture considered pointless. Furthermore, neurofilmology allows Catholics to reevaluate certain controversial scholars, such as Taddei ("Father Taddei's method is confirmed by neuronal facts, no less" we can read in a recent portrait of the Jesuit).[125]

The reasons why cinema was considered dangerous by Catholic culture now appear very clearly. By activating internal processes (which the Church had been controlling for five centuries), cinema forges a kind of viewer that is antithetical to the one promoted by Catholic culture, at least in relation to two main points:

1. While Catholic culture invokes conscientious reactions, the cinematographic experience has to do with a pre-reflexive reaction. In moral theology, internal sin occurs at the very moment when the subject adheres to a forbidden impulse or sensation, that is to say, when he/she assents to it through a rational stance. The embodied paradigm, conversely, implies a viewer that is extraordinarily similar the one that Catholic discourse tries to avert: a passive viewer who is subject to automatic responses.

2. While Catholic culture claims that occasions of sin should be avoided, the cinematographic experience is based on the constant search for new sensations. The central role accorded to subjective intention and to voluntarism in the Catholic penitential model has progressively elicited

---

125 Massimo Pampaloni, p. 496.

growing consideration of anything preceding empirical sin:
the act of sin has come to be situated in the very intention
of sinning. Therefore, the "avoiding the possibilities"
has become a sort of preliminary command, governing
the virtuous Catholic's lifestyle. While moral theology
forestalls the threshold of guilt, modernity pushes ahead
that of stimulation, shaping its public on the model of the
sensation seeker.

These, in my opinion, are the two main causes of conflict
between the Church and modernity, as constituted by cinema.

The Church had been defending itself (and its publics) from
the embodied simulation inscribed in obscene images for many
ages. The emergence of cinema, with its ability to create complex
sensorial experiences, brings this conflict to an unprecedented
degree of tension:[126] what was consequently at stake was, on the
one hand, the penitential model elaborated by the Counter-
Reformation, and on the other, the possibility to channel and
govern one precise feature of modernity, that is, its search for
sensation.

---

126 In the mid-Sixties Francesco Angelicchio initiated a period of consultation
     that was designed to reform review procedures. Among others, he sought
     advice from Ferdinando Lambruschini, then professor of Moral Theology
     at the Pontifical Lateran University in Rome, and future Archbishop of
     Perugia. According to Lambruschini, "excluded" films were subject to the
     "traditional clause of Holy See ministries, according to which the faculty
     to read prohibited books can be granted, with the exception of obscene
     books"/"la clausola tradizionale nei Dicasteri della S. Sede nel concedere
     la facoltà di leggere i libri proibiti, la quale pur nella concessione più
     ampia, esclude sempre e per tutti […] i libri […] osceni." Furthermore,
     Lambruschini underlined the necessity to "declare that the CCC's list
     was the only and absolute regulation, such that its violation will put the
     viewer in a condition of mortal sin."/"dichiarare normativa e assoluta la
     classifica data dal CCC […] in modo che la violazione di essa costituisca lo
     spettatore in stato di peccato mortale" [Ferdinando Lambruschini, study
     enclosed in Francesco Angelicchio, letter to the members of the National
     Review Committee, February 9, 1963, ACEC Archive (DB: ACEC 483)].
     The lists of excluded films are compared here to the lists of prohibited
     books. As was traditionally the custom for the latter, generous exceptions
     could be made but not for obscene texts, therefore making this evidently
     the most dangerous category.

10. *The Fall of Taboos related to Obscenity*

For the Catholic world, the very way in which cinema worked was potentially pornographic: this is clear in Andrea Carlo Ferrari's reflections, elaborated at the beginning of the twentieth century. In the guise of Archbishop of Milan, Ferrari was one of first prominent members of ecclesiastical hierarchies to articulate a stance on cinema – which he described as a tool of "moral depravation."[127] In fact, for Ferrari young people were "tyrannized by their uncontrolled passions" because of "obscene pictures [and] of lewd scenes screened in movie theatres."[128] He was not referring to the first pornographic movies, born along with cinema but forced to remain underground and to face a great deal more difficulty in circulation than pictures and flyers.[129] Nor was he reffering to any particular film, but to cinema in general, as the conveyor of a certain lifestyle. In 1909 Ferrari drafted a list of means that devised to "spread immorality among the people:" "theatres, public and private entertainment, walks, conferences, the cinema, photography, pornographic postcards, and most of all the press, the evil, blasphemous, shameless press that derides what is most sacred and saint in religion."[130] The presence of the press and conferences along with pornographic postcards is relevant, and it corroborates Walter Kendrick's claim that the problem was the very circulation, the spread, the uncontrolled movement of information. The protagonists of the anti-pornographic campaign at the end of the nineteenth century "at bottom feared nothing so much as the universal distribution of information. The prospect called up nightmarish images of a world without structure, where all barriers had been breached and all differences levelled. It was appropriate that

---

127 Rivista Diocesana Milanese, January 1910, p. 7; cit. in Dario E. Viganò, *Un cinema ogni campanile*, p. 21.
128 *Ibid.*
129 Mauro Giori, "Quadri piccanti e spettacoli indecentissimi: la ricezione dell'osceno come attrazione," in *Estetica della fruizione. Sentimento, giudizio di gusto e piacere estetico*, ed. by Maddalena Mazzocut-Mis (Milano: Lupetti, 2008), pp. 267-91.
130 Foglio Ufficiale Ecclesiastico, August (1909), pp. 82-84; cit. in Dario E. Viganò, *Un cinema ogni campanile*, pp. 18-19.

sex should become the focus of such nightmares, since long
before the modern threat arose, sex already stood for loss a
control."[131] The Church moreover feared that the new medium
would excite the viewer's senses. In the Adamite vision of the
fallen man, burdened by original sin and struggling daily with
the temptations of the flesh, this issue, which Ferrari perceived
immediately, was fundamental, and would remain so for the next
hundred years: "all of the artistic refinements, all the scientific
industrial discoveries are made to increase, to bolster and to
glorify the most ignoble instincts of mankind."[132]

As long as the Church succeeded in devising and implementing
ways to control it, in synergy with state institutions, such fears
were counterbalanced by the belief that cinema could also be
used in a positive way. In the forties, for examples, cinema was
considered in some cases a way to distract audiences from "the
most dangerous form of entertainment, that is, dance."[133] These
are the words of a preoccupied "priest from the mountains,"[134]
who in 1947 wrote to the archbishop of Milan asking for help
to open a cinema, his aim being to diminish the erotic drive
of the souls entrusted to his care. In those years, obscene
images still occupied a marginal position in the films shown
in Italian cinemas, to an extent that justified the belief that
cinema would help to counterbalance the sensations excited
by dancing.

Later on, between the end of the fifties and the beginning
of the sixties, cinema became the object of a significant social,
political and institutional confrontation. This confrontation was
social insofar as cinema represented the new social habits – for
example beach life – that were supplanting traditional ones. It
was *institutional* since cinema was often the cause for conflicts
between institutions, for example between State censorship
and the magistracy, which began to sequester movies that had

---

131 Walter Kendrick, *The Secret Museum. Pornography in Modern Culture* (New
     York: Viking, 1987), pp. 144-145.
132 Rivista Diocesana Milanese, n. 7, July (1916), p. 195; cit. in Dario E.
     Viganò, *Un cinema ogni campanile*, p. 26.
133 Velio Ancini, letter to Ildefonso Schuster, June 1, 1947, ASDMI, Fondo
     Schuster, 8469: "divertimento più pericoloso [...] e cioè quello del ballo."
134 *Ibid.*: "parroco di montagna."

obtained regular censorship visas. It was *political* because the social-democrats first, and later the socialists, began to demand an increasingly active role in the strategic control of entertainment. What caused this open confrontation? What led to the harsh debates on *La dolce vita* and *Rocco e i suoi Fratelli*? The Church's acceptance of cinema (and of modernity in general) cannot be considered as a linear progress, from Ferrari's anathema to a gradual loosening of censorship. The relation between the Church and modernity, as represented by cinema, was a much more complex process: it alternated between trust and misgivings and it underwent phases of radical refusal, such as during the early sixties, when all Catholic cinematic institutions became engaged in an open conflict due to the sudden acceleration in the dimishing of taboos related to obscenity.

A seemingly quiet decade, the fifties were actually full of fears and terrors, which erupted like a volcano in 1960 with *La dolce vita*. First and foremost was the fear of the bikini, an issue that concerned the Rimini and Riccione branches of the ACI as well as the Vatican Secretariat of State. On April 20, 1953, the Vatican asked Andreotti to intervene against a cinema magazine.[135] This episode is relevant, and indeed emblematic of the course of events in Italy for a number of reasons. First of all, for the high ranks of the persons involved: on the one side Angelo Dall'Acqua, Pius XII's right hand man (in his institutional capacity as Substitute to the Vatican Secretariat of State), on the other De Gasperi's right hand man (in his institutional capacity as Undersecretary to the Presidency of the Council). Secondly, it was significant for the object of the scandal: a film magazine that included several photographs of picture of voluptuous women in bikinis, which was dangerous since was distributed for free outside of movie theatres. In fact Andreotti had been pre-warned a few days earlier via the following note: "Excellency,

---

135 Angelo Dall'Acqua, letter to Giulio Andreotti, April 20, 1953, ACS, Presidenza del Consiglio dei Ministri, 1948-1950, 3.2.6, 32227.1 (DB: ACS 106): "Your excellency, allow me to signal to your excellency the entire leaflet that, I'm told, is being distributed at the 'Sistine' Cinema, even to young men." / "Eccellenza, mi permetto di segnalare a Vostra Eccellenza l'unito foglietto che mi si dice viene distribuito al Cinema 'Sistina', anche a giovanetti."

just this morning I received with my mail the first issue (year 1, April 12, 1953) of ECOFILM, which contains pictures that have triggered protest from 'certain families', as I read in the letter enclosed with the magazine. Thus reads the text: 'We trust in your intelligence to have images of women in this state removed from certain magazines. How are we supposed to restrain our boys? Even under fascism such magazines would not have been permitted."[136]

A tangible sign that things were changing, in the country and in some areas of DC leader's perception, was Andreotti's removal from the General Film Office. The reasons for this are well-known. Andreotti had always believed that films which offer a positive image of social conflict were more dangerous than those which tested the boundaries of sexual representation, as he himself stated in his typically convoluted style, in an interview released during the eighties: "In fact – and there were discussions in our group – I was – and still am – concerned by violence and evil more than by a certain liberality in…sentimental matters, so to speak."[137] Andreotti's diaries from those years provide further confirmation: "attack from Scalfaro during yesterday's Governing Council. Says I shouldn't be in charge of Entertainment any more, as I am unfit to restrain its immorality."[138] In fact, after a brief stint in which Entertainment was entrusted to Teodoro

---

136 Luigi Traglia, letter to Giulio Andreotti, April 15, 1953, ACS, Presidenza del Consiglio dei Ministri 1948-1950, 3.2.6, 32227.1 (DB: ACS 104): "Eccellenza, proprio stamane mi è giunto per posta il numero primo, anno primo (12 aprile 1953) di ECOFILM, contenente delle fotografie che hanno suscitato la protesta di "alcune famiglie," come leggo nella lettera che accompagna il giornale. Eccone il testo: "Ci rivolgiamo alla Sua intelligenza affinché si possa togliere su certi giornali figure di donne in questo stato. Come si possono frenare i ragazzi? e pure al tempo del fascismo non vivevano giornali simili."

137 *Intervista all'ex sottosegretario Giulio Andreotti*, in *Neorealismo. Cinema italiano 1945-1949*, ed. by Alberto Farassino (Torino: EDT, 1989), p. 77. See also Giulio Andreotti, "Il cinema italiano non è comunista," *Oggi*, a. VIII, n. 42, October 16, 1952, p. 4.

138 Giulio Andreotti, *1953. Fu legge truffa?* (Milano: Rizzoli, 2007), pp. 137-138. See also *ibid.*: 161. Following the attack, Andreotti, though he remained Undersecretary, was obliged to surrender Entertainment, against his will, to Teodoro Bubbio (*ibid.*: 198-200).

Bubbio first, and then to Giuseppe Ermini, it was Scalfaro himself who took over, with often disappointing results.

The sixties were the years of the *Inter Mirifica* conciliar decree (1963) and the creation of the World Communications Day (1967), through which the Church institutionalized its extraordinary engagement in the media. However, in same years the Italian Church was shaken by widespread tensions: the decade opened with *La dolce vita*, after which nothing remained the same; cinema was put under the CEI's strict surveillance; and, at the same time, the press was also put under the hierarchies' control.[139] The representation of what was once considered obscene took up increasingly – and relentlessly – more space, generating panic among those who, in the fifties, had believed that they could control the circulation of information, above all with regard to the representation of sexuality. While the CEI regularly received (increasingly alarmed) reports concerning the Venice Film Festival (which had not been the case in the fifties, when there was little need for such a reaction), the sexual question, not surprisingly, became central to the Church's policy. In July 1968, with the promulgation of *Humanae Vitae*, Paul VI disowned the conclusions reached by the committee put in charge of settling the matter, and unequivocally condemned the use of contraception. Some weeks later, on September 18, the same Paul VI publicly voiced his disappointment that the OCIC's prize had been awarded to Pasolini's *Teorema*, which, in his opinion, was guilty of having compared the theme of the sacred to that of sex.[140]

The habit of informing bishops about the Venice Film Festival was one of the many consequences of the generalized panic that seized all Catholics engaged in the field of cinema in the wake of *La dolce vita*. The first informant was Emilio Lonero, the Festival's most contested Director ever. He was nominated to

---

139 Notoriously, in 1968, due to its weak financial situation, the *Avvenire d'Italia* was taken over by *L'Italia*. The two newspapers later merged into *Avvenire*.

140 See Italo Moscati, *Pasolini e il teorema del sesso. 1968: dalla mostra del cinema al sequestro. Un anno vissuto nello scandalo* (Milan: Il Saggiatore, 1995); and Tomaso Subini, *"Teorema" e la fine del mondo*, in *Pasolini e l'interrogazione del sacro*, ed. by Angela Felice and Gian Paolo Gri (Venezia: Marsilio 2013).

the role on February 27 by Minister Umberto Tupini following
the ACI leaders' request, just a few days after Scalfaro's famous
"Basta!" article in *L'Osservatore Romano*.[141] At the end of the
Festival Lonero submitted a *Final Report* to CEI leaders, written
on Biennale stationary, in which he focused on the boycott
of his directorship by the "unified front of communists and
paracommunists."[142] These episodes could be considered the
second part of an imagined screenplay, first drafted in 1948 during
an equally crucial moment. At that time Lonero's role was played
by Morlion (whom Andreotti had wanted on the Festival's jury)
and *La terra trema* was in *Rocco e i suoi fratelli*'s place. Similarly, in
1948 too the Vatican leaders had been reassured of (communist)
Visconti's failure: "among nine members of the jury there were
many communists, others who were indifferent, and a minority of
committed Catholics. [...] After a lengthy altercation, the value
of the prize awarded to Visconti's *La terra trema* was downplayed
by the qualification 'for its stylistic and choral value'."[143] But,
while in 1948 these disputes had no real consequences, in 1960
they led to the removal of Lonero from his office.

Reports about the following editions of the festival were written
by Francesco Angelicchio and Enrico Baragli. In 1961, "the left-
wing press, united in one front, supported and defended morally
negative films and violently attacked the few positive ones [...],
while the Catholic press has been dangerously confused, and has
not always focused adequately on the moral aspect of films."[144]

141 [Editorial, presumably Oscar Luigi Scalfaro], "Basta!," *L'Osservatore
     Romano*, February 8-9, 1960, p. 2.
142 Emilio Lonero, *Relazione conclusiva*, enclosed to Emilio Lonero, letter to
     Alberto Castelli, September 17, 1960, CEI Archive (DB: ACEI 1; ACEI 2):
     "fronte unico dei comunisti e paracomunisti."
143 Félix Morlion, memorandum enclosed to Antonino Silli, letter to
     Giovanni Battista Montini, July 27, 1949, Archivio Generale della Curia
     Generalizia OP (General Archive of the Dominican Order), XIV. 951
     PRO.5 (DB: AGOP 2): "su nove membri della giuria vi erano diversi
     comunisti e indifferenti e solo una minoranza di cattolici convinti. [...]
     Dopo una dura lotta la premiazione del film di Visconti *La terra trema* è
     stata limitata con la formula 'per i suoi valori stilistici e corali'."
144 Francesco Angelicchio, *Nota informativa sulle iniziative cinematografiche
     estive svoltesi a Venezia*, enclosed to Francesco Angelicchio, letter to Alberto
     Castelli, September 25, 1961, CEI archive (DB: ACEI 66; ACEI 3): "la
     stampa di sinistra ha sorretto e difeso, compatta i film moralmente negativi

In particular, Angelicchio voiced concerns about the presence of a "certain trend in current productions, which tend to justify homosexuality."[145] The following year Baragli lamented the fact that among filmmakers "homosexuality seems to have become a hallmark. The screening of *Mamma Roma* at the Excelsior turned into a gathering of these wretched people, and some of them, deep into the night, were shamelessly seducing people who were merely passing by; one even showed up to the hall in the Palazzo del Cinema wearing lipstick and earrings."[146] In 1966, Angelicchio observed the following, apparently irreversible fact: "What was quite apparent at the festival was the increasing amount of nudity, which is now accepted almost entirely without censorship."[147] In 1968, the situation was irreversibly compromised:

The panorama that the majority of films provide was – at least from a religious and moral point of view – bleak and depressing. In form and content, new cinema enhances the process of the desecration and dissolution of man, family and society. With their horrible wickedness and cynicism, the issues and phenomena which find representation in the films of young auteurs merge into a preoccupying moral vacuum, where sex, brutality, violence, Marxism, neurosis, obscene language, irreligiousness, anarchy,

---

e ha attaccato violentemente i pochi positivi [...] la stampa cattolica ha denotato pericolosi sbandamenti e non sempre ha puntualizzato il lato morale delle opere."

145 DB: ACEI 66; ACEI 3: "un certo filone produttivo che tratta l'argomento dell'omosessualità con intenti giustificativi."

146 Enrico Baragli, *Relazione sulla XXIII Mostra Internazionale d'Arte Cinematografica Venezia 25 ag / 8 sett. 1962*, enclosed to Francesco Angelicchio, letter to Alberto Castelli, October 12, 1962, CEI Archive (DB: ACEI 4; ACEI 9): "ottiene sempre più diritto di onorata cittadinanza l'omosessualità. Pare che all'Excelsior, nella serata di *Mamma Roma*, si sia celebrato una specie di convegno nazionale di questi poveretti, alcuni dei quali, alle ore piccole della notte, non si vergognavano di adescare i passanti; uno poi si sarebbe mostrato nella hall del Palazzo del cinema con le labbra dipinte e gli orecchini."

147 Francesco Angelicchio, *Rapporto sulla XXVII Mostra Internazionale d'Arte Cinematografica di Venezia*, enclosed to Francesco Angelicchio, letter to Andrea Pangrazio, September 19, 1966, CEI Archive (DB: ACEI 6): "Quel che si è potuto osservare nella rassegna [...] è la presenza sempre crescente del nudo che pare ormai ammettersi senza tema di interventi censori."

anxiety and any other offence to balance, responsibility and
human dignity coalesce. [...] Save a few gatherings with limited
access, which I promoted, [...] it has not been possible to organize
meetings of the Catholics attending the Festival, due to the several
rivalries among them, which risked creating an even harsher
division and the occasion for scandal in public opinion.[148]

Linda Williams has defined 1972 as the "*annus mirabilis* of
screening sex," and indeed that year two films, *Ultimo tango a Parigi*
and *Deep Throat*, radically altered "the expectations of [...] movie
audiences of what sort of sexual feelings they might experience at
the theatre."[149] Shortly after, in 1978, the first cinema dedicated
specifically to pornographic films opened in Milan. Ortoleva has
stressed the "rapidity and intensity of a process that, [...] in a
very short period of time (1966-1972) triggered the shift from
the first infringements of taboos concerning the representation
of naked bodies to hard core movies. Elsewhere, for example
in France and northern Europe, the same process took much
longer. Rather than a gradual loosening of norms, the Italian
context was characterized by their subversion: as if, with few,

---

148 Francesco Angelicchio, *Rapporto sulla XXIX Mostra Internazionale d'Arte
     Cinematografica*, enclosed to Francesco Angelicchio, letter to Andrea
     Pangrazio, September 16, 1968, CEI Archive (DB: ACEI 7): "Il panorama
     che ci è dato di vedere in numerose pellicole è stato – dal punto di vista
     religioso e morale – quanto mai squallido e deprimente. Il nuovo cinema
     esaspera nella forma e nei contenuti il processo di dissacrazione e di
     dissoluzione dell'uomo, della famiglia e della società. Le problematiche
     e le fenomenologie rappresentate sugli schermi dai giovani autori,
     mostrano con agghiacciante empietà e cinismo, un pauroso vuoto
     morale dove si addensano magmaticamente sesso, brutalità, violenza,
     marxismo, nevrosi, turpiloquio, irreligiosità, anarchismo, angoscia e
     ogni altra offesa all'equilibrio, alla responsabilità e dignità umana. [...]
     Sull'insistente tema del sesso, vale la pena di segnalare il progressivo
     abbandono del pudore da parte delle cinematografie dei paesi socialisti,
     un tempo proverbialmente castigate. [...] Ove si escludano alcune
     riunioni ristrette, promosse dal sottoscritto [...], non è stato possibile
     organizzare una riunione più vasta dei cattolici presenti al Lido [...] a
     causa delle numerose rivalità esistenti fra loro e del pericolo che esse
     potessero risolversi in elemento di maggior divisione e di scandalo per
     l'opinione pubblica."
149 Linda Williams, *Screening Sex* (Durham/London: Duke University Press,
     2008), p. 21.

hesitant warnings, a seemingly unbreakable dam suddenly gave
way."[150] Ortoleva also focuses on the Church's role, wondering if
"pornography established itself in Italy with that time frame and
in that way not only bypassing the resistance of the Church, but
also, in part, as a consequence (of course, an unwanted one) of
the latter's choices."[151] Among other things, Ortoleva also notes
how "pornography imposed itself in Italy without a comparable
debate (be it fruitful or not) to that which characterized the
fall of taboos in the Anglo-Saxon world and, partly, in northern
Europe. The Church did not want such a debate to happen and
certainly did not favour it in any way, it being a theme which would
probably bring to light its internal divisions."[152] This had already
happened in the debate about contraception and was ongoing
thanks to debate surrounding divorce. Ortoleva thus reaches the
conclusion that "the impending presence of the Church in our
country has indeed hindered liberalization in one period, but
in another it also conditioned its developments, paradoxically
leading to a deregulation that turned out to be much wilder than
elsewhere."[153]

11. *Administrative Censorship*

At the end of the fifties, the Catholics lost the political control
over the General Film Office that they had exerted since 1948.
This happened in July 1958, when Amintore Fanfani appointed
social-democrat Egidio Ariosto to the position of undersecretary
of the Presidency of the Council of Ministers for Entertainment.
The Catholic associations that were active in the sector, and first
and foremost Gedda's Catholic Action, did everything they could
to avoid what they felt would be a traumatic change. On June 23,
1958, ACEC president Francesco Dalla Zuanna received alarming
news: "Monsignor Galletto tells me that the Honourable Ariosto
has presented his candidacy quite decisively, and what's more has

150 Peppino Ortoleva, *Il secolo dei media. Riti, abitudini, mitologie* (Milano: Il
     Saggiatore, 2008), pp. 170-171.
151 *Ibid.*, p. 181.
152 *Ibid.*
153 *Ibid.*, p. 182.

a very good chance, since the DC is likely to accept the request concerning Entertainment so as not to surrender Education. Which means that we have now reached the stage that we've been dreading so long: bartering. Monsignor Galletto has confidentially informed me of a measure taken by prof. Gedda "sua sponte" with the [Vatican] Secretariat of State, to prevent Entertainment from being handed over to a Socialist-Democrat [...]. Lonero has inquired after our position on the topic. I informed him of your intention to write to the Honourable Gui."[154] The following day, Dalla Zuanna did indeed write to Luigi Gui, then leader of the DC parliamentary group in the Chamber of Deputies, reminding him of the "great importance of that undersecretariat:" "The Marxist world in general, and the Social-Democrat Party [PSDI], also Marxist, in particular, have been trying to get hold of this important and delicate sector: fortunately, their attempts have failed. [...] Gino dear, we are going through a very interesting moment for entertainment: in fact, very soon we shall have to prepare to renew the entire legislation on cinema: I'm sure you realize quite how important it is that this sector should not be subjected to bartering, it being so delicate and in such crucial phase."[155] This time, however, as Gui himself had to admit in

---

154 Silvano Battisti, letter to Francesco Dalla Zuanna, June 23, 1958, ACEC Archive (DB: ACEC 612): "A quanto mi ha detto Mons. Galletto, lo on. Ariosto ha posto decisamente la sua candidatura, e sembra con buone probabilità di successo in quanto la DC, per non cedere il settore della Pubblica Istruzione, accetterà forse la richiesta per quello dello Spettacolo. Siamo cioè arrivati al punto che abbiamo sempre paventato: il baratto. In via riservata, Mons. Galletto mi ha informato di un passo compiuto "sua sponte" dal prof. Gedda presso la Segreteria di Stato perché il settore non sia assegnato ad un socialdemocratico [...]. Lonero mi ha chiesto il nostro orientamento in merito. L'ho informato della Sua intenzione di scrivere al riguardo all'on. Gui."

155 Francesco Dalla Zuanna, letter to Luigi Gui, June 24, 1958, ACEC Archive (DB: ACEC 613): "grande importanza [...] che riviste quel Sottosegretariato [...]. Da qualche anno il mondo marxista in generale e il [Partito Socialista Democratico Italiano] PSDI (pure marxista) in particolare, ha cercato di avere in mano questo importante e delicato settore: per fortuna non vi è riuscito. [...] Siamo, caro Gino, in un momento di estremo interesse per lo Spettacolo: infatti dovranno essere subito messi i ferri a fuoco per il rinnovo di tutta la Legislazione Cinematografica [...]: tu ti rendi certo conto quanto necessario sia,

his reply to Galletto, "for reasons that are even graver"[156] the Catholic monopoly on Entertainment was coming to an end, and a new phase in the Church's relationship with the Republic's cinematographic institutions was beginning.

As Dalla Zuanna foresaw, this new phase – in which the Catholics had less power and were forced to negotiate on many issues that they could previously settle on their own – was characterized by a debate on censorship that resulted in a new law on cinema. Unlike previous legislation, the 1962 law adapted to guidelines contained in the Constitution, which had been disregarded until then, and significantly downsized the powers of administrative censorship, limiting its scope. With the new law, the board of censors could prohibit the public screening of a film "exclusively" if it was "offensive" in the terms indicated in the last paragraph of Art. 21 of the Italian Constitution. This meant (at least theoretically) that only obscenity could be censored.

The 1962 law moreover abolished the censorship of theatre: this caused much concern in the Catholic world, where the measure was seen as conducive to the abolition of film censorship too. This can be gathered from the minutes of the meeting of the CEI's Committee for Social Communication, held April 27-28, 1965, at the Domus Mariae in Rome. On that occasion, after reporting, "in his capacity as president of the national review Committee, [...] on the momentous moral condition of Italian cinema and its causes,"[157] Angelicchio remarked that "the Italian Socialist Party and the entire lay block will almost certainly argue against current censorship regulations and demand the complete abolition of film censorship, as has already happened for the theatre. We will have to be vigilant and ready to propose alternative laws. In this event we will also have to prepare plans and solutions that, should

---

soprattutto per questo motivo non barattare un settore così delicato in un momento di così grave interesse."

156 Luigi Gui, letter to Francesco Dalla Zuanna, July 23, 1958, ACEC Archive (DB: ACEC 614): "ragioni di ancora maggior peso."

157 Commissione CEI per le Comunicazioni Sociali [CEI's Committee for Social Communication], minutes of the meeting held on April 27-28, 1965 at the Domus Mariae, Rome, ACEC Archive (DB: ACEC 984): "nella sua qualità di presidente della Commissione nazionale di revisione, [...] sulla gravità della situazione morale del cinema italiano e sulle cause che la determinano."

the current system for pre-emptive censorship be overturned, will ensure the preservation of morals [...] through the appropriate intervention of the magistracy."[158]

The new law and the subsequent weakening of film censorship motivated Angelicchio to consider the possibility of agreeing with the abolition of State censorship, so as to hand it over to the magistracy, from 1963. On January 18, 1964 he wrote to Siri, denouncing the

> total inefficacy of current regulations that, as you may well remember, were the result of a political compromise within the DC itself. In particular, the very composition of review committees, where the producers' interests were massively represented [...] is such that the law remains unenforced and contradictory, so much so that 'decency' [...] is not preserved, not even by resorting to its legal meaning, which limits judgment to the sphere of obscenity. At this stage, we should seriously consider promoting a form of legislative revision whereby, in order to safeguard the protection of minors, the moral order of entertainment should be handed over to the magistracy, thus removing censorship from the prerogatives of executive powers, which have proven unable to ensure this fundamental act of defense, and which are more susceptible to political and moral influences from outside.[159]

---

158 DB: ACEC 984: "rileva che quasi certamente il Partito Socialista Italiano e tutto lo schieramento laicista, proporranno la denuncia dell'attuale ordinamento censorio chiedendo "tout court," come già per il teatro, la completa abolizione della censura per il cinema. Occorrerà in proposito essere vigilanti e tener pronti dei controprogetti legislativi. In questa eventualità si rende necessario predisporre studi e soluzioni che tenendo conto anche di un eventuale superamento dell'attuale sistema della censura preventiva assicurino la tutela del buon costume [...] per efficaci interventi della Magistratura."

159 Francesco Angelicchio, letter to Giuseppe Siri, January 18, 1964, CEI Archive (ACEI 173): "assoluta inefficacia delle disposizioni vigenti, le quali, come ben ricorderà, risultarono frutto di un compromesso politico nella stessa sede democristiana. Soprattutto la composizione delle Commissioni di revisione, con la presenza massiccia degli interessi dei produttori, [...] rende purtroppo inoperante e contraddittoria l'applicazione della legge, al punto che lo stesso 'buon costume' [...] non viene praticamente salvaguardato neppure secondo l'accezione penalistica che restringe il giudizio alla sfera dell'osceno. Al punto in cui siamo c'è veramente da considerare l'opportunità di farci promotori di una revisione legislativa che, salvaguardando la tutela dei minori [...]

The Catholic world, most probably with the Secretariat of State's approval, drafted a *Proposta di aggiornamento della legge sulla revisione degli spettacoli cinematografici* [*Proposal to Update the Review Law Concerning Films*], which proposed the abolition of censorship in view of one very simple consideration: "We must acknowledge that the means of censorship have proven totally incapable of fulfilling the aims for which they were established, that is, its pre-emptive action; in actual fact they have even complicated the enforcement of control."[160] This argument is structured on one main premise and three further points. The premise is an awareness of the loss of control of the administration of censorship. The three further points have a convincing logic.

Point one: censorship has failed. Four years have passed since *La dolce vita*, the watershed in this story. On that occasion, the film was considered to be undeniably a work of art, which made it possible for themes that had previously been repressed to receive the seal of approval from the censorship board. Fellini's film was the work of an avant-garde director who paved the way for the ground army of Italian cinema, "which is nowadays more than ever engaged," as we read in the aforementioned *Proposal*, "in a [...] challenge to appeal to the lowest human instincts and to represent extreme erotic situations."[161]

Point two: not only does censorship fail to do what it should, but it also hinders other people from doing it. According to the *Proposal* drafted by the Catholics, "the magistracy has intervened

---

affidi alla Magistratura [...] la protezione dell'ordine morale in materia di spettacolo, sottraendo così la censura alla competenza del potere esecutivo che si è dimostrato incapace di assicurare questa essenziale difesa, e che più facilmente è suscettibile di influsso politico e morale esterno."

160 Project enclosed in Angelo Dell'Acqua, letter to Francesco Angelicchio, April 22, 1964, CEI Archive (DB: ACEI 55). A copy of the project is also preserved at the ACEC Archive (DB: ACEC 152): "Dobbiamo [...] riconoscere che lo strumento censorio si è rivelato all'attuazione pratica assolutamente incapace di realizzare quei fini di prevenzione per cui era stato istituito ed ha anzi reso più difficile perfino la realizzazione del fine repressivo."

161 DB: ACEI 55; ACEC 152: "impegnato oggi – si legge nella già citata *Proposta di aggiornamento* scritta dai cattolici – come non mai in una [...] gara a sollecitare gli istinti più bassi dell'uomo e a rappresentare situazioni erotiche sempre più spinte."

only on exceptional occasions, since, rightly or wrongly, it did not feel directly or primarily responsible for the protection of its community in this area, there being another public body which sought to preserve decency, and which had been established with this very aim."[162]

Point three: "It therefore would seem productive to suppress an institute that has so little merit, and defer to the magistracy – which can provide greater guarantees in terms of independence, competence and efficacy – the duty to review all cinematographic films and ascertain as to whether they violate fundamental rights and are therefore sanctionable by law."[163] N.b.: all films. This had to be done in advance, before the screening. Pre-emptive censorship would therefore leave through the door and sneak back in through the window. The difference lay in the fact that, in the Catholics' *Proposal*, censorship would no longer be administered by representatives of the profession. Producers would have to send magistrates "a copy of their films fifteen days before its screening date."[164] Handing over prevention to magistrates might appear contradictory, but it was promptly justified: "In cases such as these, doctrine refers to 'attempted crimes'. There is no doubt that whoever produces cinema does so with the aim of distributing it, and this aim becomes even clearer when the producer is forced to send a copy to the public prosecutor."[165]

---

162 DB: ACEI 55; ACEC 152: "l'autorità giudiziaria ha solo eccezionalmente preso iniziative in questo campo non sentendosi, a torto o a ragione, direttamente e primariamente investita della tutela della collettività in questo settore per il fatto che altro organo pubblico creato specificamente per questa finalità operava per la tutela del buon costume."

163 DB: ACEI 55; ACEC 152: "sembra pertanto utile la soppressione di un istituto che tante poche benemerenze ha da vantare ed il deferimento all'autorità giudiziaria – che dà maggiori garanzie di indipendenza, di competenza e di efficacia – dell'esame di tutte le pellicole cinematografiche per accertare se esse violino diritti fondamentali penalmente sanzionati."

164 DB: ACEI 55; ACEC 152: "una copia della pellicola 15 giorni prima della programmazione."

165 DB: ACEI 55; ACEC 152: "La dottrina parla in proposito di reati a consumazione anticipata. Non è dubbio che chi produce un film lo fa al fine della diffusione, fine questo che non può essere assolutamente dubbio nel momento in cui si giunge a presentare copia d'obbligo all'ufficio del PM."

Catholics therefore devised an extraordinary diversion tactic: precisely by meeting the demands that the front for the freedom of expression had been soliciting for a long time, the Catholics aimed to re-establish control over censorship through new means. This tactic seems to have been successful: in a joint document signed by the DC and the PSI in October 1965, the two major parties in government agreed that public censorship should be abolished.[166] However, while the two fronts apparently agreed on this fundamental step, they soon realized that this as driven by radically different motives. For this reason they would end up defending an imperfect machine, one which nobody liked, but which nevertheless served to constrain the actions of the enemy.

There is a general tendency to believe that censorship is the target of a conflict, between people defending freedom of expression and those defending neo-medieval control of information. In fact, the positions of the two sides often overlapped from a tactical point of view, and censorship became the negotiating middle-ground. Censorship was established in the second decade of the twentieth century on the request of film producers directly, who sought to elude the discretionary power of prefects and chiefs of police. Fifty years later, it continued to mitigate repressive actions.

12. *Film Reviews for Parish Movie Theatres*

The second line of action implemented by Catholics to censor obscenity consisted in reviewing films by its own means. *Vigilanti Cura* entrusted a National Office in every Catholic country to review every distributed movie, classifying them from a moral point of view. In Italy this activity was conducted by the CCC (under the supervision of first ACI and subsequently CEI) with great zeal, especially during the post war period, to such an extent that it has been defined as "parallel censorship."[167]

---

166 Document agreed upon by members of the DC and of the PSI, on October 22, 1965, ACEC Archive (DB: ACEC 502).

167 Giacomo Manzoli, "La censura parallela. Il Centro Cattolico Cinematografico," in *Italia Taglia* ed. by Tatti Saguineti (Ancona/Milano: Editori Associati, 1999), p. 233.

In fact the process of Catholic film reviewing was strictly connected to administrative censorship from 1947 when, with "highly confidential measure,"[168] Andreotti authorized two CCC representatives to sit on State censorship boards. A letter written in December 1947 by Ferdinando Prosperini allows us to establish a *terminus post quem* to date the beginning of a practice which explains how the CCC succeeded in reviewing the majority of films distributed in Italy at that time: "Finally good news: just today (but please, don't let it leak, otherwise someone will be happy to put a spoke in our wheels) we have made a deal with the General Film Office [...] for our participation in the meetings (that is, in the screenings) of the State Censorship Board, as viewers. [...] There's an achievement!"[169]

When Angelicchio was nominated Ecclesiastical Consultant of the Ente dello Spettacolo, he sought advice from his predecessor. In his response, Galletto outlines to him the "way in which the Review Committee worked during the twelve years of my office."[170] Not only does this valuable document thus allow us to grasp the precise terms of the deal between Andreotti and the CCC. In fact it also indicates the reason why, at a certain point, there was a perceived need to distinguish between pre-emptive and final reviews: "All films destined to be screened in public cinemas were first viewed on the government censorship board (courtesy of the Ministry) by our lay board members (normally two). This was indeed a privilege (albeit not entirely legal) compared to other countries; one which allowed us to map out all of the films before

---

168 Giulio Andreotti, letter to Giovanni Battista Montini, November 9, 1948, Giulio Andreotti Archive at the ASILS, envelope 178 (DB: ASILS 224): "provvedimento riservatissimo."

169 Ferdinando Prosperini, letter to Francesco Dalla Zuanna, December 5, 1947, ISACEM Archive, Prosperini papers, envelope 1, folder 5 (DB: ISACEM 98): "finalmente una buona notizia: proprio oggi (ma non la lasci trapelare, se no qualcuno ci mette i classici pali fra le ruote) abbiamo concluso con la Direzione Generale della Cinematografia [...] per la nostra partecipazione alle sedute (cioè alle visioni) della Commissione Ministeriale di Censura, come spettatori. [...] È veramente un successo."

170 Albino Galletto, letter to Francesco Angelicchio, 1961, ACEC Archive (DB: ACEC 176): "il funzionamento della Commissione di revisione durante i 12 anni della mia Consulenza Ecclesiastica all'Ente dello Spettacolo."

they were distributed. After the screening, the lay board members had to communicate their pre-emptive (and therefore indicative) opinion to the Secretariat of the Board of Review. Within three days, they had to send in a report containing a synopsis of the film along with their aesthetic and moral evaluation, typed out on the appropriate form. Films viewed at the Ministry were subsequently solicited from the various production companies, and reviewed by ecclesiastical members in the CCC's theatre."[171]

The roles were evidently well defined. The reviewing process proper was carried out by "ecclesiastical members," while the lay members' opinion was considered as merely pre-emptive, pending approval (or the lack thereof) from the clergy. Paradigmatic in this sense is the case of *La dolce vita*: lay members saw the film together with the administrative censors and declared it "not recommended" (but not "excluded"). Between the viewing by lay members and the publication of the final report, the film was screened in the CCC's movie theatre in the presence of Galletto, who then revised the preliminary indication on the film from "not recommended" to "excluded."[172]

While it is possible that, in the case of *La dolce vita*, the two lay CCC members may have been influenced by the other members of the administrative censorship board which hosted them, the contrary is also possible: in many cases the CCC members may just as well have influenced the State's censors. Informing Montini in 1948 of this "highly confidential measure," Andreotti specified: "I have authorized (through a highly confidential measure, known

---

171 DB: ACEC 176: "Tutti i film destinati alle pubbliche sale venivano anzitutto visionati in sede di censura governativa (per cortese concessione del competente Ministero) da Commissari laici (normalmente due). Si tratta di una situazione di privilegio (anche se non strettamente legale) rispetto agli altri paesi; situazione che consente di reperire alla fonte tutti i film, prima che siano messi in programmazione. I Commissari laici, dopo la visione di un film, dovevano comunicare subito per telefono alla Segreteria della Commissione di revisione il giudizio preventivo (e cioè orientativo) da loro dato. Entro tre giorni dovevano inviare una relazione con la trama del film, la valutazione estetica e quella morale, scritta su apposito formulario. I film visionati al Ministero venivano quindi richiesti alle rispettive Case Cinematografiche e revisionati collegialmente nella saletta del CCC dai Membri Ecclesiastici."

172 On these events, see Tomaso Subini, "L'arcivescovo di Milano e 'La dolce vita'," *Bianco e Nero*, a. LXXI, n. 567, May-August 2010.

only to the most trustworthy managers of relevant offices) the continuing participation of two representatives from the CCC in all sessions of the Review Committee, explicitly agreeing on the fact that, although they will not be allowed to cast a vote, their opinion will be taken into consideration; and in any case they will inform me every time a decision is made that they do not consider morally satisfactory."[173] The influential power of the representatives from the CCC must clearly not be underestimated.

To what extent could this measure remain truly confidential? What was the real extent of the "invisibility policy" which became the hallmark of Andreotti's office? According to Luigi Chiarini, "while having control to the tiniest detail on film policy, in the world of cinema Andreotti represented the Great Invisible, the Authority, his Highness; in other words a power that sat well above the contemptible and mortal hassle of the film industry, which appeared only on very rare, special occasions."[174] In much the same way, Lorenzo Quaglietti underlines how Andreotti would move behind the curtain, relying on men that he himself had put into positions of power.[175] A document preserved at the ACEC archive indicatively provides further evidence for this portrait. It is a note about the aforementioned arrangement, written by a someone at the CCC: "To avoid the situation where the State censorship board may express a positive judgment on morally negative films, the CCC members present shall inform – promptly and strictly <u>confidentially</u> – Dr. Del Ciglio of their negative opinion, so that the board can proceed to a more accurate review of the film."[176]

---

173 DB: ASILS 224: "Ho autorizzato (con provvedimento riservatissimo, e noto solo ai più fidati dirigenti dei competenti uffici) la costante partecipazione di due rappresentanti del Centro Cattolico Cinematografico a tutti i lavori delle Commissioni di revisione, con la esplicita intesa che, pur non potendo essi esercitare un diritto di voto, il loro parere sarebbe stato tenuto nella debita considerazione; e comunque essi possono informare lo scrivente ogni qualvolta stia per essere adottata una decisione che non sembri moralmente soddisfacente."

174 Luigi Chiarini, *Cinema quinto potere* (Bari: Laterza, 1954), p. 84.

175 Lorenzo Quaglietti, *Storia economico-politica del cinema italiano 1945-1980* (Roma: Editori Riuniti, 1980), p. 52 ss.

176 *Risultati dell'incontro col dr. Del Ciglio* [Outcome of the meeting with Del Ciglio], November 9, 1948, ACEC Archive (DB: ACEC 756): "Ad evitare che la commissione ministeriale di Censura esprima parere favorevole su pellicole moralmente negative, sarà opportuno che gli osservatori

If the CCC board members disagreed with the State censors' judgment, they were not to voice their disagreement publicly, but only with Del Ciglio (Andreotti's personal secretary). The latter would then forward a warning to the board, who in turn would revise its decision according to more restrictive criteria. With this in mind, Catholic film review was much more than a mere parallel form of censorship: the documents we have quoted illustrate that in reality it merged with administrative censorship, influencing it in a devious yet concrete way (at least until 1958).

In addition to the CCC review board (supervised by the Ecclesiastical Consultant of the Ente dello Spettacolo and established at a national level), from 1953 onwards the Church established local Catholic committees. Their jurisdiction was restricted to certain films: those classified as "for all," "for all with discretion," "for adults" by the national review board, and thus admitted to parish cinemas. At that stage, the majority of films had already been labelled by national review board as "for adults with discretion," "not recommended" or "excluded" and thus blocked.

In the middle of the fifties, the Italian Catholics had implemented a complicated process of reviewing that was characterized by three different levels of intervention.

To be screened in a parish cinema a film had to pass the CCC review, which meant not being classified as "for adults with discretion," "not recommended" or "excluded."

The same film had then to undergo review by the regional board (which included several dioceses). If the CCC classified the film as "for all," there would normally be no problem at the local level. The regional review mostly addressed films that were "for adults," which were typically permitted only after some abridgment.

As explained in a 1955 circular letter, parish cinema's managers would then "have the strict obligation to proceed with the advised cuts (concerning scenes that should not be shown) and with

---

del CCC facciano conoscere tempestivamente e <u>riservatamente</u> al Dr. Del Ciglio il loro parere contrario, in modo che la commissione possa essere chiamata ad una più attenta revisione e valutazione della pellicola incriminata." Emphasis in the original text.

others, too, if necessary for specific reasons, bearing in mind that the managers' opinion can only be restrictive."[177]

It is worth re-emphasizing this latter part: the obligation concerned specifically the cuts recommended by the regional review board, though the priest-cum-manager of the parish movie theatre was free to make further edits, "if necessary for specific reasons." As a whole, therefore, Catholic censorship following a strict hierarchy of stages: the second could be more restrictive than the first and the third could be more restrictive than the second, but never the other way around. The regional review board could not admit a film blocked by the national review board (CCC); in the same way, the manager of the parish cinema could not allow what the regional review board had forbidden.

Establishing regional boards helped practically to make the relevant changes that were necessary to make the film screenable. If the report issued by the national review board required cuts in order to sanction the film for parish cinemas, the negotiating power that the CCC hoped its reports could wield would be diminished. With the publication of *Segnalazioni Cinematografiche*, the Church aimed to pressure production companies to improve their moral standards. For this reason, it was important to obviate the risk of two versions of the same film in circulation – one in commercial cinema, the other in parish cinemas. In Salvatore Canals' words: "allowing films to be corrected at the national level would diminish our negotiating power with film studios, since they have no interest in cutting their film for the entire market."[178] And yet this was what ultimately happened. Nevertheless, for strategic reasons, Catholic reviews had to take place at two different levels: nationally, impacting (at least theoretically) both commercial and parish movie theatres; and locally, where impact was limited to

---

177 Direzione Generale Opere Don Bosco, RE: Centro Salesiano Spettacolo Educativo, confidential circular letter, February 24, 1955, ACEC Archive (DB: ACEC 162): "è obbligo grave di fare i tagli suggeriti (scene da omettere) ed altri, se occorre, per ragioni particolari, ricordando che il giudizio del Direttore è ammesso solo in senso restrittivo."

178 Canals' opinion is reported in a document dated November 30, 1965, unsigned, preserved at the ACEC Archive (DB: ACEC 186): "ammettere in sede nazionale che i film siano correggibili ridurrebbe l'influenza diretta sulla produzione in quanto i produttori non avrebbero interesse a modificare il film per l'intero mercato."

parish cinemas. While national reviews were widely advertised, cuts required by regional reviews were confidential, and reports drafted by local commissions were considered for internal usage only.

In such a strictly regulated mechanism, films made "for adults with discretion" represented the real grounds for negotiation, within the Catholic world, between two different stances: one promoting an open and confident attitude towards the audience (after all, we should not forget that it consisted of adult viewers) and another characterized by constant and uncompromising closure. In 1960, the year of *La dolce vita*, the rank-and-file began demanding that films "for adults with discretion" be admitted to parish cinemas.[179] The demand was reiterated in 1966 and discussed, again, in 1967, in a meeting with the Secretary of the CEI Commission for Social Communication: things were beginning to change. Finally, on January 1, 1969, new regulations were introduced that allowed regional review boards to select films within the group "adults with discretion," under the condition that they should be amended to some extent.

Let us consider just one instance of how a regional committee worked. A useful instance is the regional review board of the dioceses of Emilia Romagna, which was established, somewhat belatedly, at the very time when films for "adults with discretion" were admitted to the local review process. The condition that would allow adults to watch Sergio Leone's *C'era una volta il west*, was to "dramatically shorten the love scene at the end of the seventh reel."[180] This is the most frequent kind of cut requested.

---

179 The ACEC Archive possesses an anonymous document drafted for a meeting with Carlo Maccari, which took place in Mondovì on January 30, 1967 (DB: ACEC 185). Among others, the document discusses the issue of "admission of AR in parish cinema," which is thus summarized: "request first submitted in 1960/reasons: raising the standard of film shows, more engag films and therefore more effective pastoral action/ request again presented in 1966, proposing some cautionary measures to admit AR in our theatres."

180 Commissione Regionale di Revisione dell'Emilia-Romagna [Emilia-Romagna regional review board], 1969, ACEC Archive (DB: ACEC 163). The regional review board of the dioceses of Lombardia arrived at same conclusion. See Commissione Regionale Spettacolo per le Diocesi Lombarde [Lombardia regional review board], 1969, ACEC Archive (DB: ACEC 535): "IV reel: delete the woman protagonist's line, where she says to the bandit 'lay me over the table...'; VI reel: shorten the scene

In 1969, the committee reviewed 53 films classified for "adults with discretion:" of these, 13 were not admitted. Of the remaining 40, 18 were admitted only for "urban adults" (rather than all adults) and 16 underwent the following cuts: "the scene where the protagonist finds himself in the girl's room;" "the scene of the German soldier in the prostitute's room;" "the scene where we see the general and the woman undressing in the tent;" "the scene where the landlady is seduced;" "the scene in which the doctor entertains himself with prostitutes;" "the two protagonists' scene on the train;" "the love scene between the commander and his female assistant;" "the two protagonists' love scene in the shed;" "the dialogue with the future bride;" "the bed scene;" "the scene with the doctor;" "the scene with the two protagonists' love effusions when locked inside the room;" "the scene with outlaws in indecent clothes, and their love effusions."[181] Only two interventions did not concern sexuality. This took place in 1969, when taboos related to pornography were about to subside.

13. *Three Different Groups of Catholics*

As Richard Webster remarked, in one of the first studies of the relations between Catholicism and Italian society in the twentieth

---

of violence on the female character'; IX reel: shorten as much as possible the sensual sequence of the woman and Frank in bed." / "IV rullo: togliere battuta della protagonista al bandito 'sbattetemi sul tavolo…'; VI rullo: abbreviare scena di violenza sulla donna; IX rullo: abbreviare il più possibile la sequenza sensuale della donna e Frank a letto."

181 Commissione Regionale di Revisione dell'Emilia-Romagna [Emilia-Romagna regional review board], 1969, ACEC Archive (DB: ACEC 505): "la scena in cui il protagonista si trova nella camera della ragazza;" "la scena del soldato tedesco nella camera della prostituta;" "la scena in cui si vede il generale e la donna che si spogliano nella tenda;" "la scena di seduzione della padrona di casa;" "la scena in cui il medico si intrattiene con una donna di vita;" "la superflua sequenza del balletto nel night;" "la scena che si svolge sul treno fra i due protagonisti;" "la scena d'amore con cui si conclude il primo tempo;" "la scena d'amore tra il comandante e l'ausiliaria;" "la scena d'amore dei due protagonisti nella capanna;" "il dialogo con la futura sposa;" "la scena sul letto;" "la scena con il medico;" "la scena di effusioni amorose dei due protagonisti chiusi in camera;" "la scena di effusioni amorose dei banditi in abbigliamento sconveniente."

century, "it is always a mistake to write of Catholics, in Italy or elsewhere, as a bloc. Within the general limits of obedience to the Holy See there is room for all but the most radical differences."[182] The field of social communication in post-war Italy saw the emergence of three groups of actors, which can be defined (i) on the basis of the connection between its members, that is to say, of the closeness of their relationships inasmuch as can be documented; (ii) on the basis of their cohesion, that is, the consistency of their positions on the main issues of film policy; (iii) on the basis of the distance between their own stances and theose of the other groups. In fact, we should speak of three 'poles' rather than groups, around which different people converged without following strict rules. The three poles can be defined as follows:

1. Catholics active in the Vatican as well as Italian ecclesiastical institutions (Gedda, Galletto, Lonero, Angelicchio, Taddei, etc.);
2. Catholics with governance responsibilities in Italian state institutions (Andreotti, Scalfaro, Ammannati, Rondi, etc.);
3. Catholics outside the institutions (Mazzolari, De Piaz, Turoldo, Fabbretti, Bedeschi, etc.), that have no institutional power but significant spiritual authority, and a long-term influence which would have concrete consequences in the years of Vatican II.

The reasons for conflicts between the three groups are easy to understand. Catholics active in ecclesiastical institutions (those belonging to the first group) had to drive the institutional Church and its political agenda, and therefore accept the inevitable compromises imposed by this responsibility. In a more dramatic way, the Catholics active in state institutions (those in the second group) had to negotiate dual identities as Catholics and as political leaders. Catholics outside the institutions (the third group), instead, were free from any institutional duties, and could

---

182 Richard Webster, *The Cross and the Fasces. Christian Democracy and Fascism in Italy* (Stanford: Stanford University Press, 1960); also published with the title *Christian Democracy in Italy* (London: Hollis & Carter, 1960), p. 20.

therefore raise idealist issues and avoid all forms of compromise. Their position allowed them to unmask the contradictions that characterized the first two groups. The price for their attitude was doubtless high with regard to setting a possible agenda for the present; still, the prestige to be gained in spiritual and religious terms was even higher.

The most significant compromises were, of course, made by Catholics working in Italian state institutions: Giulio Andreotti's film policy – which was the result of his daily negotiation between the General Film Office, Parliament and the Vatican – illustrates very clearly the dangerous contortionism that was required to deal with cinema as Catholic political leader.

What distinguished the three groups was the different measures used when negotiating their religious identity with the real world, on the one hand, and the conflict they experienced with other Catholics (due to that very difference) on the other. An interpretative model of this kind, therefore, accounts not only for the palpable demands for harsher censorship made by representatives of the first group to those of the second, but also for various related facts that would otherwise be hard to frame. I refer, for example, to the closing of the Corsia dei Servi Cineforum in Milan, a crucial site of dialogue for prominent members of the third group, thanks to an inspection ordered by the Vatican Secretariat of State after the publication of an openly anti-Andreottian interview with Camillo de Piaz; or to violent articles written by Primo Mazzolari, Lorenzo Bedeschi and Nazareno Fabbretti against *Don Camillo*. The scheme (which will be discuss in the next three sections) therefore allows us to account for a diversification of positions on crucial phenomena like censorship, religious cinema and Neorealism.

14. *Catholics in Ecclesiastical Institutions: "the Pope's Cinema" and the Baroque Model*

Between the end of the thirties and the beginning of the forties, when policies were implemented to support religious cinema and, on a more ambitious level, a genuine, Catholic production, the CCC started its first experiments, leading to the production of *Pastor Angelicus*. Watching the film now, one is amazed at the predominance of footage dedicated to the sacred art that characterized Christian Rome, and the Vatican in particular. However, this amazement subsides when considering the nature of the body that promoted these first experiments in production: the *Peregrinatio ad Petri Sedem*, established by Pius XI at the end of the 1933 Jubilee as a continuation of the Central Committee that administered the Jubilee. The Committee's mission was to organize the spiritual and material accommodation of the pilgrims that came to Rome to visit the Petrine See. The duty of its "Centro di studi e produzione cinematografica" (subsequently the CCC) was to shoot footage for *Jubilaeum* (1935, material lost). The close connection, at least in this initial phase, between the *Peregrinatio* and the CCC is attested by the fact that the two bodies had the same president and a shared budget.

In 1936, immediately following the dissemination of *Vigilanti Cura*, a new project started which was soon discontinued, probably due to Pius XI's worsened health. The project created a bridge between *Jubilaeum* and *Pastor Angelicus*, under the supervision of Giuseppe Pizzardo. The latter requested permission to shoot from the Governor of the Vatican, describing thus the aims of the film: "to spread the glories of the Roman Church and show the attractions of the Vatican and of the Sacred Apostolic Palaces, to excite in believers devotion and attachment to the Vicar of Jesus Christ."[183] *Pastor Angelicus* was also conceived within this framework, as a religious experience made possible by a mediated pilgrimage, that to excite positively the same internal reaction, that otherwise immoral cinema perverted. In Gedda's words: "Whoever sees the film cannot help but think of Catholics living far away, especially those who will never be able to come to Rome, save in their wishes."[184]

---

183   Giuseppe Pizzardo, letter to Camillo Serafini, October 13, 1936, Secretariat of State, S. RR. SS. Historical Archive, AA. EE. SS., Ecclesiastical States, position 445, folder 426, sheet 14r, quoted in Gianluca della Maggiore, *La Chiesa e il cinema nell'Italia fascista*, p. 199: "diffondere le glorie della Chiesa Romana e far conoscere le bellezze della Città del Vaticano e dei Sacri Palazzi Apostolici onde eccitare la devozione e l'attaccamento dei fedeli al Vicario di Gesù Cristo."
184   Luigi Gedda, "Pastor Angelicus," *Rivista del Cinematografo*, a. XV, nn. 11-

The verb "to excite" (from Latin *excitare*, to push outside) is used by Pizzardo with the meaning of "to arouse," "to provoke," "to stimulate," "to encourage," "to incite." "To excite," as intended by Pizzardo, therefore means to induce certain actions through a stimulus.

The expression used by Pizzardo (that is, "to excite devotion") has a long medieval tradition. Its first occurrence (to our knowledge) is in a passage of *Glossa ordinaria* (written between 1241 and 1263) to *Decretali* by Gregorio IX (1234) in which the Papacy distinguished between *ludos lasciviae* (prohibited) and *ludos compunctionis* (permitted), including within the latter the tradition of "repraesentare praesepe Domini [...] ad devocionem excitandam" [representing the Lord's manger to excite devotion] (*Glossa ordinaria*, lib. III, tit. I, cap. 12). The same expression is used by Aquinas in *Summa Theologiae* (1485) in reference to sacred music and theatre. The function of sacred music is spiritual edification. To the objection that sung words are less easy understand, Aquinas replies that the words are less important than the religious feelings aroused by music: "Et eadem est ratio de audientibus, in quibus, etsi aliquando non intelligant quae cantantur, intelligunt tamen propter quid cantantur, scilicet ad laudem Dei; et hoc sufficit ad devotionem excitandam" [The same is true of the hearers, for even if they do not understand what is sung, they understand why it is sung, namely, for God's honor, and this is enough to excite their devotion] (II-II 91.2).[185] Between the seventeenth and eighteenth centuries, the expression "ad devocionem excitandam" can be found in several treatises on music and theatre. Lamberd Alard, *De veterum musica*, Schleusinga, 1636, used it even in an internal title (cap. XVII): *Musicae melodiae ad devotionem excitandam.*

Devotional excitement is an effect that the Church began to exploit (not coincidentally) in the aftermath of the Council of Trent, together with the intimist penitential model based on the control on pleasure and the confession of lust: "Behind the

---

12, November-December 1942, pp. 121-22.

185 What devotion was for Aquinas was explained in a presentation by Carla Bino at the conference *Contemplata aliis trader. Lo specchio letterario dei frati predicatori*, held at the Convento di S. Maria Sopra Minerva on January 23-27, 2017 (the proceesings are forthcoming at the time of writing).

magnificence of Counter-Reformation Baroque lay the conviction that only the beauty of external works of art would appeal to man's sensibility enough to inspire an act of faith. In 1642, with the *Sacrosancta Tridentina*, Urban VIII stated that the aim of art was to 'increase cult and veneration, and to fuel devotion and piety'."[186] Indeed, during the Counter-Reformation, the Catholic Church adopted the strategy of using religious images not only to legitimate the Papacy as a secular power, but also to favour the emergence of sacred art, in the strict sense of the word. This strategy was designed and implemented first and foremost as a response to criticism coming from reformed churches: "The new doctrine of justification by faith alone made pious donations of or for images superfluous. The whole concept of the votive image collapsed, and with it the Roman church's claim to be an institution that dispensed grace and privileges visibly embodied in its relics and images."[187] While reformed churches embraced a desensualized religion ("The empty walls of the Reformed churches were visible proof of the absence of the 'idolatrous' images of the papists. They symbolised a purified, desensualised religion that now put its trust in the word),"[188] the Roman church, on the contrary, ended up increasingly sensualizing its religious message. The outcome of such a process was the grandiose period of the Baroque that inaugurated a new relationship with the beholder, who was welcomed into the work of art to live a sensorial experience.

Secular culture tends to consider art in its autonomy and therefore hinders a comprehension of the Baroque as we intend it here: that is, as a theoretical and ideological framework established first during that epoch, yet that centuries later would inform Catholic film patronage, too. While the autonomy of art can never be absolute, since art is always part of a wider context, this premise is nonetheless strenuously defended by art historians, who consider art's historical context as limited to the travels of the artists and the circulation of their works. These two facts have the advantage of being historically ascertainable, without

---

186 Lucetta Scaraffia, *Il giubileo* (Bologna: il Mulino, 1999), p. 74.
187 Hans Belting, *Likeness and Presence*, p. 15.
188 *Ibid.*, p. 458.

depriving the work of art of its autonomy. Much more dangerous the conditions that relate to patronage and the ways in which works of art were used. These, rather, are the very terms through which the Baroque is accused of being insincere, especially in writings inspired by Protestantism, which denounced artists for something that is crucial to our discourse: that is, of giving voice, with unprecedented efficiency,[189] to the Papacy's values.

The Baroque is an essentially Roman phenomenon, or rather, a phenomenon of "European opening"[190] that nevertheless had its centre in the Rome of Jubilees and the Counter-Reformation: "Speaking of a Baroque Italy or of a Baroque Europe is possible only if we consider not the entire artistic production of the period, but the part that relates to the artistic language elaborated in Rome."[191] Montanari's definition of the Baroque is based on three elements: 1) the centrality of the beholder, 2) whose senses are deceived, 3) through naturalist illusionism. The Baroque resumes the lesson of the Renaissance (where the beholders are invited to access the work through their gaze, captured by perspective[192]) though it pushes this process to extreme consequences. Thanks to a new, architecture-oriented notion of the work of art, the Baroque favoured the emergence of a more immersive, theatrical art, where the viewer is engaged not only through their gaze, but with their whole body: it is a sensual and "exciting" art.[193]

When Pizzardo highlighted "devotional excitement" within his request for permission to film to the Governor of the Vatican, he was returning to the tradition of the most effective form of

---

189 On the Papacy's artistic policy in the Sixteenth Century see Massimo Firpo, Fabrizio Biferali, *"Navicula Petri." L'arte dei Papi nel Cinquecento* (Roma-Bari: Laterza 2009).

190 Tomaso Montanari, *Il Barocco* (Torino: Einaudi, 2012), p. 11.

191 *Ibid.*, p. 12.

192 Hans Belting, *Florenz und Bagdad. Eine westöstliche Geschichte des Blicks*, C. H. Beck, München 2008; English trans. *Florence and Baghdad. Renaissance Art and Arab Science* (Cambridge, Mass./London: Belknap Press of Harvard University Press, 2011).

193 An emblematic instance is Bernini's Cornaro Chapel in Santa Maria della Vittoria (Rome), built between 1647 and 1651. Its central group of sculptures, in which Teresa of Ávila is transverberated by an angel, has become "the symbol of Baroque art as a whole." See Tomaso Montanari, entry n. 30.

art at the service of Catholic Church. However, this raises a clear question: is there any real evidence that *Pastor Angelicus* generated "devotional excitement"? What indications can we gather from the documents available?

With the intention of supporting propaganda on occasion of the electoral campaign that, in the early months of 1948, opposed the democratic front of Communists and Socialists to the Catholics led by Alcide De Gasperi, Gedda had four vans equipped with film projectors, speakers and microphones sent to southern Italy. Each van was run by a technician, whose job was to manage the projection, and by a trained propagandist, who was to follow up the film screening with a suitable conference and write reports containing evidence that the film was perceived as a devotional object, with the power to perform miracles. In the three months preceding the 1948 election, the vans visited around 130 areas,[194] mostly within the southern region of Lucania. The propagandist's report of the screening in Montalto Uffugo, a small village in the province of Cosenza, states for example that *Pastor Angelicus* triggered "a case that stunned everyone. While a Communist militant circulated among the crowd that filled the huge square [...], telling his followers not to give any sign of disapproval, the Secretary of the Communist Section, less intelligent than the former, said indecent words to one of his close companions and made a vulgar gesture when the majestic figure of the Holy Father appeared – and was welcomed by a thunderous ovation – which scandalized the good people. When he got home, he felt acute pain in his groin and his right hand was suddenly paralyzed. He has not been able to vote, and doctors fear that they will not be able to save him, since they suspect he has cancer. We are trying to save his soul, at least."[195]

---

194 For a complete list see Mario Casella, *18 aprile 1948. La mobilitazione delle organizzazioni cattoliche* (Galatina: Congedo, 1992), pp. 213-30.

195 Gaetano Mauro, letter to Presidenza Generale [General Presidency], April 23, 1948, ISACEM Archive, PG VI, envelope 54 (DB: ISACEM 42): "Un caso che ha sbalordito tutti. Mentre un Attivista Comunista andava in giro fra la folla che gremiva l'immensa piazza [...] dicendo ai suoi seguaci di non dare nessun segno di riprovazione, il Segretario della Sezione Comunista invece, meno furbo del primo, quando apparve la maestosa figura del S. Padre, fra gli applausi più fragorosi, disse delle parole indecenti ad un suo vicino compagno e fece un gesto poco bello

As mentioned earlier, when faced with the new sensorial experiences of cinema, secular culture felt the need to "negotiate a fruitful balance between the sensory shock produced by the medium and the social need to control and regulate it, at least by means of sublimation."[196] The secular world's engagement in the legitimization of artistic cinema aimed to "channel and exploit the power of sensory excitation [...] transfiguring the original and obscure core of *sensation seeking* films, that was typical of modern life, into something more controlled and contemplative: aesthetic sentiment."[197] In other words, the secular response to cinema sought to control sexual excitement by shifting it into an aesthetic dimension. The Catholic world, on the other hand, made no such concession: sexual excitement had to be countered with equally powerful devotional excitement. While the former strategy relied on a concrete negotiation with modernity, the latter, especially under Pius XI's and Pius XII's pontificates, was evidently maximalist, and related to modernity in an exclusively instrumental way. The aim of religious cinema, as it was designed and implemented by ecclesiastical leaders (and I stress this: by ecclesiastical leaders, sublimate not by the whole Catholic world) was to exploit the intrinsic excitement of cinema's embodied, simulative experience for the Church's specific purposes, that is, the exaltation of the Pope.[198]

Any attempt that did not fit within such framework opposed to the logics of "modernization without modernity."[199] The biggest failure, in this sense, was Gedda's attempt to go beyond *Pastor Angelicus*, that is, beyond a film which had been explicitly created for devotional excitement. In a policy document drafted in the first months of 1943, Gedda has explained how in the subsequent project, that would soon lead to the foundation of the Orbis,

---

notato dai buoni con indignazione. Appena tornato a casa lo sorprende un dolere acutissimo all'inguine e gli si assecca la mano destra. Non ha potuto votare ed i medici disperano di salvarlo perché pare si tratti di un cancro. Stiamo cercando di salvargli almeno l'anima."

196 Silvio Alovisio, *L'immagine prima della coscienza*, p. 88.
197 *Ibid.*, pp. 88-89.
198 Conversely, as we have seen, the attempt to exploit the potential of cinema to promote other models of sanctity, instead, was much more problematic.
199 Daniele Menozzi, "Cristianesimo e modernità," p. XXXV.

"besides a production that we may define 'official', and entrusted to the Catholic film company (i.e. propagandistic apostolate films) [...], we should envisage – and here lies the main point of the present document – productions made by another company [...] which – with the Church becoming major shareholder and controller – should produce films that, in spite of seeming profane [...], will be infused with Christian feelings [...]. These productions will be our Trojan horse into the enemy's field."[200] The following conflicts between the managers of the production companies established by Gedda, on the one hand, and Galletto, who feared that the real Trojan horse would be secular culture entering parish cinemas, on the other, are emblematic of the contradictions generated by the attempt to go beyond the model of film that sought devotional excitement.

Let us consider the case of *Fabiola*, the third movie (after *Daniele Cortis* and *La terra trema*) produced by Silvio D'Angelo with Catholic capital (Universalia). Its content and the persons involved sparked a debate around the film, which illustrates fruitfully the inherent contradictions in Catholic entertainment production. Two opposing ideas of *Fabiola* are described in a letter written by Vittorino Veronese (then President of Italian Catholic Action) to Giovanni Battista Montini (then substitute to the Vatican Secretariat of State):

> Galletto, who had personally seen *Fabiola* and communicated his negative judgment to the film producers, has since been pressure [...] for example by Earl Dalla Torre, who phoned him to announce his intention to resign from his position within the Società Film-Universalia if *Fabiola* should be classified as "for adults with discretion" by the CCC's Censorship Committee. [...] The

---

200 Programmatic document, presumably drafted by Luigi Gedda, 1943, ISACEM Archive, PG XV, envelope 2, folder 7 (DB: ISACEM 447): "Accanto alla produzione, che chiameremo ufficiale, fatta dagli organismi cattolici (film di propaganda e di apostolato) [...] si dovrà provvedere – ed è qui il perno di questo programma – ad una produzione eseguita da un altro organismo [...] il quale – assorbito nella sua maggioranza azionaria e controllato dai competenti organi della Chiesa – produca tutti quei soggetti che, pur sembrando di carattere profano [...], siano invece permeati di sentimenti cristiani [...]. Questa produzione dovrà essere il cavallo di Troia nel campo avversario."

screening of the film for the CCC's Censorship Committee was also attended by other consultants: I was there myself. We all agreed that the classification as "for adults with discretion" was right, far too generous [...]. The negative evaluation is due, in equal part, to the dangerous structure of the film's social arguments [...] and by the intolerable concessions to sensuality, lewdness, and the horrid. [...] At the end of the screening I was sadly and deeply disappointed about such a challenging yet missed opportunity, and for such an enormous technical and financial effort that has turned out to be so misplaced from a spiritual point of view.[201]

Classified as "for adults with discretion," and thus excluded from parish movie theatres, *Fabiola* is a good example of the vain ambitions in film production nurtured by the Catholics of the first group. Universalia survived only a few years more, which were characterized by an increasingly problematic relationship with the CCC.[202] The Church thus missed the opportunity to sublimate with art (as secular culture had done) cinema's sensory shock, fearing that such mediation would actually open a fracture that would let in the values of modernity. The sensory

---

201 Vittorino Veronese, letter to Giovanni Battista Montini, March 4,1949, ASILS, Vittorino Veronese papers, series Azione Cattolica Italiana, envelope 8, folder 62, subfolder 2 (DB: ASILS 345): "Galletto, avendo avuto in personale visione il film *Fabiola* ed avendo espresso ai produttori l'impressione negativa riportatane, è stato oggetto di pressioni [...] interessate fra le quali una telefonata del Conte Dalla Torre che – in via confidenziale [...] – gli annunciò la sua intenzione di dimissionare dalla Società Film-Universalia se il film *Fabiola* fosse stato qualificato 'per adulti con riserva' dalla Commissione di censura del CCC. [...] La visione del film da parte della Commissione di censura del CCC si è svolta [...] con l'intervento anche di altri consulenti: io stesso vi ho partecipato. Il giudizio è stato unanime nel ritenere che la classificazione 'per adulti con riserva' fosse da ritenere di stretta misura [...]. Il giudizio negativo è basato in equa parte fra la pericolosa impostazione della tesi sociale [...] e le intollerabili concessioni alla sensualità, alla lubricità e all'orrido. [...] Io sono uscito dalla visione del film con la pena profonda per un'occasione così impegnativa e così amaramente delusa e per l'enorme sforzo tecnico e finanziario così mal diretto dal punto di vista spirituale."
202 On the abandonment of production plans see Mariagrazia Fanchi, *The "Ideal Film,"* and Mariagrazia Fanchi, "Pastore di anime. Monde catholique e médias des années Cinquante aux années Soixante," in *Il cinema si impara? Sapere, formazione, professioni,* ed. by Anna Bertolli, Andrea Mariani and Martina Panelli (Udine: Forum, 2013).

shock could not be negotiated or transfigured; it could only be exploited. For this reason, the only films produced by Gedda that were met with positive reactions in ecclesiastical hierarchies were those that Gedda himself defined as 'propagandistic apostolate films', produced following the guidelines set by Pizzardo in the thirties, that is, those designed to excite devotion.

15. *Catholics in State Institutions: Gian Luigi Rondi and the Double Morals Logic*

Andreotti's strategies to achieve his goals, acting behind the scenes, are hard to reconstruct in detail. One is often forced to work with clues alone, as I have sought to do in reconstructing the stages of one of his most ambitious projects (which he shared with Morlion), that is, reforming Neorealism by grafting Christian content onto it. It is perhaps more productive, in terms of stable results, to follow the progress of another "Catholic active in Italian state institutions" (i.e., in the second group): Gian Luigi Rondi. In the shadows of his movements, we can distinguish the silhouette of his prompter from behind the scenes.

How did Rondi negotiate his identity as a Catholic, in relation to his institutual assignments? To answer this question, I have drawn from both archival sources and Rondi's diary, which was published very recently.[203] On October 18, 1949, Rondi wrote in his diary:

---

203 Gian Luigi Rondi, *Le mie vite allo specchio. Diari 1947-1997* (Roma: Edizioni Sabinae, 2016). In the preface, Rondi himself traces the origin of his diaries back to Andreotti's suggestions: "when he [Andreotti] saw me taking on the difficult oath of public life, he recommended I write a diary entry every night, 'because', he underlined, 'you'll certainly need it. Some events do vanish with time, details become confused, and you'll often have to clarify, to remember, speaking to other people, and this might not always happen in favourable times. Noting down everything, therefore, is in some cases almost a necessity'" (*ibid.*, p. 5). One wonders whether the political character of Rondi's diaries has changed with the passing of time, having been published when the author was still alive and under his supervision, meaning that he was able to review, veil and at times censor the texts. Part of their political drive has probably been lost for these very reasons. What remains is, in many regards, very interesting. However, Rondi's diary remains a tricky document, and one that should

Andreotti, who seems to be showing me that he's my friend, has
asked me to organize a symposium with a film journalists trade
union, to gain their support with some motions. I succeeded in
having them vote for these motions, and as a reward he had me
nominated to the jury at Venice. My first time! And at my age! But
then, to favour the co-productions with France that are underway,
he had Clouzot's *Manon* put in the running, and he let us
understand that he wouldn't mind if the film won the Golden Lion.
Done. Though actually the film has disappointed many people in
officially demure milieus, for its apparent immorality. Hence the
advice (which I received quite explicitly), to write that I had prized
art at an international festival but now, in Italy, censorship had to
perform its duty. Needless to say, this led to a general uproar, and
even a Jesuit magazine picked on me by denying the possibility of
two morals. And, secretly, I agree. But politics, apparently, functions
with different laws, and I'm just starting to realize this.[204]

Between these two laws – one of religion, the other of politics
– Rondi would always choose the latter, without hesitation. He
knew very well that they were mutually exclusive, the Jesuits
of the Centro San Fedele did not need to remind him of that.
Still, the lesson that Rondi learned on that occasion was that by
being shrewd one could justify any kind of compromise. The
description of the prize-giving process is illuminating in this
regard: Andreotti asked, Rondi executed. In fact, Andreotti's
ability to act on different fronts, pulling the strings from behind
the scenes was extraordinary: he was the one who had films win

---

be approached with caution. Rondi maintains that, writing his diary, he
"never thought that they might one day be read by someone other than
me" (*ibid.*, p. 6). But actually, a good many pages of this presumed diary
are the first drafts of texts that he published at a later stage: sometimes
they are just notes, written down quickly to be subsequently expanded
for publication in one of the many magazines with which Rondi
collaborated. Sometimes one has the impression of reading a genuine
record of conversations with actors and film directors; at others entries
are the outcome of long and elaborated reflections which are in no
way extemporary. Therefore, scholars working on Rondi's diaries are
constantly faced with the need to double check, by means of archival
evidence, each and every piece of information, in order to assess the
truth behind the passage in question.

204 *Ibid.*, p. 84.

prizes and be censored at the same time. And yet, officially, none of this was him. In a note dating from few months after the Venice episode (March 11, 1950), we read: "Been at Andreotti's. [...] He's recommended me to RAI president Ridomi, that I be nominated radio critic, and he's mentioned my name to Gonella, to help Giovanni Sangiorgi, with whom he has entrusted the establishment of a cultural foundation."[205] These brief mentions, dating back to the very early stages of Rondi's career, are significant enough to outline the uniqueness of his experience: we are in the presence of a young Catholic intellectual, who gained recognition in the cinema and TV institutions controlled by the DC thanks to his political relationship with Andreotti.

Having outlined Rondi's political position, at this point we can turn to a brief overview of his religious identity. Rondi's Catholicism took shape in two institutional contexts: Pius XII's Vatican (whose rituals are the object of extensive description in Rondi's diaries), and Jesuit spirituality. Rondi's religious zeal reached its peak in the mid-fifties: while this period is not covered in his diaries, significant evidence of that time is found in archival documents. The latter illuminate a very relevant event in Rondi's trajectory, that is, his attempt to join the Society of Jesus. He describes this process in a letter to Taddei, dated June 6, 1955: "Last year the Lord wanted to rescue me from murky lake, I obeyed, then I misunderstood his call and was tempted by vocation. When I finally succeeded in overcoming this, thanks to the Lord's help more than to my own endeavours, I was left with little or no reason to live. I realized that my original ambition of an apostolate within the Society of Jesus had faded: I still believed in it, but in a vague way, as though it had been part of the illusions that I had to overcome."[206]

---

205 *Ibid.*, p. 95. The reference is to the Fondazione Premi Roma.
206 Gian Luigi Rondi, letter to Nazareno Taddei, January 6, 1955, ANT (DB: ANT 105): "Un anno fa il Signore ha voluto tirarmi su dal lago tenebroso [...], io gli ho obbedito, poi ho frainteso e mi son fatta venire la tentazione della vocazione. Quando son riuscito a vincerla, più in grazia degli aiuti che il Signore mi ha dato che non per mio merito, me ne son rimasto lì senza più molte ragioni di vita [...]. Il disegno che avevo tracciato di un apostolato in Compagnia mi sembra quasi superato: ci credevo ancora, ma in modo vago, quasi anche quello avesse fatto parte delle illusioni che avevo dovuto vincere."

Once he had long since given up on the "temptation of a vocation," in the sixties, Rondi defined it as a "mystical infatuation."[207] This sort of 'ebbing phase' is evidenced in remarks of this sort: "Been to Father Gentiloni. I asked him to help me to mechanically perform the gestures of faith anyway, hoping, as St. Ignatius suggests, to regain faith in that way. No emotion, no sensibility."[208] Or: "Been to Mondragone to hold a *cineforum* on De Sica's *Tetto* for Frascati Catholic associations. These trips back to Mondragone always provide me with an occasion for reflection – and not always in positive terms – on myself. The times of my first spiritual exercises […]. The times […] of spiritual exercises with Father Rotondi and the conference-sermons for "a Better World." […] Father Bruno in Villavecchia and the solid spiritual comfort provided by good Father Mesini. The time, let us call it that, of Gian Luigi the 'glory of Catholic laity', as Gedda used to say."[209]

How did the world of cinema impact on Rondi's religious identity? And how did Rondi relate, more specifically, to religious cinema, i.e. a kind of cinema that, by centralizing religion as its key theme, interrogates the viewer's religious identity? The episode that best illuminates the compromises that Rondi had to make is concerns Ken Russell's *The Devils*. The first attempt to nominate Rondi as Director of the Venice Film Festival dates back to 1963, and the second one to 1966. At the time of the latter, Rondi writes: "Almost dawn at Rumor's. Andreotti told me about Venice. If we can get rid of Chiarini, the DC might recommend me…"[210] However, it was not until 1968 that the DC managed to get rid of Chiarini, thanks to the student protests. Then, when things cooled down, in 1971 (once he had been waiting for eight years) Rondi finally managed to be nominated Director. Though he was the official DC candidate, he was actually endorsed by all actors involved: from the socialist minister who nominated him, to the communist fraction that (as Rondi explains in detail in his diaries) obtained in return the election of Mario Gallo to the

---

207   Gian Luigi Rondi, *Le mie vite allo specchio,* July 8, 1963, p. 231.
208   *Ibid.,* January 18, 1963, p. 172.
209   *Ibid.,* April 20, 1963, p. 198.
210   *Ibid.,* July 29, 1966, p. 402.

presidency of the Ente di Gestione. A letter from Visconti prepared the ground within Leftist milieus, as Rondi writes: "Lunch [...] with Antonello Trombadori. [...] Says he will explain his position on my case to the Chief of the Cinema Department of his party, Napolitano. He will tell him that he endorses my nomination, because it is 'the best from a technical point of view'. He will also nudge Visconti into writing a letter to make this point."[211] This was the moment of the ultimate compromise: in fact, we might even suggest that the 1971 edition of the Festival was directed by Rondi together with the board that selected films under Visconti's guidance, as is further evidenced by a recently published letter. Visconti wrote to Rondi on July 27, 1971: "I know the Canadian production that you would like to screen for the press only.[212] It is not so bad, after all. Of course, it is somewhat distressing, but not more than *Devils*, which seems to me the most violent film so far [...]. It is a comedy that I saw two years ago on Broadway, and the film is definitely more moderate, compared to the play. But, I repeat, it is less upsetting than *Devils*. [...] I'm not in favour of dividing Venice into subfestivals: Venice I, Venice II etc."[213] The letter continued on with the same assertive tone, making it clear, during that year, that decisions would be taken jointly.

Still, Russell's film was not *Manon*. Not only did it raise decency issues – which could easily resolved through Andreottian shrewdness – but it was also problematic from a religious point of view, and in Venice there were not only "Catholics active in state institutions" (i.e. the second group), but also "Catholics active in ecclesiastical institutions" (i.e. the first group). Rondi solved what for him was a purely political problem by seeking institutional support from the Patriarch of Venice. His report reads as follows:

---

211 *Ibid.*, February 17, 1971, p. 460. On February 16, 1971, Visconti wrote a letter to Giorgio Napolitano, then in charge of the PCI Cultural Commission. The letter is preserved at the Gramsci Institute in Rome, in Luchino Visconti papers, series 16, subseries PCI Archive, UA 2.

212 *Fortune and Men's Eyes*, by Harvey Hart.

213 Luchino Visconti, letter to Gian Luigi Rondi, July 27, 1971, in Gian Luigi Rondi, *Tutto il cinema in 100 [e più] lettere*, ed. by Simone Casavecchia, Domenico Monetti and Luca Pallanch (Roma: Centro Sperimentale di Cinematografia/Edizioni Sabinæ, 2015), pp. 201-04.

The film was reported to the Festival Working Committee [...] through confidential messages sent to Franco Zeffirelli, Luchino Visconti, Vittorio De Sica [...]. An English copy of the film was sent to Rome at the end of June and viewed by the Working Committee almost in full force, and it gained everyone's consent [...]. Personally, I was bewildered; and yet, while I did not fail to voice my reservations and objections, I realized that the other members on the Committee [...] would not allow me to censor anything [...]. So I joined my colleagues in voting for the film in August; but when I went to Venice for the first time, I immediately sought out the Patriarch for advice, and informed him that the programme featured some films which I had not been able to oppose, since the entire Committee had accepted them, although this had inspired my perplexity.[214]

Relying on political support from the Patriarch, Rondi was better prepared to face the criticism that he was likely to receive. The harshest words of course came from "Catholics active in ecclesiastical institutions" (the first group):

Don Claudio Sorgi, representative of the Centro Cattolico Cinematografico Italiano, issued a protest that was published by the ANSA press agency, which was not restricted to a moral criticism of the film, but also contained a personal attack on me that read as follows: 'This severe episode might affect, from this very moment, our general opinion of the direction of this 32nd edition of the Festival. The political alchemy regulating nominations within Italian Cinematographic institutions is already deplorable in itself; all the more so – which really puzzles us – if the Catholics' seat should be taken by someone who, while bearing the title of Christian, actually demonstrates, in exercizing the very task with which he has been entrusted as a Catholic, to disregard the set of values that he is supposed to represent.[215]

To award the prize to *Manon* in 1949, Rondi had to comply with the double morals logic. He did so then by overcoming the personal resistances that he mentions in his diaries. This time, in 1971, there was no religious issue to be settled: the ground

---

214 Gian Luigi Rondi, *Le mie vite allo specchio*, September 15, 1971, pp. 475-76.
215 *Ibid.*, pp. 476-77.

for negotiation was solely institutional: "The following day, in the afternoon, I spoke with the Patriarch on the phone. He told me that he had talked, over lunch, with Father Sorgi and that he had voiced his discontent over the personal attack against me."[216] The matter was settled, therefore, by shifting the discourse from principles and values to political opportunity. This, however, did not hold for the Catholics from the Centro Studi Cinematografici (a Catholic cultural film association) led by Sorgi. After a few weeks, the Centre voiced its discontent over the confirmation of the "former glory of Catholic laity" as Director of the Venice Film Festival. As we can read in the Centro's minutes (signed, among others, by Francesco Ceriotti, Marco Bongioanni, Giuseppe Fossati and Emilio Mayer): "The C.S.C.'s stance against Rondi's nomination as Director of the Venice Film Festival is made explicit."[217]

16. *Catholics outside the Institutions: Religious Cinema in the Opinion of Nazareno Fabbretti*

The meaning of religious cinema, in the opinion of "Catholics active in ecclesiastical institutions" (the first group), is clearly represented by the CCC's list of "films that have a religious character." What it meant for "Catholics active in state institutions" (the second group), is a question to be asked to Gian Luigi Rondi, who always addressed the issue from a political point of view. In 1950 he collaborated on the production of *Francesco giullare di Dio*, knowing very well that Rossellini certainly was not involved at a religious level, but that the film served the political project of the Christianization of Neorealism. Pasolini's *Il Vangelo secondo Matteo*, when it was released years later in 1964, was met with the opposite reaction from Rondi, as attested by an entry in his diary written after its screening at the Venice Film Festival: "I am perplexed by Pasolini's *Il Vangelo secondo Matteo*. [...] Audience at the Patriarch's. Chiarini not there (he does not

---

216 *Ibid.*, p. 477.
217 Consiglio federale del C.S.C., Milan, October 16-17, 1971, proposed minutes, ACEC Archive (DB: ACEC 1783).

mingle with priests), while not only many priests present but also many "official" Catholics, members of several […] international organizations. Almost all of them in favour of Pasolini and his film. […] Therefore twice perplexed. Especially when I think of Angiolillo and of the spite he always vents on Pasolini. Once he said: "I accept faggots, I even accept communists, but a communist faggot…never, never!"[218]

Ultimately, each of the groups had its own agenda, which corresponded to a specific list of good films. Let us consider, for instance, the different stance that the groups took on two emblematic films – *Francesco giullare di Dio* and *Don Camillo* – both classed as having "religious character" on the CCC's list (the first group) and both rejected, without any hesitation, by "Catholics outside the institutions" (the third group). The vicissitudes of the third group are more difficult to reconstruct, for obvious reasons. It was a dissenting group that had not been institutionalized, and forced to act covertly. As such we know very little of its true composition nor of its internal debate. However, we know for certain that one of its meeting places was the Corsia dei Servi Cineforum in Milan (led by Camillo De Piaz, David Maria Turoldo, Nazareno Fabbretti and Morando Morandini). Andreotti managed to have it closed, by reporting a reckless interview to the Secretariat of State in which Dal Piaz had dared to comment: "The famous 'dirty linen'? Seeing them drying in the open air is for me a great joy. Especially since dirty linen is never really country-specific."[219]

At stake was Neorealism. Neorealist films, with their focus on social conflict, were dangerous and to be condemned, especially when "heavily exploited by the Left," that is, "when they became the hallmark of political conflict, which, during the Cold War, could take on menacing tones."[220] Evidence provided by Andreotti, even after many years, emphatically supports the claim that Neorealism was perceived by "Catholics active in state institutions" (the second group) as dangerous, first and foremost

---

218 Gian Luigi Rondi, *Le mie vite allo specchio*, September 4-5, 1964, p. 345.
219 Antonio Pitta, Ettore Capriolo, penultimate page.
220 Aldo Bernardini, *Cattolici e cinema italiano*, in *Bianco e nero. Gli anni del cinema di parrocchia*, ed. by Gianfranco Gori and Stefano Pivano (Rimini: Maggioli, 1981), p. 64.

from a political point of view: "I [...] gave a political interpretation and my feeling was that the whole of Italian cinema was drifting towards the left."[221]

Andreotti understood quickly that the best approach to waging war against Neorealism was laterally, that is, by proposing alternative models, since at that moment Neorealism had established itself at international level and a frontal attack would prove self-defeating with the media. For this reason Andreotti waited for five years before officially declaring war. In 1948, his strategy consisted in a slow campaign of attrition. In order to be subverted from within, Neorealism had first to be blandished: "We must encourage," Andreotti stated, answering a question in parliament in November 1948, "genuine, moral and at the same time alluring productions, which could fit into the current of new Italian cinema that I have just mentioned, that are a credit to our national cinema and are envied abroad. Therefore, I think our task is to give value to Neorealism, by having this formula take on a spiritual significance, too, which I believe is possible."[222] The actions taken by "Catholics active in state institutions" (the second group), under Andreotti's guidance, alternated censorship and intimidation with a series of attempts to promote alternative models that could combine certain aspects of Neorealism with "spiritually inspired" content. These demands were met by films written by Morlion and directed by Rossellini between the end of the forties and the beginning of the fifties.

Andreotti revealed his true intentions only in 1952, finally adopting an explicit stance when reprimanding De Sica for "rendering a very bad service to his country," leading "the world [...] to believe that the Italy of *Umberto D.* is that of the the mid-twentieth century."[223] With this comment Andreotti translated into political language (in a weekly DC magazine, that is, i.e. in the appropriate venue), in the best political moment (that is, when Neorealism had already lost its drive) the thoughts and

---

221 Paolo Conti, "Andreotti: Rondi? Bravo a stroncare 'Mani sulla città'," interview with Giulio Andreotti, *la Repubblica*, June 6, 2008.

222 Giulio Andreotti, "I film italiani nella polemica parlamentare," *Bianco e Nero*, a. IX, n. 10, December, 1948, pp. 62-63.

223 Giulio Andreotti, "Piaghe sociali e necessità di redenzione," *Libertas*, n. 7, February 28, 1952, p. 5.

reflections that had already been widely circulating in those ecclesiastical institutions engaged in the field of cinema like the CCC or the ACEC (the first group). Let us consider only one example, taken from a the weekly of a curia: "America sends us optimistic films and rightly so, since they want to let us know that over there everything is going right, even when it is going badly. Still, considering the fact that one should not wash his dirty linen in public, we should do exactly as they do: improve from within, and keep the less nice things to ourselves."[224] Of course, the point about not washing one's dirty linen in public was just a pretext. The "Catholics active in ecclesiastical institutions" (the first group) appealed to the inconvenience in representing "less nice things" in order to gain negotiation power with "Catholics active in state institutions" (the second group), but their primary concern was moral rather than political. We find an excellent instance of the kinds of concerns that "less nice things" generated for "Catholics active in ecclesiastical institutions" (the first group) in Albino Luciani's words (ten years after): "Because of the original sin, we all act as though keeping a piglet on a lead. You can probably imagine what tricks the piglet will play on the farmer who keeps him on a leash. Just imagine, when they pass by a bush of cyclamens or carnations, the piglet won't even see them; however, when they pass a ditch, the piglet will jump in it, growling merrily, and if the farmer doesn't tug at the lead, his little beast will come back to him all soiled and covered with mud. [...] I just meant that our soul sometimes tends to behave like the piglet: it does not see noble, beautiful things but it throws itself, driven by desire, into things that are not good, and it is the tug of our will that must restrain it and keep it clean. And when it comes to cinema: one has to make a sacrifice and stay home, since it is a ditch, from which one returns with a soiled soul."[225]

A few days after the publication of the open letter to De Sica, the "Catholics active in ecclesiastical institutions" (the first group) thanked Andreotti for his belated but nevertheless

---

224   Carlo Trabucco, "Se ci rubano la bicicletta la colpa è di De Gasperi," *L'Eco di Bergamo,* May 20, 1950.

225   Albino Luciani, "Paterne esortazioni dei nostri vescovi," *Informazioni della Commissione Regionale dello Spettacolo per le Diocesi Venete,* anno IV, n. 1, January 1961 (DB: PER 235).

clarifying stance in an article signed by Mario Milani (one of the managers of the consortium of Lombard parish cinemas) in *Nuovo Cittadino*, the daily of the Genoan diocese. The article, entitled "Cinema italiano nemico della patria" [Italian cinema, enemy of the nation], reads: "We are not talking about the aesthetic quality of movies that have enjoyed varied success. We are talking about their content: and we must say straight out that the content of the Italian films labelled as 'Neorealist' has been quite dirty. In fact, this quality seems to represent more and more the essential, unchangeable feature of Neorealism. Read 'Neorealism', understand 'Italian misery', 'Italian criminality', 'Italian filthiness'. This is how far have we come."[226]

However, this reaction to Andreotti's letter was not ubiquitous in entire Catholic world. Here I refer, of course, to the Catholics belonging to the third group, among whom the promoters of the Corsia dei Servi Cineforum in Milan: Camillo De Piaz, David Maria Turoldo, Nazareno Fabbretti and Morando Morandini. Parallel to his activity at the Cineforum, the latter was in charge of the cinema column of the *Ordine*, the daily of the curia of Como. He was therefore able to provide his daring (in view of the venue) interpretation of Neorealism: "We often read letters that reprimand our directors for providing the foreign public with what is considered a slanderous image of our country. Well, such an opinion is hypocritical: the truth – not only the material truth but also the human truth – of our films has been highly appreciated abroad."[227] The small group of subverters that gathered around De Piaz entrusted young Morandini with the task of responding to Milani's article in the pages of the Como curia daily: "We will not deny it: there are miserable people. But many other people – and probably many more still – may have thought: there's someone who has the guts to confess, there's someone whose faith in life is so strong that it can also be narrated in its bleakest and saddest aspects and episodes."[228]

---

226 Mario Milani, "Cinema italiano nemico della Patria," *Il Nuovo Cittadino*, April 8, 1952; then *L'Ordine*, May 28, 1952.

227 Morando Morandini, *L'Ordine*, December 19, 1951.

228 Morando Morandini, "Patrie vere e Patrie false," *L'Ordine*, May 28, 1952.

As we have seen, Andreotti (or someone on his behalf) succeeded in having the Corsia dei Servi Cineforum closed down, by reporting the pro-Neorealism interview with Camillo De Piaz to the State Secretariat. The same De Piaz provided his own account of the vents: "In an interview for our friend Guido Aristarco's *Cinema Nuovo* I defended Neorealist cinema. If I remember well it was February 1952. Andreotti, who was then Undersecretary to the Presidency of the Council, thought that Neorealism misrepresented Italian society, and he set the State Secretariat in motion. The Vatican therefore sent Prior General of the Servite Order Alfonso Benetti, who came on an exceptional canonical visitation to inquire about me: I was the victim of a typical collusion between political and ecclesiastical power."[229] De Piaz's reconstruction actually requires some corrections. In the controversial interview with *Cinema* – not *Cinema Nuovo* – De Piaz did not limit himself to "defending Neorealism" but in fact he also violently attacked *Francesco giullare di Dio*, voicing an explicit criticism of Morlion's work and of Andreotti's policy. In fact, his attack was addressed to "Catholics active in state institutions" (the second group), and their plan to re-found Neorealism: "When inspired and under a good star, Rossellini is a great director; but this [*Francesco giullare di Dio*] is a bad and ambiguous film, as always happens when a certain culture and a certain society deals with themes such as Franciscanism and the likes […]. Rossellini should have the decency not to lecture us on the Franciscan message, and his complaisant ecclesiastical advisors should be brave enough not to let him be so self-conceited. He's completely incapable of embracing that message in a spiritual and lively way!"[230]

While *Francesco giullare di Dio* was considered by "Catholics active in the ecclesiastical institutions" (the first group) suitable film for screening in parish movie theatres, and it was appreciated by the "Catholics active in state institutions" (the second group) as a political occasion to Christianize the contents of Neorealism, the film was judged negatively by "Catholics outside institutions" (the

---

229 Camillo De Piaz in Giuseppe Gozzini, *Sulla frontiera. Camillo De Piaz, la Resistenza, il Concilio e oltre* (Milano: Scheiwiller, 2006), p. 137.
230 Antonio Pitta, Ettore Capriolo, pp. 353-354.

third group), who challenged its significance from a genuinely religious point of view.

Andreotti was not wrong when he identified a criticism of his policy in De Piaz's interview, and therefore reporting the fact to the Vatican Secretariat of State – who in turn got in touch with the leaders of the Servite order. This resulted in the closure of the Corsia dei Servi Cineforum and in a potentially successful, internal, opposing faction being crushed in its very early stages. Consequently De Piaz's work around cinema came to an end. Morandini understood that if he wanted to be a professional critic he would have to change milieu. Fabbretti and Turoldo continued to pursue their interest in cinema, and very often got into trouble as a result. The group, overall, disbanded.

Don Camillo is another emblematic film that signals how the three different groups positioned themselves in the field of cinema. If the aim of "Catholics active in state institutions" (the second group) was to replace Neorealism with politically harmless films, *Don Camillo* proved to be fit for the purpose. We know that the project of *Don Camillo* took its first steps precisely in the second group. Indeed, it was Morlion who wrote the first treatment of the film.[231] The "Catholics active in state institutions" sided with this film to the point of defending it from a presumed attack from the Holy Office.[232] On behalf of Andreotti (who received a copy of the letter), Nicola De Pirro informed the Vatican Secretariat of State, Angelo Dell'Acqua, of Rizzoli's fears of a possible "intervention by the Holy Office regarding *D. Camillo*."[233] Dell'Acqua was asked to take "those steps that he deemed right, considering the huge interests revolving around the film, which are not just of a material nature [...] but also concern the peculiar political moment (elections) that we

231 Félix Morlion, Note per una eventuale elaborazione di un soggetto cinematografico tratto dal volume "Don Camillo" di G. Guareschi [Preliminary notes for a screenplay inspired by Guareschi's *Don Camillo*], October 17, 1950, Giovannino Guareschi Archive (DB: AGG 9).

232 See Benny Lai, "Il Don Camillo sarà messo all'indice?," *La Gazzetta del Popolo*, February 1, 1953.

233 Nicola De Pirro, letter to Angelo Dell'Acqua, February 26, 1953, Giulio Andreotti Archive at the ASILS, Serie Vaticano, envelope 120 (DB: ASILS 268): "intervento del S. Uffizio a proposito del D. Camillo."

are going through. The second movie should be out in time for the electoral campaign."[234]

"Catholics active in ecclesiastical institutions" (the first group) seemingly gave their full support to the film, which was even listed among those that "the Ecclesiastical Consultant of the CCC considers as having 'religious character'."[235] Furthermore, the *Rivista del Cinematografo* and diocese dailies reviewed it enthusiastically: "*Don Camillo* is an outstanding film."[236] The film was even defended from within the group when the *Legion of Decency* expressed certain misgivings.[237] During the shooting of the second film (*The Return of Don Camillo*), Fernandel was even invited for a special audience with the Pope[238], which is, of course, a highly symbolic gesture within Vatican rituals.

The "Catholics outside institutions" (the third group) held a radically different position. Fabbretti defined the film as "a fundamental misunderstanding, a banal film [...] that has thrown into raptures those who know nothing of communism – and even less of Christianity."[239] However, we should not be misled by the venue of his opinion. It was hosted by a newspaper of the first group – the daily of the Milanese curia – as a dissenting voice within a debate on religious films: "Lugaro reassures me that the film is 'exquisite and funny, and profoundly human'. Indeed. Still, people having fun do so behind the back of a priest, who is only in part a priest. For the rest of the time he is a rather vulgar man, irreverent and rash."[240]

---

234   DB: ASILS 268: "quegli eventuali passi che reputasse più opportuni, data l'importanza degl'interessi connessi al film, che sembrerebbero non solo di ordine materiale [...] ma relativi anche allo straordinario periodo politico (elezioni) che attraversiamo. Infatti il secondo film dovrebbe uscire in tempo utile per il periodo elettorale."

235   DB: ACEC 3.

236   Giorgio Santarelli, "Don Camillo," *Rivista del Cinematografo*, a. XXV. n. 5, May 1952.

237   Albino Galletto [?], letter to Patrick Masterson, June 19, 1952, ACEC Archive (DB: ACEC 19).

238   See. s.n., "Panoramica," *Rivista del Cinematografo*, a. XXVI, n. 2, February 1953, p. 24.

239   Nazareno Fabbretti, "Un film su Gesù?," *L'Italia*, September 6, 1952.

240   Nazareno Fabbretti, "Cinema religioso? Invito alla discussione," *L'Italia*, September 23, 1952.

Fabbretti's opinion can be read together with that of Primo Mazzolari (a prominent figure for the group), who, throughout his whole life, wrote just three articles on cinema, all of them dedicated to *Don Camillo*. The articles had the clear purpose of denouncing its status as a comedy, and emphasizing the distance between the film and its religious reference: "Don Camillo is no priest, just as Peppone is no communist. [...] I know for it has been my job to be a country priest, I know what it means. [...] The public must not be disturbed when having fun...Communists, non-communists, people of Catholic Action, they all rush to the cinema, and they laugh. They go to the movies to laugh."[241]

An article by Fabbretti, published in 1954 is emblematic of the third group's theoretical stance on religious cinema. The piece clearly originated in the experiences and the debates that took place within the group itself, and thus implicitly accounts for its identity. The screening of *The Robe* (Henry Koster, 1953) provided Fabbretti with the occasion to summarize his thoughts on religious cinema. The article clearly opposed the general trend of debates on religious cinema within the Catholic world, and characterized the third group in opposition not to the secular world, but rather to other Catholic groups active in the field of cinema. The heart of the matter was stated directly:

> Catholics remained silent over one of the greatest misunderstandings, one concerning religion, in the history of cinema. I am referring to the pretense of dealing with the figures of Christ, of the Holy Virgin, of the Saints, by placing them in their original context, thus producing a 'visual' history of their lives. [...] There has not been enough opposition to banal and inane films, such as *Mater Dei* and *La Tunica*. The former film deserved to be put on the Index for the sake of faith and art: and yet it was only marginally criticized, and it is remembered in popular opinion as a good film, only because it told the story of the Holy Virgin. [...] Emilio Cordero – the director of *Mater Dei* – is shooting dozens of films in southern Italy [...] among which many are on Jesus Christ's life. Even a brief examination will show that such films, in the past just as today, are devoid of any genuine spiritual and religious value, to such an extent that they tried to capture Christ's look,

---

241 Primo Mazzolari, "Addio Don Camillo," *Adesso*, July 15, 1952.

242 Catholicism and Cinema

his smile and his voice (ah! Ruggeri's voice in *Don Camillo*) and his physiognomy in a very straightforward way.[242]

Fabbretti voiced his irritation with many of the titles that would soon feature, together with *Mater Dei*, *La tunica* and *Don Camillo*, on the CCC's lists of religious films. The few films that Fabretti saved were those that refused "religious historicism" and that represented "religious values in men's and women's lives:"[243] precisely those films that we classified in the second line of production, the one Gedda wanted (without success) to place alongside the "Pope's cinema." It is no coincidence that the two titles that Fabbretti presents as positive models, and as possible inspiration for Italian cinema, did not feature on the CCC's lists: John Ford's *The Grapes of Wrath* (1940) and Edward Dmytryk's *Give Us This Day* (1949).

---

242 Nazareno Fabbretti, "Equivoci e speranze del cinema religioso," *Studium*, a. 50, March 1954, pp. 156-157.
243 *Ibid.*, p. 160.

Printed by
STARlog – Asti (AT)
September 2020